T0355331

Belisarius & Antonina

BELISARIUS & ANTONINA

Love and War in the Age of Justinian

DAVID ALAN PARNELL

OXFORD
UNIVERSITY PRESS

Oxford University Press is a department of the University of Oxford. It furthers
the University's objective of excellence in research, scholarship, and education
by publishing worldwide. Oxford is a registered trade mark of Oxford University
Press in the UK and certain other countries.

Published in the United States of America by Oxford University Press
198 Madison Avenue, New York, NY 10016, United States of America.

Library of Congress Cataloging-in-Publication Data
Names: Parnell, David Alan, author.
Title: Belisarius & Antonina : love and war in the age of Justinian /
David Alan Parnell.
Other titles: Belisarius and Antonina
Description: New York, NY : Oxford University Press, [2023] |
Includes bibliographical references and index.
Identifiers: LCCN 2023004753 (print) | LCCN 2023004754 (ebook) |
ISBN 9780197574706 (hardback) | ISBN 9780197574720 (epub)
Subjects: LCSH: Belisarius, approximately 505–565. |
Antonina, approximately 484-approximately 565. |
Byzantine Empire—History—Justinian I, 527–565. | LCGFT: Biographies.
Classification: LCC DF572.8.B4 P37 2023 (print) | LCC DF572.8.B4 (ebook) |
DDC 945/.7010922—dc23/eng/20230202
LC record available at https://lccn.loc.gov/2023004753
LC ebook record available at https://lccn.loc.gov/2023004754

DOI: 10.1093/oso/9780197574706.001.0001

Printed by Sheridan Books, Inc., United States of America

Contents

Illustrations

Figures

Maps

Acknowledgments

I HAVE BEEN extremely fortunate to be supported in many ways, by both institutions and individuals, in the writing of this book. Credit for the idea for this book goes to my friend and graduate-student colleague Vincent Ryan, who many years ago suggested I write a monograph on Belisarius. The research and writing of this book would have been impossible without the steadfast support of my institution, Indiana University Northwest. The combination of a travel fellowship and sabbatical leave in Spring 2020 allowed me to conduct research in Rome, which was sadly cut short by the outbreak of the COVID-19 pandemic in Italy. I also received from my university additional research funding in Summer 2021, which allowed me to complete the majority of the writing. I am enormously grateful for the support I have received from Indiana University, which values the research of its faculty. As this book came together, I was blessed to have many of my historian colleagues read portions or the entirety of the manuscript and offer suggestions. I would like to particularly thank Michael Stewart, Conor Whately, Christopher Lillington-Martin, Geoffrey Greatrex, and Michael Bonner for their time and expertise. I also benefited from the passion and insight of other acquaintances interested in Belisarius and Antonina, including Toby Groom of Epic History TV and John Yelland of Judicator. I am sincerely grateful for the assistance of my editor at Oxford, Stefan Vranka, and the comments of the anonymous reviewers of both the proposal and manuscript. Finally, I am so appreciative of my wife, Bethany, who has been supportive of her academic spouse for more than ten years now. Authors write about what they know. Who is to say how much of my decision to write a book about a married couple was inspired by my own marriage? This book is dedicated to her.

D. A. P.

Introduction

ALTHOUGH THEIR NAMES may not quite resonate with the public today, Belisarius and Antonina were titans in the Roman world some 1,500 years ago. Belisarius was the most well-known general of his age, victor over the Persians, conqueror of the Vandals and the Goths, and, as if this were not enough, wealthy beyond imagination. His wife, Antonina, was an impressive person in her own right. She made a name for herself by traveling with Belisarius on his military campaigns, deposing a pope, and scheming to disgrace important Roman officials. Together, the pair were extremely influential, and they arguably wielded more power in the Roman world than anyone except the emperor and empress themselves. This unadulterated power and wealth did not mean that Belisarius and Antonina were universally successful in all that they undertook. They occasionally stumbled militarily, politically, and personally—in their marriage and with their children. These failures knock them from their lofty perch, humanize them, and make them even more relatable and intriguing as subjects of study.

This book is an exploration of the marriage and partnership of Belisarius and Antonina. A dual portrait of this type has not previously been attempted, although there have been many biographies of Belisarius alone. What sets this book apart from, say, a military biography of Belisarius as general is that here the focus is on the relationship between Belisarius and Antonina, and how that partnership enabled each of them to reach heights of power and success. For Belisarius and Antonina were not merely husband and wife, but also partners in power. This is a paradigm that might seem strange. We reflexively imagine that marriages in the ancient world were staunchly traditional in that each partner had gendered roles, the husband in the public sphere and the wife in the domestic. But Antonina was not a reserved housewife, and Belisarius showed no desire for Antonina to remain in the home. Their

Belisarius & Antonina. David Alan Parnell, Oxford University Press. © Oxford University Press 2023.
DOI: 10.1093/oso/9780197574706.003.0001

private and public lives blended as they traveled together, sometimes bringing their children, and worked side-by-side.[1]

Belisarius and Antonina lived in the Roman Empire. By the time they achieved prominence in the sixth century, the Roman state was already incredibly ancient. Counting from the legendary founding of the city of Rome in 753 BC, the Roman polity was 1,282 years old by the time Belisarius became a general in 529 AD. Of course, the Roman world of 529 AD looked nothing like that of 753 BC. Over the course of centuries, Roman society had evolved from a small city-state, overlooking the Tiber River in central Italy, to a sprawling empire that stretched from the Atlantic Ocean to the Euphrates River, from northern Britain to southern Egypt. By 529, that empire had contracted, losing its western half, but remained quite substantial in size. Similarly, the Roman government had evolved over the centuries, from monarchy to republic, and then into an empire that was at first cloaked in republican language and later more nakedly autocratic. In 395 AD, that government was divided for the last time between two different emperors. The line of emperors ruling in the West, from Italy, was extinguished in 476 AD. The line of emperors ruling in the East, at Constantinople, remained unbowed and unbroken stretching back through the centuries to Augustus, acknowledged as the first of the Roman emperors. Though they lived in Constantinople rather than Rome, these were Roman emperors who ruled over Roman citizens and were the heads of state of a Roman government. This empire is sometimes called "Byzantine" after the original Greek city at the site of Constantinople, named Byzantium, rather than Roman. However, modern historians disagree on a starting point for a "Byzantine Empire," and some recently have argued that the term should not be used for any period of the medieval Roman state's history. In this book, the term "Byzantine" will not appear, the empire under discussion will be described only as the Roman Empire, and Belisarius and Antonina will be styled as Romans.[2]

One other significant aspect of the ancient Roman society's evolution over the course of these many centuries is the rise and triumph of Christianity. While this religion began in the first century AD as a small sect, persecuted by both Jewish religious authorities and, sporadically, by the Roman government itself, belief in Christ gained toleration and instant respectability with the conversion of the Emperor Constantine I (r. 306–337 AD). From this point, Christianity began to spread and displace ancient forms of polytheism across the Roman world. This process was still underway in the sixth century, and some pagan holdouts remained, but it does not seem that Belisarius and Antonina were among them. Their Christian faith is confirmed by, among other evidence, a papal letter referring to Antonina as a "most Christian" daughter of Pope Vigilius (r. 537–555 AD) and a casual reference to Belisarius fasting prior to Easter 531. Belisarius and Antonina therefore were a part of the Christianization of Roman society, a process that did not come without growing pains and disagreements among believers.[3]

Belisarius and Antonina's sovereigns were the Emperor Justinian I (r. 527–565 AD) and the Empress Theodora (r. 527–548), who are themselves justly famous. Over the course of a 38-year reign, Justinian presided over building projects and revisions of the law code, mediated between Christian factions, and launched many wars. His wife Theodora was at his side for 21 of these years, and like Antonina with Belisarius, she was known for her partnership with Justinian in government. Theodora inspired legislation, had a say in the selection of government ministers, and sheltered Christian dissidents. The empire that Justinian and Theodora ruled may have been smaller than in its heyday before the division between East and West, but it was still massive: the Romans governed southeastern Europe south of the Danube, Anatolia (roughly corresponding to modern Turkey), and the Near East bending from Syria south to Egypt. Even though this may seem like quite enough to rule, Justinian and Theodora also believed it to be their Roman and Christian duty to consider the safety and quality of life of Romans outside of their authority, to the West in formerly Roman Italy and North Africa, and of Christians to the East near and beyond the empire's borders with the powerful Persian Empire.[4]

Justinian and Theodora knew Belisarius and Antonina personally. It is hard to say exactly how close of friends these couples were, but the intricate operations that they pulled off in concert with one another point to a degree of trust. When they were all on the same page, these four ruled the Roman world and sought to fulfill great and difficult ambitions including the conquest of other kingdoms and the reordering of the Roman government and of the Christian Church. When they occasionally quarreled, it was inevitably Belisarius and Antonina who fell from favor. They were, after all, the pair without the crowns. This happened just frequently enough to give a whiff of drama to the relationship between Belisarius/Antonina and Justinian/Theodora, which was, over the long haul of their lives, mostly stable.

Now that we have been introduced to Belisarius and Antonina, to Justinian and Theodora, and to the Roman world they called home, we need to become familiar with one more character who must of necessity be an integral part of this book. Procopius of Caesarea was the most prominent historian of the century. Born in Caesarea (in modern Israel), he received a first-rate classical education, becoming a lawyer. When Belisarius received his first significant military command in 527, he hired Procopius to be his legal adviser (*assessor*) and personal secretary. This was an important position for the young Procopius. Working for a powerful military officer, he could expect entry into the rarified air of the upper levels of the Roman administration. The position became even more of a bonanza for Procopius when his employer Belisarius was promoted to general in 529, becoming one of the most important men in the Roman army. For the next eleven years, Procopius followed Belisarius and Antonina around the Mediterranean, from posting to posting. Probably in 540, Procopius left the service of Belisarius and settled in Constantinople to become a historian. He first began work on a massive history he called the *Wars*, which was to be a military history of the wars of Justinian, with a significant focus on the role played by Belisarius, who is frequently portrayed as a heroic protagonist. Writing this massive work took years. The first seven books of the *Wars* were probably completed and distributed in 551, and the eighth and last book followed in 554. While working on the *Wars*, Procopius also wrote a shorter, scandalous book, which is known as the *Secret History*. This is a libelous screed that savagely critiques Justinian, Theodora, Belisarius, and Antonina for the way they governed the Roman world. Procopius wrote it in the late 540s and stopped work on it, unfinished, around 550. The historian also wrote a book entitled *On Buildings* to praise Justinian's building projects, which he probably worked on, although possibly left incomplete, in 554.[5]

Readers of this book who are satisfied with this brief introduction of Procopius and eager to get into the remarkable story of Belisarius and Antonina may wish to proceed directly to Chapter 1. Readers who are curious that Procopius, who knew Belisarius and Antonina personally, would portray them so differently in the *Wars* and the *Secret History* may wish to read on to learn why this was the case. Because we have no surviving documents that Belisarius or Antonina wrote themselves, and because Procopius knew them personally, the books that he wrote are our most detailed and knowledgeable contemporary account of the couple. Writing a history of Belisarius and Antonina without the works of Procopius would be virtually impossible. This means that any attempt to write about Belisarius and Antonina must grapple with the contrasting accounts of Procopius. In the *Wars*, Belisarius is often (but not always) portrayed as a heroic and successful general, and Antonina is shown as an intelligent, compassionate, and active spouse. In the *Secret History*, Procopius describes Belisarius as a submissive weakling completely dominated by his powerful wife, paralleling the author's negative portrayals of

Justinian and Theodora. Antonina controls Belisarius with spells to the extent that he at first fails to notice and then fails to punish her for having a sexual affair with their adopted son. No whisper of these outrageous accusations appears in the *Wars* or any other surviving source. Full examples of these two contrasting presentations of Belisarius and Antonina will of course be found in the remainder of this book, but as a preview one might consider the different ways the two works portray the retreat of Belisarius from a campaign on the Persian front in 541. In the *Wars*, Belisarius has his army withdraw from Persian territory for valid military reasons, while in the *Secret History*, Belisarius withdraws in order to rush to confront Antonina over her alleged affair with their adopted son.[6]

To write a history of Belisarius and Antonina is therefore partially about reconciling Procopius with Procopius, the *Wars* with the *Secret History*. We can begin to do that by considering the nature of each of the two works and their intended audience. The *Wars* is a military history in the style of the *Histories* of Thucydides, which recounted the Peloponnesian War (431–404 BC). Procopius shows that he was familiar with the writing of Thucydides and numerous other ancient writers by incorporating many classical allusions to their texts into the *Wars*. Procopius intended this book to make him famous as a historian. This means that he wrote the *Wars* to be distributed and read by a wide audience. Because of the nature of literacy in the period, this audience was probably limited to the elites of the Roman world, and the book would have perhaps appealed most to those who worked in the military or civilian government. Most importantly, this audience would have included Justinian, Belisarius, and their wives. Procopius implies in *On Buildings* that he had received favor from the emperor, and this favor was likely bestowed by Justinian for the completion of the *Wars*. Since Belisarius and Antonina would have had access to the *Wars*, it seems likely that most if not all of the characterizations of these individuals and their actions in that book would have been acceptable to them. This does not mean that every description of Belisarius and Antonina in the *Wars* is historical truth, or on the other hand political propaganda, only that the words in it often aligned with the couple's own view of how the events unfolded. In addition, the author's depiction of relations between the genders, such as the relationship between Antonina and Belisarius, was probably considered normal by most of the readers of this work. In other words, the depiction of the active role of Antonina in her relationship with Belisarius is presented as something typical, and the elites of the period would not have been surprised by what they read in this work.[7]

The *Secret History* is, however, a very different beast. It is not strictly a work of history, but rather an invective. In the *Secret History*, Procopius seeks to make Justinian, Theodora, Belisarius, and Antonina look bad by coming up with the most outrageous and salacious accusations against them. It resembles a hyperbolic legal argument that might have been made against these powerful people by those who felt wronged by them. Because the purpose is invective rather than history, we should not expect all of the charges in the *Secret History* to be historical truth, any more than we might expect modern, vitriolic political campaign advertisements to reflect the exact truth. Since the *Secret History* is so harsh on some of the most powerful people in the Roman world, it stands to reason that its audience was intended to be quite smaller than that for the *Wars*. Far from expecting the *Secret History* to be read widely, Procopius intended it for only extremely limited distribution and only in particular circumstances. It is possible that Procopius wrote the *Secret History* in anticipation of a revolution that would overthrow Justinian and those closest to him, such as Belisarius and Antonina. In the event of that revolution, the scurrilous pamphlet would prove to the new ruler that Procopius was not actually any longer aligned with his former employer Belisarius and the Emperor Justinian, and therefore was not a threat to the new regime. In this way, the *Secret History* served as insurance against the possibility that Procopius might be swept out with the old order by the new emperor. Under these circumstances, Procopius would have every reason to make the invective in the book as outrageous as possible, while also still making it convincing enough that the new regime would buy it as something more than simple fiction. However, the revolution that Procopius imagined never came to pass, and there is no evidence that the author outlived Justinian. Given this, it seems likely that very few, or perhaps even none, of Procopius' contemporaries read the *Secret History*. It was perhaps left in storage and discovered after the author's death. The earliest certain reference to the text in another surviving work is in the *Suda*, an encyclopedia compiled in the 10th century.[8]

It should be said that not all modern historians would accept these characterizations of the nature of the *Wars* and the *Secret History*. Scholarship on the works of Procopius continues to evolve, and consensus is difficult to achieve. However, these characterizations of the works of Procopius allow us to create a framework for the purpose of examining the lives of Belisarius and Antonina. In general, in this book I will treat accounts of Belisarius and Antonina in the *Wars* as descriptions of which they would approve, or at least not violently oppose. This does not mean, however, that we should take every description of the couple in the *Wars* at face value. In particular, because it was written for an audience that included Belisarius and Antonina, some of the anecdotes about them in this work downplay or ignore their failures. Individual episodes in the *Wars* still need to be scrutinized for their accuracy. In general, I will approach the *Secret History* as invective rather than history, but will treat that invective as though it is based on a kernel of historical truth. Invective is more effective when it is based in truth, which a talented writer like Procopius would have realized while composing this work. In order to make the invective believable to the hypothetical new regime, Procopius would have wanted to make sure that the accusations could at least in part be verified by common knowledge or other sources. Therefore, many of the slanderous tales told about Belisarius and Antonina in the *Secret History* may in fact have a basis in historical reality that was then exaggerated by Procopius to make the couple look as bad as possible. For example, consider the way that Procopius' sexual slander of Theodora in the *Secret History* is probably grossly exaggerated, yet rooted in common knowledge of the empress' background as an actress. This framework underpins the analysis of the works of Procopius in this book and helps to bring to light Belisarius and Antonina, who were not always as successful as the *Wars* makes them seem, but were not as terribly villainous as the *Secret History* would have it either.[9]

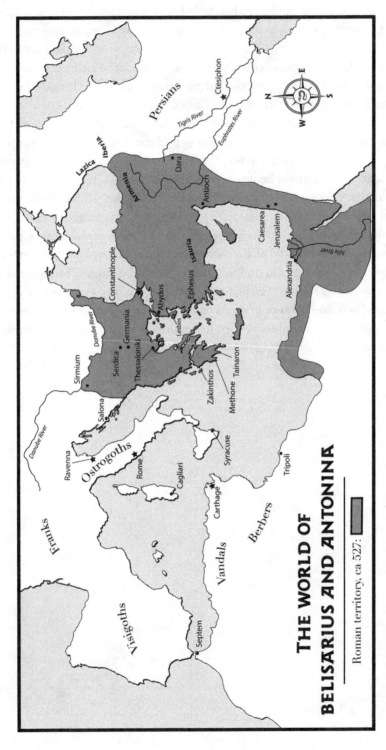

MAP 1 The World of Belisarius and Antonina (the Mediterranean in the sixth century). Created by John Wyatt Greenlee.

Persians

Ctesiphon

Tigris River

Euphrates River

Iberia

Lazica

Armenia

Dara

Antioch

Caesarea

Jerusalem

Isauria

Alexandria

Nile River

Constantinople

Abydos

Ephesus

Lesbos

Germania

Danube River

Thessaloniki

Tainaron

Serdica

Zakinthos

Sirmium

Methone

Salona

Syracuse

Danube River

Ravenna

Ostrogoths

Rome

Cagliari

Tripoli

Franks

Carthage

Berbers

Septem

Vandals

Visigoths

THE WORLD OF
BELISARIUS AND ANTONINA

Roman territory, ca 527:

I

The World of Antonina

THE STORY OF one of the greatest and most unusual marital partnerships of the ancient Roman world begins with the birth, sometime near the end of the fifth century of this era, of a baby named Antonina. Almost nothing is known of the circumstances of her birth, but the historian Procopius, while refusing to name her parents, does at least record their occupations: her mother was an actress and her father a charioteer. This revelation opens a window onto the world into which Antonina was born. Roman cities of this period including the capital, Constantinople, were completely swept up by enthusiasm for public entertainment. There were two chief forms of spectacle, which Antonina's parents just so happen to represent through their professions: performances in theaters and chariot races in large arenas known as hippodromes.[1]

The theater of the sixth century was bawdy, raucous, and fun rather than stately, serious, and intellectual. It was completely dominated by dancing pantomimes, backed up by singing choruses. The pantomimes were the stars and lead performers, while the choruses were made up of nearly anonymous backup singers. Their performances were often informed by ancient myth and contained a healthy dose of lewdness and sexual situations. For instance, Procopius claims that the Empress Theodora, in her days as an actress in the theater, was famous for an act in which she lay on her back, scantily attired, and allowed geese to peck grains of barley off of her body. This act has been identified as a satirical reference to the tale in Greek mythology in which Zeus, in the form of a swan, rapes the princess Leda. Although Procopius tells this story, and others, about the actress Theodora in an attempt to discredit her, it is clear that such acts were immensely popular, and that Procopius himself had personal knowledge of their contents. Roman society, despite the growing importance of the Christian church, was not prudish. Plays with a focus on

Belisarius & Antonina. David Alan Parnell, Oxford University Press. © Oxford University Press 2023.
DOI: 10.1093/oso/9780197574706.003.0002

adultery were not uncommon: Euripides' *Hippolytus*, in which a married woman lusts after her stepson, was particularly popular in both art and theater at the time. Some indication of the massive popularity of theatrical shows comes from the fact that a ban on pantomimes could be considered a significant punishment. In 522, the Emperor Justin I banished such performers across the empire after a major riot in Constantinople. Theatrical shows aroused such excitement and passions that they themselves could spark riots, which could, again, invite bans, as happened in Antioch in 529.[2]

When not jamming into theaters to leer at pantomime acts, urban Romans crowded into the local hippodrome to watch intense chariot races. These races were typically held on special event days, during which there would be between eight and twenty-four separate races. In a race, four chariots pulled by teams of four horses each would compete. The rules of the standard race would have been familiar to modern observers: the chariots began in starting boxes whose gates were opened at the same moment. The first chariot to cross the finish line after a lap around the track was crowned the winner. There were some variations. A popular one was the *diversium*, in which after the first race, the charioteers exchanged horses and chariots, and then raced again. This provided an opportunity for the winning charioteer of the first race to prove that he won because of his skill, not because of his horses and equipment. Charioteers were immensely popular individuals. The best were cheered by their fans, and jeered by the fans of their opponents, by name. They might also be honored by statues, inscribed with a record of their victories, and erected inside the race track for all to see. Porphyrius was perhaps the most popular and successful charioteer of the sixth century and was honored by at least seven statues. Charioteers enjoyed considerable mobility, sometimes moving to a different city or team, much like modern superstar athletes. The hippodromes in which these races took place were elliptical-shaped arenas, and some could be quite large. The largest one was the Circus Maximus in Rome, but hippodromes could also be found in most large cities across the Mediterranean, including Alexandria, Antioch, and Thessaloniki. At the time of Antonina's birth, the most important hippodrome was that of Constantinople. It stood in the southeastern portion of the city (today's Sultanahmet Square), directly adjacent to the Great Palace, the home of the emperors. The massive structure was some 118 meters wide and 450 meters long. Its capacity was enormous: about 100,000 people.[3]

The two seemingly disparate public entertainments of theater and hippodrome were tied together by the professional athletic teams that historians call the factions. These organizations were originally four in number: the

Blues, Greens, Whites, and Reds. However, by the sixth century the Whites and Reds had been absorbed by the Blues and Greens respectively. In a chariot race, one chariot bore each of the four team colors, but there were only the two administrative structures of the Blues and Greens. Originally private organizations, the Blues and Greens were bureaucratized in the fifth century. The government paid and organized the teams to provide free public spectacles for the people in the name of the emperor. The Blue and Green factions not only administered and put on the chariot races, but were also responsible for hiring pantomimes, dancers, and singers, and organizing theatrical shows. Thus employees of the factions ran the gamut from actresses to charioteers and all the assorted support staff required. The Blues and Greens inspired intense fandom, comparable to modern football clubs and their supporters. The most extreme and dedicated fans were known as partisans. They were a radical minority who were the loudest and rowdiest spectators both in the hippodrome and in the theater. Most fans were not so extreme, but it does seem that almost all inhabitants of major cities did identify as fans of one faction or another. This mania for the Blues and Greens and public spectacle as a whole coexisted uneasily with the powerful Christian church. Clergy generally disapproved of both chariot racing and theatrical performances, seeing these as rivals that lured the people away from church and connected them to ancient pagan traditions. Ecclesiastics criticized these spectacles quite openly. The ecclesiastical historian John of Ephesus described a hippodrome as a "church of Satan." The contemporary bishop Severus of Antioch railed against those "who look on the vile gyrations of the dancing madness with their many turns, and in the thought of their heart wander as in deep darkness." Condemnations like these did little to dampen the popularity of such entertainments.[4]

This urban Roman landscape of massively popular public entertainments was the world of Antonina's parents. If Procopius is to be believed, of the two of them Antonina's mother had the less exalted position. The author introduces her as "one of those types who whore themselves on the stage." This unflattering description reveals the disdain that Procopius had for those who acted, an attitude that was shared by other elite Romans. Actors and actresses, although they might attract large crowds and become quite popular, were considered inappropriate and unrespectable by the rich and prominent. Actresses in particular were associated with prostitution, a point that Procopius drove home with excruciating detail in his slanders against Theodora. The term that Procopius uses about the location of the work of Antonina's mother—the stage (*thuméle*)—is a hint at the type of actress she was. During performances, she sang from the orchestra portion of the stage, as a member of the chorus. This was the lowest position an actress could hold and was less important, less glamorous, and probably less lucrative than the pantomimes who took the lead roles in theatrical productions. Still, it was a job, and women in poor families usually had to work in the Roman world. Antonina's father, on the other hand, had a more important and lucrative job. Procopius says that "her father and grandfather were both charioteers, who had performed professionally in Constantinople and Thessaloniki." The wording of the sentence does not make clear whether Antonina's father and grandfather both raced in both cities, or one raced in Constantinople and one raced in Thessaloniki. It was common for charioteers to experience geographic mobility, so it should not be surprising if her father raced in both cities. As already mentioned, charioteers were immensely popular individuals. They were also far better paid than chorus singers like Antonina's mother. While salary information for the sixth century is not available, by the tenth century charioteers were eligible to receive cash bonuses from the imperial government that were in the same range as those given to junior palace officials and subdeacons of the great church Hagia Sophia. Despite a comfortable salary and their popularity with the masses, charioteers were, like actresses, despised by the elite. Entertainment of any kind was not considered a respectable occupation in the sixth century, or in any period of the Roman Empire for that matter. By explaining that Antonina's parents were a charioteer and an actress, Procopius is not simply providing biography, but arguing that her ancestry was base and unrespectable. Such denigration of the target's family background was a standard technique of ancient invective. Procopius is setting the stage for a long, slanderous critique of Antonina that unfolds throughout the rest of the *Secret History*. While there are reasons to doubt aspects of that critique, there is no particular reason to doubt Procopius' claim here that Antonina's parents were a charioteer and an actress. However, that Antonina's mother literally prostituted herself need not be believed—there is no reason to think Procopius would have any personal knowledge of the lifestyle of Antonina's mother. He simply equated all actresses with prostitutes, which says more about his general assumptions of acting as a profession than it does about his particular knowledge of Antonina's family.[5]

Because of the claim that Antonina's father could have raced in both Constantinople and Thessaloniki, it is impossible to know for sure in which city he met her mother or where Antonina was born. It is almost certain that Antonina found herself in Constantinople later in her life, for neither her future husband Belisarius nor her future friend Theodora are known to have ever

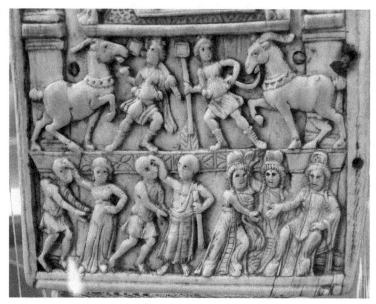

FIGURE I Dancers and actresses on the diptych of Flavios Anastasios Probos. Wikimedia Commons.

been to Thessaloniki. So, in order to meet these two individuals, Antonina would have had to be in Constantinople. But she could have easily been born and raised in Thessaloniki and only moved to Constantinople as an adult. Or perhaps her parents met in Constantinople and she was born and raised there. Both options are just as likely. Thessaloniki was an important city in the sixth century. It was the capital of the prefecture of Illyricum and therefore the second-most-significant city in the Roman Balkans (after Constantinople). Thessaloniki had a palace, which had been built for the Emperor Galerius in the third century, a hippodrome, and several important churches. It was by no means a sleepy, provincial backwater. It did, however, take second place to Constantinople, which by the sixth century was the greatest city in Europe. Constantinople housed a population of about 500,000. It was well protected by the Theodosian Walls, built in 413 during the reign of Theodosius II. In addition to the hippodrome described earlier, Constantinople was home to the Great Palace of the emperors, dozens of churches, and monuments beyond count. Starting with Constantine's re-founding of the city of Byzantium as the New Rome in 330, emperors and other members of the imperial family had built it up, seeking to put their own stamp on the city. It was a loud, raucous, vibrant place, full of contradictions. The rich walked down the same market streets as the poor. Churches stood near, and coexisted uneasily with, both hippodrome and theaters. The same men who hooted at a pantomime performance, or rioted at a chariot race, might the next day find themselves in somber worship in a church next door. Enormous amounts of food were shipped into the city, and yet some still went hungry. Men and women from across the Roman world, and beyond, could rub shoulders at the docks and in the great markets of the city. Constantinople was truly a marvel, both wondrous and terrible to behold.[6]

Antonina was probably born in one of these two cities, Thessaloniki or Constantinople, to a mother who was an actress and a father who was a charioteer, but beyond that nothing is known for certain about her birth. In particular, the year of her birth is a bit of a mystery. This does not mean that there is no evidence for it, however. In the *Secret History*, Procopius claims that in 544 Antonina was "already past sixty years old." If taken literally, this would require Antonina to be born no later than 484. There is good reason to doubt this is accurate. In the full passage, Procopius is clearly attempting to make Belisarius look ridiculous for loving an older woman: "He was so extraordinarily infatuated with her, and this despite the fact that she was already past sixty years old." Given the nature of the *Secret History* as invective, and Procopius' inclination to use hyperbole as part of his slander, it seems unreasonable to take this claim of Antonina's age literally. Besides, other clues to Antonina's age that Procopius drops are incompatible with a birth in 484. For example, Procopius claims that Belisarius and Antonina's daughter, Ioannina, was betrothed to Theodora's grandson Anastasios in 543. Presumably the reason that this was only a betrothal and not yet a marriage was because Ioannina was not old enough to marry at the time. But the age of consent for marriage was only twelve years old. For Ioannina not to have been old enough to marry in 543 means the earliest Ioannina could have been born was 531. If Antonina was actually born in 484, that would mean she gave birth to Ioannina when she was forty-seven years old, which is extremely unlikely. This suggests Antonina could not have been born as early as 484. On the other end of the range of possibilities, Antonina had to have been old enough to have a granddaughter who might be wooed in 545. In that year, Procopius reports that the General Sergios was a suitor for the hand of Antonina's granddaughter. These considerations bound the birth of Antonina: she was young enough to give birth to a daughter of her own in 531, but old enough to have a granddaughter of marriageable age in 545. Therefore, a reasonable guess is that Antonina was born between 495 and 500.[7]

As with her birth, nearly nothing is known of Antonina's childhood. Two very different childhoods are possible. In one scenario, Antonina's mother and father were married, or at least co-habiting, and Antonina had the emotional and financial support of both her parents. In this situation, Antonina would have grown up in some comfort. As a charioteer, her father would have made a salary well above subsistence level, and if very successful in his career might have even become wealthy. The family would have a comfortable home, and food would have been plentiful. This stability would have allowed Antonina the luxury of not finding a job herself, of perhaps receiving some basic education, and potentially finding a respectable husband when she grew up. In the second possible scenario, Antonina's father was not a part of her life. Antonina was raised by a single mother, whom Procopius claims was one of the lowest-ranking actresses of the theater. In this situation, her childhood would have been quite different. Very possibly she would have frequently gone hungry. It is very likely that she would have needed to start working at a young age to help support her small family. Procopius provides a good idea of what such a childhood might have looked like for the daughter of an actress in his description of the early life of Theodora. She started work before she reached puberty and her first job was to follow her older sister Komito around and carry a stool on which Komito stood when she danced. When Theodora reached puberty she joined the theater, presumably as a chorus singer. Later, she moved up in the hierarchy and became a pantomime. Procopius, ever eager to associate acting with prostitution, also provides descriptions of the sexual services Theodora offered at each stage of this work, beginning before she even hit puberty. Thus, Antonina's early life as a child would have been quite different depending on whether her father was involved in her life, or at least supported her with his income. It is not possible to know which of these two scenarios gets closer to the truth of Antonina's childhood. At least we can be relatively certain about the language Antonina grew up speaking: whether she lived in Thessaloniki or Constantinople, and whether she grew up in financial comfort or not, she was likely to have spoken Greek. Greek was the chief language in both Thessaloniki and Constantinople at that time, as well as the most common language throughout the sixth-century Roman Empire as a whole. This is not to say that use of Latin was nonexistent in these cities: it remained an important language in law and administration in the empire of the time, and there was a substantial, and influential, Latin-speaking minority in Constantinople. But it is unlikely that the circles Antonina ran in would have either required or encouraged her to learn Latin.[8]

The Adult Life of Antonina

Beyond the information about her parents' occupations and cities of residence, Procopius makes two remarks on Antonina's early life that are worth examining. He claims that,

> Before marrying Belisarius, this woman had lived a wanton life and had never learned to show any restraint. She had also spent time with sorcerers and poisoners from her parents' world and had learned from them many things that were useful to her.

These remarks have sometimes been interpreted to mean that Antonina became an actress, as her mother before her had been. But this is by no means certain. For one thing, Procopius does not come right out and say that Antonina was an actress (as he does about her mother), and it would have been exceptionally easy for him to do so. Procopius does accuse Antonina of leading a sexually unrestrained life, and we know from what the author wrote about Antonina's mother and Theodora that he equated such a lifestyle with acting. However, even if it is true that Antonina was sexually promiscuous, she would not be required to be an actress to have that sort of lifestyle. The accusation is vague enough anyway that Procopius evidently did not feel like the theme was worth developing as part of his invective. The second claim of the passage is that Antonina learned from *pharmakeusi*—literally sorcerers or poisoners. The suggestion that these were people "from her parents' world" is meant to make this knowledge seem even more illicit and scandalous to an elite Roman. This accusation could be a twisted report of Antonina having received an education at some point in her childhood. More likely, it is a slander invented to set up her alleged use of charms and spells to control Belisarius later in the *Secret History*. It was a common ancient trope that women might use sorcery to control men. Even if the claim that Antonina learned such things is true, it does not necessarily mean that she was an actress. She could have learned from people her parents knew as she grew up without herself becoming a paid worker in their world. There is evidence from later in Antonina's life that she did have some interesting knowledge. For instance, Procopius suggests that she knew how to keep water from spoiling in the hot sun on a long sea voyage. Could this have been one of the lessons she learned in her early life associating with the various officials of the faction for which her parents worked? What Procopius calls sorcery or poison might instead have been herb lore or rudimentary chemistry.[9]

The last thing that Procopius says about Antonina's life before she met Belisarius is easier to verify. He writes in the *Secret History* that "she became the lawful wife of Belisarius, though she was already the mother of many children." The wording of the sentence makes it clear that Procopius intends this as a criticism, and that he is perhaps trying to subtly imply that these children were born out of wedlock (as he contrasts her status as their mother with her status as Belisarius' *lawful* wife). Procopius leaves out in this sentence that Antonina was actually married before she met Belisarius, but he lets that information slip out in a passage in the *Wars* that describes Photios as her son by a previous marriage. So Antonina was married before she met Belisarius and she became the mother of many children, which is exactly what would be expected of a Roman woman who had been previously married. However, this does not prove that all of the children Antonina had were born within the confines of her first marriage, nor does it prove that she had only one marriage before Belisarius. As with Antonina's childhood, multiple scenarios can fit the evidence of Procopius in regard to Antonina's prior relationship(s) and children. Antonina is firmly credited with at least two children born before she met Belisarius: a son named Photios and an unnamed daughter. Photios, who later served in the army with Belisarius, is described in 535 as "a young man wearing his first beard." This description suggests that he was perhaps born about the year 520 at latest. He is the only child of Antonina attested by sources other than Procopius—both the western writer Liberatus of Carthage and the eastern historian John of Ephesus confirm him as a son of Antonina. Much less is known about the unnamed daughter of Antonina. Her existence is confirmed by Procopius in the *Wars* when he describes Ildiger in 534 as the son-in-law of Antonina. So this daughter had to be old enough to be married by 534. Likely, Ildiger was married to Antonina's daughter earlier than this mention. He would have probably had to marry her before Antonina and Belisarius departed for Africa in June 533. This suggests that the unnamed daughter could have been born, at the latest, around the same time as Photios in 520. However, as previously mentioned, Antonina had a granddaughter old enough to be wooed by the General Sergios in 545. If this granddaughter were the child of Ildiger and the unnamed daughter, then the unnamed daughter could perhaps have been a few years older, born around 515. Alternatively, the granddaughter could have been the child of another of Antonina's adult children for whom we have no evidence in the sources. As quoted above, Procopius says that Antonina was the mother of "many" children, though only two can be identified. It is possible that these are the only two children who survived to adulthood. Infancy was a dangerous time in the ancient world, and infant mortality was high. To have two children who survived to adulthood, Antonina might very well have had two children who died young. Thus, it is not necessary to invent additional, unreported adult children for Antonina in order to explain Procopius' claim that she was the mother of many children. There might have been at least one other adult child of Antonina beyond Photios and the unnamed daughter, and there might not.[10]

The identity of Antonina's first husband is also unclear. He is mentioned only the one time, in connection to Photios, and not named. Given that the *Secret History* is an invective, it might be expected that Procopius would have lost no time in trumpeting the low birth or unsuitability of Antonina's first husband if he was in fact unrespectable. That Procopius does not do so could be an indication that Antonina's first husband was a respectable man, in other words, not an entertainer like her parents. He is unlikely to have been one of the senatorial elite, for they were banned from marrying actresses or the daughters of actresses until a law issued in 520 or 521. It is not possible to say more than this about his identity. It is also unclear whether he was the father of all of Antonina's children or only some of them. Procopius' suggestion that Antonina had lived a wanton life might imply that she had sexual relationships and possibly children with multiple men, but it is not possible to know whether this is actually true or just hyperbolic slander. Procopius does not elaborate or provide any details, and neither does any other surviving source. Perhaps Antonina had multiple lovers before she married her first husband, or perhaps Procopius just assumed she did because she was the daughter of an actress, which the historian associated with promiscuity. Just as the identity of the first husband is unclear, it is also unclear when Antonina married him or how long the marriage lasted. The only hint is a brief statement of Belisarius in the *Secret History* in which he claims to have raised Photios, whose father died when Photios was "a baby in his wet nurse's arms." If Photios was born around 520, this would imply that his father, Antonina's first husband, died within the next couple of years. However, Procopius has Belisarius make this claim in the middle of an invented speech that Procopius could not himself have witnessed, so it is perhaps not to be taken literally. Therefore, the date of Antonina's first marriage and the length of that marriage cannot be ascertained with certainty. A strict Procopian view of her life would suggest she had many lovers as a teen (potentially having children with some of those lovers), met and married her husband (who was the father of at least Photios), and then became a widow. A revisionist possibility is that she married straight out of her father's house, had several children with her first husband (only some of whom survived), and then became a widow. In one scenario, Antonina lived a "wanton" life by the standards of the day, and in the other, she lived a much more respectable life, common for women seeking upward social mobility. It is impossible to know which is the more accurate description.[11]

This is the end of the available information on Antonina's life between her birth and her marriage to Belisarius. It leaves the modern reader with a gap of unknown size. It is not clear when Antonina's first husband, the father of Photios, died, and it is equally unclear when Antonina met and married Belisarius. Perhaps Antonina was for a time a grieving widow and single mother. If so, she might have been driven to find a powerful patron who might provide help. For a daughter of entertainers, who understood that world well, the most logical person to turn to for help in the early 520s would have been Theodora. When she married Justinian, in 522 or 523, Theodora became by far the most powerful and influential former actress in the Roman world. She was not yet empress (that would come in 527), but her husband Justinian was a general, the nephew and adopted son of the Emperor Justin I, and was already quite powerful and likely quite rich. Theodora thus would have been well positioned to offer help to other actresses or daughters of actresses who petitioned her for assistance. Later, during her time as empress, Theodora would become famous for helping widows and wives scorned by their husbands, so it is not unreasonable to imagine this tendency had begun during the 520s. It is also possible that the early relationship between Antonina and Theodora was one based on employment rather than charity. Justinian and Theodora were using the Blues as an information network to support their political machinations, and with her connections to the entertainment world, Antonina might have been a valuable asset. Either way, that Antonina sought out Theodora after the death of her first husband is completely conjecture, but it is not purposeless conjecture. Somehow, Antonina met Belisarius around this time, and it is possible that Theodora was the conduit that linked them together. To understand why Belisarius was in Theodora's orbit, we must leave Antonina for a moment to look back at the early life of Belisarius.[12]

The Early Life of Belisarius

While for Antonina, we have the occupations of her parents but no certain location for her birth, for Belisarius, we have the opposite: the location of his birth, but no information about his parents. Procopius reports that Belisarius was born in a town named Germania, which lay between the lands of the

Thracians and Illyrians. This description is typically taken to mean that the town sat approximately on the border between the Roman prefecture of Illyricum and the provinces of Thrace (which belonged to the prefecture of the East). In the 19th century, the Czech historian Konstantin Jireček identified Germania with modern Sapareva Banya in southwestern Bulgaria. The town lies in what was the province of Dacia Mediterranea, near where the sixth-century border between Illyricum and Thrace would have been. Ancient Germania was not a large place—its walls enclosed an area of approximately 180 x 140 meters. Nearby Serdica (modern Sofia) would have been the closest city. This means that Belisarius grew up in a considerably more rural setting than either of the two locations (Thessaloniki or Constantinople) that Antonina was likely to have called home. Because nothing is known of his parents or ancestors, it is impossible to know for certain in what circumstances Belisarius was born and nurtured. Modern historians have suggested that Belisarius' family was well off based on an argument from silence. In the *Secret History*, Procopius makes a big show of denigrating the heritage of Antonina, Theodora, and Justinian as lowborn and contemptible. Suspiciously, he does not do the same for Belisarius. This could be an indication that Belisarius' parents were at the very least respectable in the author's eyes (in other words, they were neither entertainers like Theodora's and Antonina's nor extremely poor like Justinian's uncle). As far as arguments from silence go, this seems like a reasonable guess. More specific hypotheses, such as claims that Belisarius had "noble blood" and "inherited a patrimonial fortune" or that his father was a decurion (a member of a town's local elite, who served as a city councilor), are just pure speculation. Unless additional information surfaces, we are completely in the dark about the identity and wealth of Belisarius' parents. This makes it difficult to imagine what the early life of Belisarius might have been like. If his parents were wealthy enough, he would have received a basic education and lived in a nicely appointed villa outside of town. Recent archaeological work in the Balkans has uncovered dozens of such villas from this period, ranging from large and fortified to small and basic. A villa of any of these types might have been a home to the young Belisarius and his family. On the other hand, if Belisarius' parents were poor, he might have started to work on a small family farm at an early age and perhaps joined the army as soon as he could to relieve his parents of an extra mouth to feed, as Justinian's uncle Justin allegedly did.[13]

It is not clear which language Belisarius would have grown up speaking. One scholar has attempted to identify the origin of his name in the ancient Thracian language, although this has not been widely accepted. Thracian was still a living language in the sixth century, but even if the name Belisarius is Thracian, that is no guarantee that he or his family spoke it. If Belisarius did grow up speaking Thracian, he would have learned at least one of the two great imperial languages of Latin and Greek alongside it. The fact that his hometown of Germania lay in the province of Dacia Mediterranea might suggest that he learned Latin first: the Dacian provinces of Illyricum were generally Latinate. However, the nearby Thracian provinces were generally Greek-speaking. But neither of these generalizations is a hard-and-fast rule, so even if Belisarius' family did live on the side of the divide where Latin was more common, they might still have spoken Greek in their household. Beyond this, the wealth of Belisarius' family might have impacted what languages he learned. If the family was wealthy enough, Belisarius would have been taught both Latin and Greek as he grew up. All of these variables mean that it is impossible to be certain which language(s) Belisarius learned first. Given his later success in the army and imperial court, we can be relatively sure he eventually gained a command of both Latin and Greek, for the former was the historic language of the army and the latter increasingly in use both in the army and in Justinian's government. When he met Antonina later, it is likely that Belisarius spoke with her in Greek, for she would have had no particular reason to learn Latin.[14]

Belisarius was probably born around the turn of the sixth century, but it is impossible to be more exact than that. No source records the specific year of his birth. The estimate is based on offhanded remarks made by two different sources. In the *Wars*, Procopius reports that in 526, when Belisarius engaged in his first recorded military action, he was a "young man wearing his first beard." By 559, during Belisarius' last military action against Zabergan, the historian Agathias twice describes the retired general as already old. To satisfy these two conditions, modern historians have estimated that Belisarius must have been born in 500 or 505, and this seems like a reasonable range. This would make Belisarius perhaps around five years younger than Antonina. In the *Secret History*, Procopius insinuates that Antonina was much older than Belisarius, so it seems likely that she was at least somewhat older than him in order for this accusation to make sense to contemporaries. Throughout the *Secret History*, Procopius takes historical facts and exaggerates them for his invective purposes, and his description of the age difference between Belisarius and Antonina is likely one of those instances. Antonina was probably older than Belisarius, because she had to be to account for the children she bore before she met him, but she was unlikely to be much more than five years older than him.[15]

Belisarius first emerges into the historical record as a young man with an extremely advantageous position: one of the guardsmen of the General Justinian, the nephew of Emperor Justin I. How the young Belisarius progressed from a childhood in Germania to employment with the future emperor, one of the most important people in the entire Roman world, is unknown. Procopius mentions Belisarius first in 526, in the context of a raid into the Persian-controlled portion of Armenia, some 1,300 miles from his hometown. According to the author, the co-commanders of the raid were Belisarius and Sittas, both guardsmen of Justinian. The Greek term used by Procopius (*doruphóro*) to describe their title and the authority of the two men over the raiding party suggests that they were not merely rank-and-file guards in Justinian's personal unit, but officers of it. Guardsmen were known in Latin as *bucellarii* (biscuit-men, after the hard bread provided to soldiers) and were an important, if small, part of sixth-century armies. Some generals employed hundreds or even thousands of these guardsmen, using them for special operations, as messengers, and as crack troops to turn the tide of a battle. The seniority of Belisarius and Sittas in Justinian's guards in 526 could be an indication that they were not new at that time and had several years of experience already. Unfortunately, no evidence survives that indicates how early Belisarius might have joined the guards of Justinian. Had he been serving with the future emperor for years before this? Did he first join a regular army unit, only to get noticed by Justinian and invited to join his guardsmen at a later date? Such questions cannot be answered. We only know that, somehow, by 526, Belisarius was an officer of the guardsmen of the General Justinian, who was shortly to become emperor. In this capacity, Belisarius and his fellow officer Sittas led a raid into Persarmenia that was perhaps ordered directly by Justinian himself. The raid was a resounding success, in which Belisarius and Sittas plundered the land and seized many captives before returning to Roman territory. Inspired by the accomplishment, the two officers tried again later in the summer of the same year, but this time were confronted by a Persian army which defeated and repelled them. These two raids are described by Procopius with extreme concision, so it is impossible to gain any idea of the size of the force Belisarius and Sittas commanded or the details of the battle during the second raid. The historian's tantalizingly brief description of these two campaigns instead serves merely as a prelude of much more to come: Belisarius has arrived, fully formed and ready for action.[16]

It is possible that, in placing Belisarius and Sittas in command of these raids, Justinian was testing their fitness for more permanent, important

FIGURE 2 Soldiers, possibly guardsmen, detail from the imperial
panel of Justinian in San Vitale, Ravenna. Photo by Steven Zucker.

commands. Those would quickly follow. Sometime in the summer of 527,
Justinian appointed Belisarius Duke of Mesopotamia (*Dux Mesopotamiae*)
with his headquarters at the great Roman fortress city of Dara (today the village of Oğuz in southwestern Turkey). The date of this appointment is uncertain, but perhaps coincided with Justinian's own accession to sole rule
on August 1. With this command, Belisarius stepped out of the cocoon of
Justinian's unit of guardsmen into a significant role of his own. It was at this
time that the new duke selected Procopius as his legal adviser (*assessor*) and
personal secretary. Procopius would work with Belisarius for more than
a decade, following him from Mesopotamia to North Africa and Italy. His
job was primarily to maintain his employer's correspondence and ensure his
legal and literary respectability. If the quality of Procopius' writing in his later
histories is any indication, this he was well qualified to do.[17]

Belisarius and Antonina

By the time of his elevation to duke, Belisarius had perhaps already met and fallen in love with Antonina. Although neither Procopius nor any other source records their first meeting, it is most likely to have occurred in Constantinople in the 520s. Antonina's family is associated with two cities, Thessaloniki and Constantinople, but Belisarius is not recorded as ever visiting Thessaloniki. He would, however, have been in Constantinople frequently. For prior to his accession as emperor, Justinian was General of the Army in the Emperor's Presence (*magister militum praesentalis*). He probably commanded his army from Constantinople most of the time, which means that his personal guardsmen, including Belisarius, would have been with him in the capital on a regular basis. There, especially once Justinian married Theodora in 522 or 523, it is likely that the young guardsman Belisarius would have run into the future empress. If Antonina had sought out Theodora after the death of her first husband, then perhaps Belisarius and Antonina would have met through Theodora. This meeting is likely to have occurred sometime after 523 and before 527, when Belisarius began to spend much more of his time in Mesopotamia. It is possible, however, that Belisarius and Antonina could have met later, during one of Belisarius' returns to Constantinople, which could possibly have taken place as frequently as every winter he was stationed at Dara. There is not enough information to be certain.[18]

The date of the wedding of Belisarius and Antonina is as unknown as the date of their first meeting. The direct evidence of Procopius is only sufficient to provide a terminus ante quem: the two had to be married by no later than June 533, when they set sail on the expedition to northern Africa. That is the earliest date at which Procopius attests that Belisarius and Antonina were husband and wife. There are reasons to suspect that the pair married well before 533, however. Most importantly, it is difficult to reconcile the estimated ages of Antonina's son, Photios, and the couple's daughter, Ioannina, with a marriage later than 530. As mentioned earlier, Photios was born around 520 at latest, but needed to be young enough when Belisarius married Antonina that Belisarius could plausibly claim to have raised him. Similarly, Ioannina's birth is estimated to have taken place around 531. It is possible that the marriage of Belisarius' comrade-in-arms, Sittas, also points to a wedding for Belisarius and Antonina in the late 520s. In 528, Sittas married Komito, the older sister of the Empress Theodora. This wedding is reported by the chronicler John Malalas, who also records that in the same year Justinian appointed Sittas General of Armenia (*magister militum per Armeniam*). The marriage to

Komito firmly allied Sittas with Theodora and, by extension, with Justinian. Perhaps Theodora arranged this marriage personally. The combination of the marriage alliance and the promotion to the rank of General of Armenia may indicate that Sittas was the more celebrated of Justinian's two former guardsmen at the time. Although no source similarly records the wedding of Belisarius and Antonina, it could have taken place in the same year as that of Sittas (528), or perhaps a year earlier (527) at the same time that Belisarius was appointed Duke of Mesopotamia, which would have mirrored Sittas earning promotion and marrying in the same year.[19]

Whenever Belisarius wed Antonina, it is almost certain that it was a match of love. The swaggering, young duke was a man of great importance in the Roman world. He had close ties to the emperor, had already earned an appointment of significance in the army, and could expect preferment to even more exalted commands in the future. He could have sought a profitable marriage alliance with one of the wealthy, elite families living in Constantinople, or perhaps tried to hold out for a marriage into the imperial family itself. Antonina, although she would later prove to be a worthy match for Belisarius, would not at the time have been considered an amazing catch by contemporaries. Her ancestry was undistinguished, her parents were merely entertainers, and she was widowed with at least two children. Antonina may already have by this point become a close friend of Theodora, which could be seen as advantageous, and perhaps the empress even encouraged the match. But since Belisarius had a close relationship with Justinian from before his accession to the throne, this could hardly have been a deciding factor in his pursuit of her hand. Belisarius simply did not need Antonina's connection to Theodora at this time. So, it was likely that Antonina had little to recommend herself according to the traditional beliefs of the time. However, elite Roman men of the period were beginning to make a habit of "marrying down," deliberately wedding women who did not have influential families that could challenge them. In choosing Antonina, Belisarius was in good company, as Justinian chose Theodora and Sittas chose Komito. This would suggest that Belisarius marrying Antonina was not at all beyond the pale. Still, it was more likely to have been motivated by love rather than political or financial considerations. Beyond this logic, the love match of Belisarius and Antonina is confirmed by Procopius, although the author sometimes frames it as a negative. Throughout the *Secret History*, he rails about Belisarius' attachment to Antonina on multiple occasions, complaining that Belisarius was "so infatuated" with her. In the *Wars*, Procopius puts it more kindly, praising Belisarius for possessing "self-restraint to an extraordinary degree, so that he never touched any woman other than his wife." Although these statements only show the tie of affection running in one direction, it seems likely that Antonina and Belisarius very much loved each other. If Belisarius "proved" his love by marrying Antonina when his situation was so much better than hers, then Antonina "proved" her love by spending a lifetime traveling with Belisarius to far-flung military postings around the Roman world, as we will see in the coming chapters.[20]

Belisarius and Antonina had a remarkable and durable love story, comparable to that which Justinian and Theodora themselves shared. Indeed, perhaps the similarities in their marital situations strengthened the bonds of the two couples with each other. Justinian and Belisarius were both military officers from rural areas of the Balkans, and Theodora and Antonina were both urban-dwellers and daughters of entertainers. It might be that the same imperial law that legalized the marriage of Justinian and Theodora also made possible the union of Belisarius and Antonina. Far more united the two couples than divided them. This was the beginning of a remarkable, quadripartite alliance that would enable the four of them to rule the Roman world and rack up impressive achievements over the course of the next 20 years or so. For Belisarius and Antonina, their wedding and their blossoming friendships with the imperial couple were the beginning of something extraordinary. Their partnership would see them use their considerable skills to catapult themselves to extreme heights of success, and their egregious mistakes would cast them to seemingly insurmountable lows.[21]

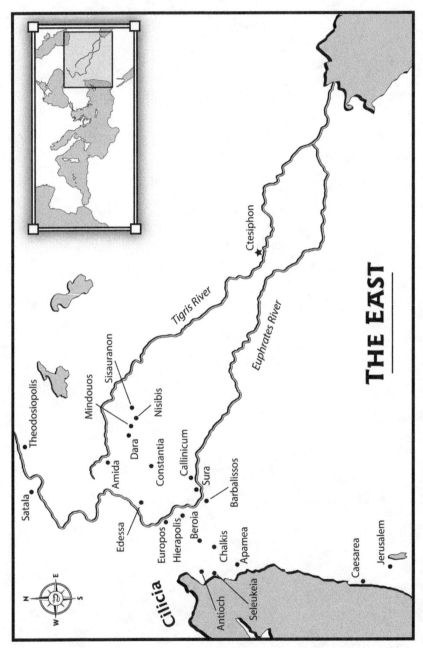

THE EAST

Cilicia

Satala
Theodosiopolis
Amida
Edessa
Europos
Hierapolis
Beroia
Antioch
Seleukeia
Chalkis
Apamea
Mindouos
Sisauranon
Dara
Nisibis
Constantia
Callinicum
Sura
Barballissos
Caesarea
Jerusalem
Ctesiphon

Tigris River
Euphrates River

N
E
S
W

MAP 2 The East: an overview of the Roman/Persian Mesopotamian frontier. Created by John Wyatt Greenlee.

2

General of the East

WHEN HE ASSUMED his command at Dara in Mesopotamia in 527, Belisarius was taking on a major role in an international relationship, at times peaceful and at times violent, that was already quite ancient. With the annexation of Syria by Pompey in 63 BC, the Romans staked out a claim in the Near East. The ruling power of Mesopotamia and Iran at the time was the kingdom of Parthia, the army of which soundly defeated the Roman general Crassus at the Battle of Carrhae in 53 BC. Thus began centuries of intermittent conflict, separated by long and prosperous periods of peace. When the Sassanian dynasty replaced the Parthians in 224 AD, they inherited the Parthians' contentious relationship with the Romans. The conflict reached a crescendo in 363, when the Emperor Julian led a Roman army to the walls of the Persian capital, Ctesiphon, but was subsequently killed in battle. To extricate the survivors of his army, his successor Jovian agreed to a peace treaty dictated by the Persian King Shapur II, in which the Romans ceded the vital Mesopotamian frontier city of Nisibis to the Persians. This proved, surprisingly, the basis for a durable peace. For most of the next century and a half, the Roman and Persian Empires maintained a respectful and peaceful relationship, punctuated only by occasional, very brief outbursts of violence, as their monarchs focused on matters elsewhere. This peace was at last ended in 502, when an overwhelming need for money to pay off the neighboring Hepthalite Huns seems to have pushed the Persian King Kavad into launching an invasion of Roman territory. The Persian army captured both Theodosiopolis in Roman Armenia, and Amida in Roman Mesopotamia. For the next couple of years Romans and Persians fought over control of Amida. The Romans won the city back in peace negotiations in 505. It was during these negotiations that the Romans began construction of a major new frontier fortress at Dara, about 16 miles northwest of Nisibis. Dara was completed by 508 or 509, and

Belisarius & Antonina. David Alan Parnell, Oxford University Press. © Oxford University Press 2023.
DOI: 10.1093/oso/9780197574706.003.0003

at that time became the headquarters of the Duke of Mesopotamia and the seat of a bishop. It was a large fortress city, and could serve both as a base of offensive operations against Persian Nisibis, and to coordinate Roman defenses in Mesopotamia. The peace negotiations were finished in 506, and a cessation of hostilities for seven years was agreed. For the next 20 years, there was peace in Mesopotamia. Although the truce technically expired in 513, neither side moved to renew hostilities immediately. Kavad was preoccupied and Roman fortifications in Mesopotamia, including the new fortress at Dara, were now formidable, which made combat there less appealing to the Persians. But renewed conflict became more likely in the 520s, when the Roman Emperor Justin I, the uncle of Justinian, refused to adopt Khusro, the son of Kavad. The Persian king had sought this adoption to guarantee Khusro's succession, so the refusal of Justin rankled. At roughly the same time, formerly Persian client kingdoms Lazica and Iberia in the Caucasus edged closer to Christianity and Roman influence, further irritating Kavad.[1]

It was in this context that Belisarius and Sittas raided Persian Armenia in 526. Perhaps their raids were intended to relieve Persian pressure on the Lazicans and Iberians. In the summer of the next year, the General Libelarios led a contingent of Roman soldiers from Dara in a foray into Persian territory around Nisibis, perhaps in response to Arab allies of the Persian king raiding in the region. He withdrew without accomplishing anything of significance and was quickly dismissed by Justinian. Shortly after this, Belisarius was appointed Duke of Mesopotamia (*Dux Mesopotamiae*), as related in the previous chapter. The position was one of considerable importance in the structure of the Roman army. He commanded the frontier soldiers (*limitanei*) of a province or grouping of provinces, in this case that of Mesopotamia. Frontier soldiers were not always of the same experience and quality as the more prestigious soldiers of the field armies (*comitatenses*), but they were still trained and professional soldiers that were vital for the defense of the borders of the empire. As Duke of Mesopotamia, Belisarius might have commanded some 9,500 of these soldiers. It was a significant command for the young officer, and an indication of the trust Justinian had in his judgment.[2]

The situation vis-à-vis the Persians that Belisarius inherited at Dara is a little opaque to us, although it must have been much clearer to him. He assumed command at a time when there was no official peace with Persia (it had expired in 513), but there was not yet exactly open warfare either. It seems as if the Roman and Persian military forces were both testing each other out, and awaiting orders from their sovereigns to engage in full-scale conflict. If the political and military situation was uncertain, at least Belisarius and his soldiers had a solid base from which to operate. By this time, Dara was nearly 20 years old. It was a large, strong fortress, and the key to the Roman frontier with Persia in Mesopotamia. This did not mean, however, that the Romans could not further improve their line of fortifications in Mesopotamia to deter Persian aggression. The impetus for further building in this area seems to have come directly from the new Emperor Justinian. In spring 528, Belisarius, at Justinian's command, set miners and craftsmen to work on constructing a new fortification at Mindouos, about 4 miles southeast of Dara. The location was significant: it straddled the road between Roman Dara and Persian Nisibis.[3]

The construction at Mindouos might have been intended as a fortlet or might have just been a watch tower, but either way it would provide the Romans with additional security for Dara in this contested region in the event of all-out war. For this very reason, the Persians were keen to prevent the completion of the project, and they warned the Romans to cease construction or face attack. When the project at Mindouos continued, perhaps in summer 528, the Persians attempted to intervene by sending a substantial army across the frontier. Having been forewarned, Justinian dispatched reinforcements to Belisarius: Proclianos, Duke of Phoenice (modern Lebanon), and Koutzes and Bouzes, brothers and Dukes of Phoenice Libanensis (modern Syria), presumably each with their own armies. There followed a fierce battle in which the Romans tried to defend the construction site at Mindouos, while the

FIGURE 3 The road leading south out of Dara. Photo by Alexander Sarantis.

Persians strove to drive off the Romans. Malalas records that the Persian army numbered 30,000 soldiers. While this might be an exaggeration, it indicates that this was perhaps a major battle, although no source offers the number of soldiers the Romans brought to bear. The battle went poorly for the Romans, who were routed. Proclianos was killed, while Koutzes and many others were captured by the Persians. Belisarius, Bouzes, and others survived by fleeing, presumably back to the safety of Dara. With the Roman army defeated and dispersed, the Persians easily destroyed the construction site at Mindouos, and then returned to Persian territory.[4]

There is no doubt that the Battle of Mindouos was a fiasco for the Romans: they were soundly defeated and had to give up their new fortification to boot. However, it is not clear who exactly is to blame because it is not easy to determine who was in command at this battle. It was perhaps Belisarius, who was after all the local duke, but it is not certain that he would have outranked the other dukes who had come to his support. If the officers could not agree on who was in charge, it is possible they shared a joint command. Although Justinian was probably not pleased to learn of the Roman loss in battle, he might not have been surprised to learn that the fortification work at Mindouos had not succeeded: he was perhaps aware that it would have been very difficult to construct a fortlet there in the face of active Persian intervention. It seems likely that, either way, Justinian did not blame Belisarius for this failure, for the emperor now chose to promote Belisarius yet again.[5]

In April 529, Belisarius was appointed General of the East (*magister militum per Orientem*). This was a post of great importance. At the time, there were only four generals of the field armies with defined regional commands in the entire Roman Empire: the generals of the East, Armenia, Thrace, and Illyricum, and two generals for the armies in the emperor's presence. As one of the six top generals of the Roman world, Belisarius was now moving in rarified air indeed. The General of the East, stationed at the time at Antioch, commanded 20,000 field army soldiers and was responsible for the region stretching from Egypt all the way north to Armenia. This increase in responsibility came with a corresponding jump in salary: the General of the East received pay about seven times as high as a duke. In his new office, Belisarius would earn about 11,500 *nomismata* (gold coins) per year. For comparison, a poverty-level wage in Constantinople at around this time was about 5 *nomismata* per year. By any standard, Belisarius now became quite wealthy, just from his military salary alone. The trajectory of Belisarius' career to this point is worth emphasizing. In the span of two years, he had gone from guardsman of the General Justinian, to Duke of Mesopotamia and then General of the East under the Emperor Justinian. To say this was a meteoric rise for a man who was probably still under 30 would be an understatement. At the same time, it was not unprecedented, even in his own time. Belisarius' companion-in-arms, Sittas, who had served among the guardsmen of Justinian as well, had become General of Armenia the year before in 528, a similarly swift rise to prominence. It is clear that the new Emperor Justinian trusted both Belisarius and Sittas, and it is likely that their promotions were the result of considera-tion of several years of their service to the emperor when he was a general (of which we are only partially aware), rather than only the result of the campaigns immediately preceding their promotions (for Belisarius, that of Mindouos). There is also a sense that Justinian was sweeping away an older generation of generals and replacing them with the men who had served him before his accession, whom he felt he could trust implicitly. In the case of Belisarius, he was replacing as General of the East Hypatios, one of the nephews of the old Emperor Anastasios (r. 491–518), who had held the post throughout much of the 520s. Hypatios had done little to check the raids of the Arab allies of the Persian king in the past two years and had been conspicuously absent from the Battle of Mindouos. Justinian probably expected Belisarius to be a more vigorous opponent to Persia and its allies.[6]

It is most likely that Belisarius traveled to Constantinople in early 529 in order to receive his new command. While no contemporary source explicitly records this journey, it can be inferred from the nature of the office of the General of the East. All of the regional generals of the field army held illus-trious (*illustris*) rank in the Roman senate by virtue of their military office. Illustrious appointments were made via imperial codicil—a document signed personally by the emperor. Because of the high rank conferred by his position, it is likely that Belisarius received his commission from Justinian in person, in a formal imperial audience. While it might seem improvident of Belisarius to have left Dara to visit Constantinople during this dangerous time after his defeat at Mindouos, the travel was facilitated by the unusually harsh winter of 528/529. This caused the Romans and Persians in Mesopotamia to agree to a suspension of hostilities over the winter, as each side hunkered down against the cold. It is likely that Belisarius only departed Dara and traveled to Constantinople after this agreement occurred. Simultaneously, Justinian dispatched several senators with their own guardsmen from Constantinople to garrison cities in the region, including Amida, Edessa, and Constantia. Belisarius was, therefore, able to enjoy his sojourn in Constantinople and the pomp of his promotion without having to worry too much about the state of the eastern front in his absence.[7]

The short stay of Belisarius in Constantinople provides us with a welcome opportunity to check in on his wife, Antonina. To be fair, neither Procopius nor any other source records Antonina's location or activity during this period. In fact, for her life between Procopius' brief remarks about her parentage and childhood in the *Secret History* (discussed in the previous chapter), and his description of her departure with Belisarius on a voyage to North Africa (discussed in the next chapter), there is no mention of her in any source whatsoever. However, using what is known of the rest of her life as circumstantial evidence, it is possible to deduce what Antonina was doing in the late 520s after her marriage to Belisarius. It is highly likely that Antonina was residing in Constantinople while Belisarius was Duke of Mesopotamia and during his early tenure as General of the East. This may be inferred from the fact that, starting in 533, Procopius explicitly noted that Antonina accompanied Belisarius on all of his far-flung military campaigns, to the extent that the historian could exclaim "she made a point of accompanying him to the ends of the earth." Yet, for the period between 527 and 531, Procopius makes no mention of Antonina being with Belisarius at Dara. So it is reasonable to assume, then, that Antonina was not with Belisarius during this period. If she was not with Belisarius, then she was most likely residing in Constantinople, where we know the couple had at least one home by 541, and there is no reason to think they did not purchase it or another earlier. Perhaps they moved into their first home in Constantinople shortly after their wedding and before Belisarius reported to Dara, and Antonina remained there.[8]

So much then for where Antonina was during this period, but it is also worth considering why she was in Constantinople instead of accompanying Belisarius, as would later become her defining tradition. The most likely reason that Antonina was not accompanying Belisarius, and that Procopius does not mention her whereabouts, is that she was dealing with personal, family issues at the time that did not impinge upon the public history Procopius was writing in the *Wars* or provide evidence of Antonina's supposed deviancy that Procopius could use in the *Secret History*. Likely, Antonina was pregnant at some time during the period 527–531. This fits, roughly, the timeline in which she would have needed to be pregnant and give birth to her daughter with Belisarius, Ioannina. As mentioned in Chapter 1, Ioannina cannot have been older than 12 in 543, which would place her birth at earliest in 531. She might possibly have been born as late as the end of 532, but it is unlikely for her to have been born any later than that: for in June 533, Antonina was able to accompany Belisarius to North Africa. It is unlikely that she would have taken this voyage while pregnant, or if she had very recently given birth, which would imply she had given birth to Ioannina early enough to have fully recovered and been able to hand her daughter over to a wet nurse when she departed in 533. This suggests that this blank period in Antonina's life, between her marriage to Belisarius in 527 or 528, and her departure with Belisarius to North Africa in 533, is one in which she gave birth to Ioannina.[9]

Of course, even taking the smaller bounds proposed here (marriage in 528 and birth of Ioannina in 531), three years is still more time than is needed for Antonina to have a single pregnancy and birth. Perhaps Antonina and Belisarius wrestled with infertility during this period, or Antonina struggled to carry her pregnancy to term. A sequence of pregnancies and miscarriages might explain why Antonina was sidelined in Constantinople throughout these years, while Belisarius built his reputation in the east. That Antonina would eventually succeed in giving birth to Ioannina (perhaps in 531 or 532) would not have made these first couple years of her marriage to Belisarius any easier. Antonina would have had to live without Belisarius for significant stretches of time, and based on what we know of her travels with him later this must have been undesirable to her. She also would have had to raise her children from her previous marriage, Photios and her unnamed daughter, all while struggling with her own fertility with Belisarius. This was a lot for a mother to deal with, although the difficulty was probably eased by the substantial wealth she and Belisarius now possessed. Antonina would have been able to hire many servants or, more darkly but just as likely, buy many domestic slaves to help ensure that the household functioned and her children were well educated. Domestic slaves in this period filled many roles, from wet nurses to tutors, all of which would have helped Antonina to manage the family and household. Speaking of those children from her previous marriage, one more potential domestic activity for Antonina during this period was marrying off her unnamed daughter, perhaps to Ildiger, and becoming a grandmother. Procopius claims that Antonina had a granddaughter of marriageable age in 545, which would mean that granddaughter had to be born at the latest in 533. This would imply that the unnamed daughter of Antonina, who would give birth to this granddaughter, must have married sometime in this period. So in addition to raising Photios, managing the household, and trying to get pregnant with Belisarius and give birth to Ioannina, Antonina was likely also trying to help her daughter transition into married life and later motherhood. She clearly had her hands full during the time that Belisarius was at Dara as Duke of Mesopotamia and later General of the East, which is more than enough explanation for why she was unable to accompany him there. Just as we have used the short stay of Belisarius in Constantinople when he was promoted to General of the East in April 529 as an opportunity to check on Antonina, so we can imagine that the new general gladly availed himself of the opportunity to spend some nights at home with his wife during this visit. Belisarius is unlikely to have followed the virtuous example of Uriah the Hittite and refused to spend the night with Antonina during this time, given the stresses that she was under and the responsibilities she was shouldering. More than this, if the pair really were struggling with infertility, it is possible to imagine that Belisarius spent the majority of the winter in Constantinople with Antonina, and perhaps returned each subsequent winter as his duties allowed him.[10]

The Battle of Dara

After a winter spent with Antonina and the exuberant emotional high of his dramatic promotion to General of the East in Justinian's presence, Belisarius would have returned to the east to assume his new command in late spring 529. He perhaps traveled with Hermogenes, the Master of Offices (*magister officiorum*), who we know arrived in Antioch on May 12, 529, on his way to the Persian court to negotiate a cessation of hostilities. The Romans had no desire for an intensive war with Persia at the moment, so there is every reason to believe that Hermogenes' mission to Kavad was genuine. When Hermogenes met with Kavad in July 529, the king made his demands: the Romans would give the Persians a sum of gold, or the Persian army would attack. The Persian king set a limit of one year for the payment to arrive. This served as a de facto additional one-year truce while Hermogenes brought this demand before Justinian, and no military conflicts emerged for the remainder of 529. This provided Belisarius with the chance to assemble his officers and meet his troops, the Army of the East, at Antioch. The city had just the year before been ravaged by an earthquake, so perhaps the general was also involved in the recovery operations as well. Beyond this, Belisarius and his army probably passed the summer of 529 in drills and gathering the arms and supplies needed to wage all-out war with the Persians. As General of the East, Belisarius was certainly now aware, if he had not been before, of the attempted negotiations with Kavad and had perhaps been advised to prepare as if the negotiations would fail.[11]

In the spring of 530, if not before, Justinian instructed Belisarius to march to Dara in preparation for war with Persia. The young general gathered together the Army of the East and marched to his old stomping grounds in Mesopotamia. This order anticipated war, for Justinian had decided not to send a payment to Kavad, and the one-year deadline set by the Persian king was approaching. Yet, Justinian still hoped to have peace without having to pay for it, and so he simultaneously sent an envoy named Rouphinos to further negotiate with Kavad if possible. Hermogenes, meanwhile, was ordered to travel with Belisarius and the Army of the East to Dara. Procopius says that Hermogenes' orders were "to set the army in order" with Belisarius. This is often interpreted to mean that Belisarius and Hermogenes shared the command of the army, and perhaps they did in terms of logistics and organizational matters, but it is unlikely that Hermogenes had input into strategic, let alone tactical, decisions. The arrival of the Army of the East at Dara caused considerable panic on the Persian side of the frontier. It was probably seen, not without justification, as a provocation. Beyond this, it must have been obvious that no payment from Justinian was forthcoming. Given the evident failure of Justinian to meet the demand, and the provocation of the army assembling on the doorstep of the frontier, the Persians decided to pre-empt whatever the Romans had planned and invade Roman territory. Procopius reports that the Persians planned to capture Dara, which would have given them a considerable bargaining chip in forcing Justinian to accede to their earlier wishes for a payment. A large Persian army under the command of Peroz set out from Nisibis in June 530 and crossed into Roman territory, eventually camping at Ammodios, some five miles south of Dara. Upon receiving word of this invasion, Belisarius immediately began to prepare by having his soldiers dig a defensive trench about a mile and a half south of Dara. It is possible that the walls of Dara were undergoing repairs at the time, and therefore Belisarius deemed it better to fight the battle in the open rather than undergo a siege in the city. The general perhaps ordered the digging of the trench as a way to support the infantry in his army, who might have been nervous about engaging the Persians in a pitched battle. By contrast, the Persians were confident, which Procopius illustrates by claiming that Peroz instructed Belisarius to prepare him a bath inside of Dara, so that the Persian general could relax there the following day.[12]

In the morning, the Persians advanced from their camp to the Roman position south of Dara. Procopius reports, probably with a little exaggeration, that the Persian army numbered 40,000. On the other side, Belisarius had assembled 25,000 men, probably some combination of the Army of the

FIGURE 4 The ruins of the fortifications of Dara. Photo by Alexander Sarantis.

East and his old frontier soldiers from the Ducate of Mesopotamia. Typically, Procopius does not provide a specific breakdown of this army's composition, but does name its command officers. Bouzes, who had fought with Belisarius at Mindouos, took up the Roman left wing, commanding an unknown number of cavalry. With him on the left was Pharas the Herul, who would go on to fight with Belisarius on other campaigns, commanding 300 of his countrymen (a Germanic people who lived north of the Danube), presumably also outfitted as cavalry. On the center-left, just ahead of the trenches, were stationed the commanders Sounikas and Aigan, with 600 cavalry, all Massagetae Huns. The center was probably manned primarily by infantry, all standing behind the trench for added safety from Persian charges. Behind the infantry, Belisarius and Hermogenes had stationed themselves, presumably with their own guardsmen units, to act as a reserve. The right wing of the Roman army was a mirror image of the left, although with many more officers. Procopius reports that the cavalry of the right wing were commanded by John (the son of Niketas), Kyrillos, Markellos, Germanos, and Dorotheos. The center-right, just ahead of the trenches, was held by more Huns: Simmas and Askan, with another 600 cavalry. Perhaps Belisarius intended to halt a potential attack by the Persian center with the infantry-manned trenches, allowing for his cavalry to sweep in from the Roman wings. Peroz, seeking to test the strength of the Roman formation, dispatched a contingent of cavalry to charge into the Roman left wing, perhaps an indication that the left wing was undersized compared to the right. Bouzes and Pharas with their men gave way to the charge, pulling back. When the Persian contingent declined to pursue them, Bouzes and Pharas' cavalry wheeled back around and fell on the Persian soldiers, causing them to flee back to the main Persian formation. This small skirmish left seven dead Persians and no dead Romans, according to Procopius. This was the extent of the large-scale conflict for the day. However, perhaps seeking a morale boost, a Persian champion rode out from the ranks and issued a challenge to the Roman army for a man to come out and duel him. None of the Roman soldiers was willing to answer the challenge of this Persian Goliath, according to Procopius, but a wrestling trainer named Andreas, who was present as an attendant for Bouzes, stepped out to accept. He easily slew the Persian champion, and then when another stepped out to take his place, Andreas slew him as well. The Persian army then broke formation and retreated back to its camp at Ammodios, and the Romans sang a victory song. This ended the first day of the Battle of Dara.[13]

On the second day, Peroz was strengthened by the arrival of an additional 10,000 soldiers who had marched to Ammodios from Nisibis. This brought the total Persian force to 50,000, according to Procopius, although we must be cautious with this number, which is probably inflated to make Belisarius' achievement more impressive. Belisarius and Peroz exchanged letters, with Belisarius urging the Persian general to withdraw to Persian territory and to allow the Roman envoy Rouphinos to speak with Kavad. Peroz refused, and both generals prepared their armies for battle the next day.[14]

The third day of the Battle of Dara was to be decisive. Belisarius addressed his soldiers in the morning as they prepared. The speech, preserved by Procopius, betrays the anxiety of the Roman soldiers, and perhaps of their commander, by acknowledging that the Romans had been defeated by the Persians before, but attempts to soothe any concern by belittling the Persian infantry as "a crowd of pitiful peasants." Belisarius urged the soldiers to "heed the orders given," suggesting that this will lead them to victory. If accurate, and it should be since Procopius himself probably helped to draft the speech, this showed considerable confidence on the part of Belisarius, who had so far as we know never commanded a force in a battle of this size, let alone won a battle of this size. After the speech, Belisarius lined up his forces along the trench south of Dara just as they had been on the first day, with one small change: Pharas, at his own request, was stationed with his 300 men behind a small hill on the far left of the Roman formation. When the Persians arrived, they drew up across from the Roman formation, with Peroz stationed in the center, and commanders named Pityaxes and Vareshman by Procopius in charge of the Persian right and left, respectively. For several hours, the two forces stared at each other. At noon, the Persians began the battle by drawing near and firing arrows. The Romans responded by firing their arrows as well. The wind blew steadily into the face of the Persian formation, which blunted the effectiveness of their arrow fire. As on day one, the hand-to-hand fighting began on the Roman left. The Persian right wing under Pityaxes attacked Bouzes on the Roman left, and his forces, as on day one, began to fall back. As probably planned in advance, Sounikas and Aigan then charged into the flank of the Persian right wing as it pursued Bouzes' retreating forces. At the same time, Pharas and the Heruls stampeded down the hill that had hidden them and fell onto the rear of the Persian right wing. Surrounded by Roman units, the Persian right wing disintegrated. Some 3,000 men were cut down, and the rest fled back to the Persian center for support. Peroz, meanwhile, had strengthened the unused Persian left wing with the Immortals, his best soldiers. Before he could order the new attack, Belisarius and Hermogenes perceived this change, but made only relatively modest preparation: Sounikas and Aigan, with their 600 cavalry, were ordered to break off from the engagement on the Roman left, and come to join Simmas and Askan, with their 600 cavalry, on the Roman center-right. Soon thereafter, Vareshman led the Persian left, with the Immortals, in a charge into the Roman right wing, which collapsed under the pressure. But as with the earlier attack on the other side of the formation, Belisarius' preparations proved more than sufficient. Sounikas, Aigan, Simmas, and Askan, with 1,200 Hunnic cavalry, immediately charged into the flank of the Persian wing and were followed by the guardsmen of Belisarius. The Persian wing was essentially cleaved in two, and the fighting became fierce around the portion that was nearly encircled now by the Romans. Sounikas slew Vareshman's standard-bearer, and then Vareshman himself. The Persians in this contingent were then thrown into confusion and fled, but not before the Romans had killed 5,000 of them. It seems that the flight of the Persian left snowballed into a general rout of the entire Persian army. Procopius records with particular glee that the much-maligned Persian infantry threw down their shields in the flight and were ruthlessly cut down by Roman pursuers. After a short pursuit, Belisarius ordered his men to break off and return to formation, unwilling to risk them stringing out and being vulnerable to a potential counterattack. The remains of the Persian army limped back to its camp at Ammodios. For Belisarius and the Romans, this was a resounding victory. Not only had the Romans won, they had won convincingly: Procopius claims that Peroz had lost more than half of his soldiers in the battle. It had been a century since the Romans had defeated the Persian army on the field in such fashion. Thus, in a day, Belisarius had made his reputation as a battlefield commander. Dara was safe, the Persians were in retreat, and Belisarius' star was rising.[15]

While Belisarius was winning decisively at Dara, his former companion and now fellow general, Sittas, was winning a victory of his own to the north in Roman Armenia. Sittas had recently been promoted to General of the Army in the Emperor's Presence, a command Justinian had held before his accession to the throne. In that capacity, he was in Armenia assisting the new General of Armenia, Dorotheos, to resist Persian encroachment. Near the time of the invasion of Peroz in Mesopotamia, another Persian army under Mihr-Mihroe invaded Roman territory from Persian Armenia, bringing 30,000 soldiers. The Romans under Sittas and Dorotheos had only about 15,000 men. While Dorotheos and the majority of the army stayed behind the walls of the city of Satala (modern Sadak, Turkey), Sittas and 1,000 cavalry hid behind a small hill nearby. As the Persian army approached and began to encircle Satala, Sittas and his men charged from behind the hill and hit the Persians in the rear, and Dorotheos and his men charged out from the city. The ensuing battle was fierce, but the Romans eventually claimed the victory and forced the Persians to withdraw to their camp. This is an indication that the triumph of Belisarius at Dara, while impressive, did not occur in a vacuum—at least one other Roman general on the Persian front was also performing well at the time, using tactics that were relatively similar.[16]

The Battle of Callinicum

The defeats suffered by the Persians brought Kavad back to the bargaining table in August 530. While the Roman ambassador Rouphinos blamed the Persians for the war, citing their invasions, the Persian king blamed the Romans for building the fortress of Dara (over 20 years ago) as a threat to the Persians. Kavad did, however, admit that he would again be willing to conclude a peace if the Romans paid him off. Justinian pondered the offer in the fall of 530 and dispatched Rouphinos back to the Persian king near the end of the year. At about the same time, Belisarius was in the east questioning some Samaritans (inhabitants of what is today northern Israel), who had been captured when crossing the border from Persia into Roman territory. The general discovered that the Samaritans had just been with Kavad, telling him of a Samaritan revolt that would give the Persian king control of Roman Palestine. Perhaps because of this, Kavad had changed his mind by the time Rouphinos returned to him at the end of 530. The Persian king decided to continue the war, either relying upon a Samaritan revolt or else hoping for a quick victory to allow him to negotiate from a stronger position. Kavad therefore commanded another Persian invasion of Roman territory in early spring 531.[17]

The new Persian incursion took a different route than the previous year, perhaps an indication that the Persian army had found Mesopotamia too well defended for their liking. On the advice of the Arab leader al-Mundhir, a Persian army under the command of Azarethes instead advanced north from Persian territory along the Euphrates into the Roman province of Euphratesia. Azarethes and al-Mundhir commanded an army about 20,000 strong, consisting entirely of cavalry, which suggests that their aim was to plunder rather than capture fortresses. The Persian army made it some distance before Belisarius was alerted. The general responded promptly, leaving some of his forces in Mesopotamia to guard against any Persian attack there, and moving westward with 8,000 men, which included 5,000 Arab allies under al-Harith. The relatively small size of this force is an indication that Belisarius brought only cavalry from Dara, in order to catch up to the Persian army as quickly as possible. At the same time, and no doubt at Belisarius' order, the dukes of the surrounding provinces also converged on the Euphrates with their own forces. Hermogenes, sent out from Constantinople by the emperor once again, also arrived in the area, perhaps in early April 531. Belisarius, Hermogenes, the dukes, and their troops moved to converge on Barbalissos (modern Qala'at Balis, Syria), again, most likely on the order of Belisarius, who as General of the East had the responsibility for coordinating this united defense. Once they were all assembled, Belisarius had about 20,000 soldiers under his command, a mix of his cavalry from the Army of the East, the Roman Arab allies of al-Harith, and the forces of the local dukes. Procopius reports that the cavalry commanders with Belisarius were the same as the ones at the Battle of Dara, so presumably they included the four commanders of the Hunnic cavalry and Pharas the Herul. Sounikas is named by Malalas as a duke, so perhaps he had been promoted to Duke of Euphratesia.[18]

The chronology of the campaign is unclear, because the two primary accounts, that of Procopius and Malalas, are at odds on many of the details. Only Malalas describes the beginning stages of the campaign. He relates that the Persian army, under Azarethes and al-Mundhir, penetrated to Gabbulon, northwest of Barbalissos and on the road to Antioch. The Persian forces sacked the town. Here, before they joined Belisarius at Barbalissos, Sounikas and his forces launched a surprise attack on a portion of the Persian army, killing some and alerting the Persians to the growing Roman response.

Perhaps at the same time, Belisarius' forces had reached Chalkis (modern Qinnasrin, Syria), primarily to prevent the Persians from continuing west toward Antioch. This caused the Persians to turn north. Belisarius and his forces therefore marched east to the Euphrates, meeting up with Hermogenes, the dukes, and their forces at Barbalissos. Belisarius there chastised Sounikas for attacking the Persians without orders. Although Hermogenes attempted to mediate between Belisarius and Sounikas, their argument presaged a growing divide between the general and his officers that would prove fatal to the campaign. However, for the moment, all of the forced marches of Belisarius and the dukes seem to be paying off. The Roman army was now positioned to cut off the Persian army deep inside Roman territory, a prospect that Azarethes and al-Mundhir did not find appealing. The Persian army therefore turned around and began to retreat south and east along the southern bank of the Euphrates, heading back toward Persian territory. One more forced march brought the entire Roman host to the north of the Persian army, about one day's travel behind it, and so for several days the Romans shadowed the Persian army as it withdrew. Procopius makes clear that this was an intentional choice on the part of Belisarius, who thought it sufficient to drive the Persians out of Roman territory without risking an open battle. However, this strategy did not appeal to everyone in the Roman army. The Persians had, after all, just plundered and sacked their way through Euphratesia and into Syria, so some Romans no doubt felt that vengeance must be exacted. Confidence was perhaps also overly high, given the victory at Dara the previous year. According to Procopius, all the soldiers and officers of the army badgered Belisarius to overtake the Persians and offer battle. This is likely an exaggeration to excuse Belisarius' eventual caving in to the demand. While it was probably not all the soldiers, it does seem likely that the principal dukes and officers must have voiced this demand, indeed probably the very same men who had helped Belisarius win at Dara such as Sounikas and Simmas. While Procopius maintains that Hermogenes agreed with Belisarius' more cautious strategy, perhaps he switched his opinion and joined those clamoring for battle, leaving Belisarius isolated. Belisarius attempted to defend his strategy in a speech, outlining the risks of battle, and asking why it was worth undertaking those risks when the Persians were already retreating anyway. But according to Procopius, both soldiers and officers responded to the speech by mutinously abusing Belisarius to his face and demanding to fight. Belisarius, perhaps fearing that the dukes would instigate their own attack, as Sounikas already had, if he continued to remain steadfast, caved to the demand and prepared for battle.[19]

With one more march, the Roman army caught up to the Persian force on the southern bank of the Euphrates, across the river from Callinicum (modern Ar Raqqah, Syria). The date was April 19, 531. It happened to be Holy Saturday, and many in the Roman army, including Belisarius, had been fasting since Good Friday, the day before. Procopius makes a point of this in a speech he places in the mouth of Belisarius, in which the general admits "all of us are fasting." If not meant rhetorically, this is a clue to the depth of Belisarius' faith: fasting while on campaign cannot have been easy. All of this meant it was not a propitious day to force a battle, but Belisarius nevertheless led the army into one. Belisarius drew his army up in formation at a 90-degree angle to the Euphrates. The Romans' Arab allies under al-Harith were on the far right, with some untested infantry next to them, and Ascan's Hunnic cavalry in the center right. On the far left, closest to the river, were more infantry under the command of Peter, a guardsman of Justinian, and on the center left were Sounikas and Simmas with their forces. Belisarius held the center with the cavalry he had brought from Dara. This formation has been interpreted as the reverse of the tactics at Dara: here at Callinicum, Belisarius hoped the center would hold even if the forces on the wings (the unreliable infantry and Arabs of al-Harith) broke. The Persian General Azarethes aped the Roman formation, placing his Arab allies under al-Mundhir on his left, opposite the Romans' Arab allies, some of his cavalry on the right, opposite the Roman infantry of Peter, and his best cavalry in the center.[20]

The battle began in the afternoon with a flurry of arrows from both sides. Then Azarethes launched a light attack on Sounikas and Simmas' position, which they repulsed with few casualties. But this turned out to have been a diversion, during which the Persian general transferred some of his best cavalry from the center to join al-Mundhir on the Persian left. Once this movement was complete, a massive assault was launched by the Arabs of al-Mundhir and the Persian cavalry onto the Roman right. The untested infantry and Arabs of al-Harith on the Roman right collapsed under the pressure of the assault and turned to flight, leaving Ascan's cavalry alone to try to protect the right flank of the Roman center. The death of Ascan put an end to that hope. Belisarius desperately reacted by having the remaining Roman units retreat back 90 degrees, placing the river to their rear, to ensure against the Persians getting behind them. The general then ordered all surviving cavalry to dismount and join the infantry in a solid formation, with interlocking shields, to offer the best defense possible against Persian cavalry charges. The Romans clashed their shields to alarm the Persians' horses, and those with arrows remaining fired from within the shielded formation, and somehow the Romans managed to hold off the Persians until night fell. Under the cover of darkness, Belisarius and the surviving Romans evacuated the battlefield and were ferried across the Euphrates to Callinicum. Having claimed the victory, the Persians stripped the dead of valuables, and then continued their retreat eastward to Persian territory.[21]

The Battle of Callinicum was clearly a defeat for Belisarius and the Romans. Part of the Roman army had routed and fled the battlefield, and the remainder of the army had only survived by hunkering down into a defensive formation until nightfall. However, it is difficult to determine the full extent of the defeat. We have no casualty totals for either the Romans or the Persians, although Procopius suggests that both sides suffered similar losses. Either way, coming so soon after the overwhelming victory at Dara the year before, the defeat at Callinicum was perplexing, for contemporaries no less than for modern observers. Justinian wanted to know how it could have happened, and so he dispatched a duke named Konstantiolos to conduct an inquiry into the conduct of the Romans at the battle. It seems that Konstantiolos heard at least two different versions of the event, and conveniently our two surviving sources each seem based on those differing accounts. Procopius presents the point of view of Belisarius, which not surprisingly sought to exonerate the general as much as possible. The account therefore emphasizes the insubordination of the Roman soldiers and officers who demanded a battle that Belisarius did not want to fight, charges that the Roman right wing collapsed because of treachery on the part of the Romans' Arab allies, and celebrates Belisarius for leading the desperate defensive infantry action to preserve the core of the army until nightfall. Malalas presents the point of view of the other Roman commanders, probably most notably of Sounikas, which places the blame squarely on Belisarius' shoulders. This account says nothing about uncertainty or disagreement over fighting the battle, implying that Belisarius and all his officers agreed to fight the Persians. While Malalas concurs with Procopius on accusing the Arab allies of treachery, his account of the end of the battle differs markedly. In Malalas' version, Belisarius got on a boat on the Euphrates and ran away across the river to Callinicum while the battle was still raging. It was therefore not the general, but the dukes Sounikas and Simmas who dismounted and fought gallantly with the infantry until nightfall, holding off the Persians to allow many of the Roman soldiers to follow Belisarius in escaping across the river.[22]

The two versions also differ wildly on the aftermath of the battle. Procopius claims, plausibly, that the Persians controlled the battlefield after the Roman withdrawal and were able to despoil the dead. Malalas' far more unlikely claim is that when the battle reached evening, Sounikas and Simmas were able to pursue the Persians for two miles, and then the Romans despoiled the dead the next day. Given all these differences between the two accounts, it is difficult to say for sure exactly what happened at the Battle of Callinicum. Modern historians have long correctly pointed out that Procopius' version is clearly a defense of Belisarius and should therefore be distrusted. But it does not follow that this automatically makes Malalas' account trustworthy in comparison, for it is clearly designed to make a scapegoat out of Belisarius while going to unreasonable lengths to make heroes out of Sounikas and Simmas. The impartiality of Sounikas, in particular, is even more called into question by the fact that Malalas admits that Belisarius and Sounikas were at odds before the battle over Sounikas attacking the Persians at Gabbulon without permission. It therefore seems likely that the commissioner Konstantiolos heard at least two main versions of the campaign and battle: one from Belisarius, perhaps assisted by Procopius, who was after all his legal adviser, and one from Sounikas and Simmas. Konstantiolos will have also talked to Hermogenes, who perhaps told him of the earlier antagonism between Belisarius and Sounikas.[23]

After conducting his interviews, Konstantiolos returned to Constantinople to report on the matter to the emperor. In the meantime, Belisarius and his fellow commanders apparently remained inactive, awaiting the results of the investigation. Although the Persian war continued in other theaters during this year, Belisarius played no further part in it. In Constantinople, the report that Konstantiolos gave to Justinian probably hewed closer to the account of Sounikas than it did to the version of Belisarius. It has even been plausibly suggested that the passages in Malalas about the Battle of Callinicum actually draw upon the official report that Konstantiolos drafted after his inquiry. Given this report by a third-party investigator, who in theory had no reason to lie to the emperor, Justinian appears to have accepted the findings. The emperor relieved Belisarius of his command and recalled him to Constantinople. Procopius tries to soften the blow for his employer by claiming, in the *Wars*, that Belisarius was recalled in order to be placed in charge of a new expedition, but this is transparently not the case. Malalas preserves the cold fact: "When [Justinian] had heard a report on the battle from Konstantiolos, he relieved Belisarius of his command." Belisarius was probably sacked in summer 531 and returned immediately to Constantinople.[24]

This was a swift fall from grace for a man whose career had seemed on a rocket trajectory straight to the top. Was it deserved? Although Belisarius had won a tremendous triumph at Dara in 530, it is not as though he had a long resumé of battle victories. Indeed, his career fighting in the east to this point had been remarkably average. As a guardsman, he conducted two raids with Sittas, succeeding in one and failing in the other. As a duke, he was defeated at Mindouos. As a general, he won at Dara but lost at Callinicum. Although Procopius, and probably Belisarius himself, could try to blame the loss at Callinicum on a variety of factors, from insubordinate officers to treacherous Arab allies and soldiers fatigued from fasting, the fact remains that at the end of the day, Belisarius was the general. It was up to him to manage these difficulties and only offer battle if necessary for a defensive purpose or if victory could be assured. A maxim in the *Strategikon*, a sixth-century handbook on military strategy, urged generals: "Risks should not be taken without necessity or real hope of gain." At Callinicum, Belisarius had failed to meet those requirements. Perhaps, if he had a long history of victories, this would have been overlooked as a fluke, but he really only had the one. It is also possible that if Belisarius were the only general to win in 530, his loss at Callinicum might have been overlooked, but Sittas and Dorotheos had won a neat victory at Satala, which might have had the unfortunate result for Belisarius of making his victory seem less unique. A final consideration: Justinian might have decided that, regardless of Belisarius' previous success, he at the moment did not have the confidence of his subordinate officers, and he should therefore be provided a change in scenery. It is impossible to know which, if any, of these factors crossed Justinian's mind as he decided to recall Belisarius. While this fall from grace seems abrupt and complete, we must be careful not to make too much fuss over the sacking of Belisarius. It was very common in the sixth century for a Roman general to be recalled after losing a battle or otherwise disappointing the emperor. Being recalled was not a permanent stain on the general and did not prevent him from being assigned a different command subsequently.[25]

Nevertheless, for Belisarius, his recall to Constantinople in summer 531 must have felt devastating in the moment. No doubt Belisarius reported to the emperor upon his arrival and probably apologized for the poor showing at Callinicum. This appears to have been sufficient for Justinian, who took no further action against Belisarius. He still held the rank of general in the Roman army, although he was now without a command. Belisarius was also permitted to retain his guardsmen, who had returned to the city with him, now battle hardened after years of campaigning in the east, but there was not much for him or them to do. The general presumably lived in Constantinople with Antonina, going to the Great Palace regularly in the hopes that the emperor would choose to honor him with a different position, or perhaps he even dreamed of being restored to his post in the east. In this state, Belisarius passed many months. Without him, the Persian war continued with Mundus temporarily in place as General of the East, but the conflict was already bending toward resolution, with the number of engagements winding down. When summer gave way to fall, Kavad died and was succeeded by his son Khusro, which made peace negotiations all the more likely. As 531 came to a close, the Romans had a real hope of securing peace with Persia, but Belisarius remained unemployed.[26]

The Nika Riot

January 532 would prove a difficult and momentous month for Belisarius, Justinian, and the people of Constantinople. On Saturday, January 10th, there was a public execution of some partisans of the Blue and Green factions who had been found guilty of murder. Unusually, the scaffold broke during the executions, and two of the convicted murderers, one of the Blue persuasion and one of the Green, survived their hanging. They were immediately rescued by bystanders and stuffed into a church for safekeeping, with the bystanders claiming that this was proof that God thought they should be spared. The church was swiftly put under guard by the men of the City Prefect Eudaemon, who had been in charge of the execution, but they were not eager to violate the sanctuary by taking the convicts out by force. A stalemate followed until Tuesday, January 13th, which was a chariot race day. Justinian was watching the races from the imperial box in the hippodrome, and the crowds assembled for the races took up a chant demanding that the emperor pardon the two murderers who had escaped the noose. Such chants were common in the sixth-century Roman world: the hippodrome was a place for communication between Roman citizens and their sovereign. Typically, citizens could expect some kind of reaction from the emperor to such pointed requests, even if the answer was "no." On this occasion, however, Justinian refused to answer or react to the chants at all. This seems to have angered the assembled spectators, and on the 22nd race of the day, fans of the Blues and Greens united with a single chant: "*Nika*." The Greek word, meaning "win," was a typical acclamation, although often shouted to encourage the charioteer of one faction or another on to victory. Now, it served as a unifying chant and a watchword for the factions to start rioting. The Nika Riot had begun.[27]

The rioting on January 13th began in the hippodrome, so Justinian and his entourage withdrew and took refuge in the Great Palace, which

FIGURE 5 The emperor and his people at the games, detail from the base of the column of Theodosius in Istanbul. Photo by the author.

was connected directly to the imperial box in the hippodrome by a stair-case. At this, the riot spilled out of the hippodrome and onto the streets of Constantinople. Driven by their request to free the two convicted murderers who had escaped the hangman, the rioters proceeded to the headquarters of the city prefect, loudly demanding the release of the prisoners. When no response was forthcoming, the rioters burned down the building and prob-ably at the same time succeeded in liberating the convicts from the church where they were under guard. Justinian responded to this action with a con-ciliatory move: the next morning, Wednesday the 14th, he attempted to restart the chariot races in the hippodrome as if nothing had happened. Perhaps the emperor hoped that, with their demands achieved, the rioting citizens would be pacified by more games and would abandon the riot. If so, he was mistaken. Perhaps still angered that the emperor had not paid them more attention during their initial requests, the people continued to riot, now setting fire to the hippodrome itself. The rioters then issued a new set of demands: they wanted Justinian to dismiss the praetorian prefect, John the Cappadocian; the city prefect, Eudaemon; and the legal adviser (*quaestor*), Tribonian. Justinian now acted swiftly. Since previously ignoring the demands of the rioters had not worked, this time he decided to grant their request immediately. The three officials were sacked and replaced by Wednesday afternoon.[28]

However, the people, by this point in no mood for backing down from their behavior, continued to riot in the streets. They were perhaps emboldened by the way Justinian vacillated between ignoring them and acquiescing to their demands. In response, by the end of the day, it seems that Justinian had vacillated again. He completely switched from a policy of conciliating the rioters to one of repressing them. The emperor ordered Belisarius to attempt to clear the crowd from the streets outside the palace by force. The choice of Belisarius for this mission is an interesting one. As far as we know, he was still in a sort of limbo—a general without an army. However, he did have with him his battle-hardened guardsmen, and it is presumably these men whom Belisarius conscripted for this crowd control operation. That Belisarius was close to Justinian in this hour of need, and that the emperor would select him suggests that no rupture had occurred in the relationship between the general and the emperor after his dismissal as General of the East. In fact, here Belisarius is practically slipping back into the comfortable clothes of his first military role, acting as a personal guardsman of Justinian, as he had been in the 520s. Justinian's selection of Belisarius for this delicate assignment, and the fact that Belisarius willingly accepted the job, are therefore evidence that their relationship remained strong despite the fiasco of the Battle of Callinicum and Belisarius' subsequent recall. Belisarius perhaps did not perceive it at the moment, but by accepting this task, he was irrevocably casting his lot with Justinian to the bitter end of the riot. In the late afternoon of Wednesday the 14th, Belisarius led his guardsmen out of the palace and into the rioting crowd. They cut down rioters throughout the rest of the day, until night fell, but were unable to quash the riot. This is not surprising, as the crowd was much more numerous than Belisarius and his guardsmen and had the option of dispersing into other parts of the city to avoid direct confrontation. In the evening, Belisarius and his men returned to the Great Palace. Perhaps Antonina and her children had also retreated to the safety of the palace by this point, if not before. If the crowd knew who Belisarius was, then Antonina would not have been safe roaming the streets of the city after Belisarius had led an attack on the rioters.[29]

The crowd was enraged by the attempt to check its activities with military force and responded with further arson. Over the course of Wednesday night, or perhaps on the morning of Thursday the 15th, rioters started fires that burned down much of central Constantinople. General unrest continued. Later in the day on Thursday, the rioters rushed to the house of Probos, a nephew of the former Emperor Anastasios, hoping to acclaim him emperor in opposition to Justinian. When they found out that Probos was not home, they set fire to his house. The riot continued into Friday the 16th of January, when people crowded around the headquarters of the praetorian prefect and burned it to the ground, destroying its archives. Although the emperor did not respond to these actions directly, Justinian must have either on Thursday or Friday given the order to have soldiers from Thrace begin marching to the capital. He clearly realized that the guardsmen of Belisarius and whatever imperial guards were on hand were not sufficient to forcibly suppress the riot, which had grown wildly since Tuesday. On Saturday the 17th, these troops arrived and skirmished with the rioters, mostly ineffectually, as they marched through the city to the Great Palace. Additional buildings in the city were burned down in this action. In the palace, Justinian and his advisors, perhaps including Belisarius, settled upon next steps. First, some of the senators who had been taking refuge in the palace—including Hypatios, the former General of the East, and his brother Pompey, both nephews of the late Emperor Anastasios—were turned out of the palace on Saturday evening and sent to their homes. This probably served to create space in the palace complex for the newly arrived Thracian troops. Second, Justinian decided to make one further attempt to be conciliatory: early on the morning of Sunday, January 18th, he appeared in the hippodrome and, holding the Gospels in his hands, acknowledged his own error in not listening to the protests of the previous Tuesday and offered the assembled rioters a pardon. This apology was not just pandering to the crowd, but a realization on Justinian's part that he had indeed erred in his earlier (lack of) interaction with the people in the hippodrome. While some cheered the emperor for this apology, others hurled abuse at him, and so he again withdrew into the palace.[30]

With the failure of this gambit, Justinian and his advisors decided that the only way to end the riot was to suppress it with force. To do so, the rioters would have to be attacked in a confined location, where they could not disperse or use their knowledge of the city to avoid the attack, as had happened when Belisarius attacked on Wednesday and the Thracian troops arrived on Saturday. Hypatios, recently expelled from the palace, would turn out to be the mechanism for assembling the rioters. After Justinian returned to the palace on Sunday morning, the rioters noticed that Hypatios was no longer in the palace, rushed to him, and acclaimed him emperor. The crowd then escorted Hypatios into the hippodrome and forcibly installed him in the imperial box, where he was again acclaimed. This was exactly what Justinian was waiting for: the rioters were gathered in a confined place and could be suppressed violently. But now, at this critical moment, the emperor wavered on whether he should stay in Constantinople for what came next, or whether he should leave the city. Leaving the city would offer two principal advantages: if the assault went poorly, Justinian would obviously be safe from reprisals from the angry rioters, and if the assault went well, Justinian would have moral cover to claim that he had no idea such violence was about to occur. Rumor that Justinian was considering flight reached Hypatios in the hippodrome, and he now began to consider that he might actually succeed in seizing imperial power. Within the palace, Theodora put an end to Justinian's thoughts of flight by passionately arguing that the imperial couple should stay put and fight for their positions. And if they should lose? "Kingship is a good burial shroud," Theodora concluded. So Justinian and Theodora decided to stay in the palace, while their trusted military men finally brought an end to the Nika Riot.[31]

In addition to Belisarius, Mundus, now the General of Illyricum, was present in the city with his son, Mauricius. Dividing the available Thracian soldiers between them to supplement their own guardsmen, Belisarius, Mundus, and Mauricius were dispatched from the palace on Sunday the 18th to suppress the rioters in the hippodrome. Just before they set out, Justinian's trusted chamberlain and steward, Narses the eunuch, moved through the hippodrome, attempting to bribe some of the partisans of the Blues to switch their allegiance to the emperor. This was perhaps an attempt to introduce some confusion into the crowd while the soldiers assembled. Of the available generals, Justinian trusted Belisarius with the most delicate mission: he was to enter the imperial box directly from the palace and capture Hypatios. It seems that Belisarius' appearance there was to be the cue for the other commanders to begin a general assault on the rioters in the hippodrome. However, when Belisarius and his forces reached the staircase leading from the palace to the imperial box, they found the way barred by guards who were unwilling to let them in—an indication that the cause of Hypatios was attracting support even from some of the palace guards, who had deserted Justinian's cause. Belisarius and his soldiers abandoned their objective, perhaps because the general deemed that fighting through the staircase would be too difficult, costly, or time-consuming. Belisarius was apparently despondent at this turn of events. Justinian, less perturbed, ordered Belisarius and his men to exit the palace, move to the north side of the hippodrome and enter through there. Mundus, Mauricius, and their soldiers had lined up at the entrances on the south side of the hippodrome. Narses also returned to lead some forces in the assault. Of all these men, Procopius makes it clear that Belisarius struck first: "he drew his sword from its scabbard, ordered the others to follow his lead, and rushed at them with a cry." The other commanders had clearly been instructed to wait for the appearance of Belisarius, which they probably had expected in the imperial box rather than at the northern side of the hippodrome. But seeing Belisarius engage, they now attacked as well. The crowd assembled in the hippodrome to acclaim Hypatios may have been rioters, and many may indeed have been experienced in urban fighting and arson in Constantinople, but they were no match for veteran soldiers and had nowhere to run. Mundus, Mauricius, Narses, and their men met no serious opposition and began to cut down everyone they encountered in the hippodrome. Belisarius and his men, who had been tasked with seizing Hypatios, were probably more narrowly focused on marching through the crowd to the imperial box as quickly as possible. It is likely that Belisarius and his guards did indeed kill many citizens, but their job at this point was not crowd control, but getting to the imperial box. There, they seized Hypatios and his brother Pompey. Two sources for the event report that Belisarius seized Hypatios and Pompey, while Procopius maintains that the would-be usurper and his brother were seized by Justus and Boraides, cousins of Justinian. It is possible to reconcile these accounts by suggesting that Justus and Boraides had joined Belisarius and his guardsmen for this operation, and that it was they who personally laid hands on Hypatios and Pompey while Belisarius and his guards fought off any supporters trying to protect them. While this drama was going on in the imperial box, the soldiers under Mundus, Mauricius, and Narses were engaged in an indiscriminate slaughter. By the end of the day, they had allegedly killed some 30,000 people, including no doubt those innocently caught up in the activities of the day as well as those who had led the riot from its beginning. To cap off the bloodletting, Hypatios and Pompey were executed the next morning as usurpers. The riot had at last come to an end.[32]

Belisarius' participation in the suppression of the Nika Riot must be acknowledged as a bloody stain on his resume and character, although a few qualifications should be allowed. It is possible to argue that Belisarius by Sunday had little choice but to follow Justinian's order in violently ending the Nika Riot. By leading an attack on the rioters on Wednesday, Belisarius had irrevocably cast his lot with Justinian: if Justinian fell, Belisarius would doubtless be killed as one of his primary supporters. It is also important to acknowledge that Belisarius himself was not necessarily directly involved in the worst of the atrocities on Sunday. After all, he was tasked with using his guardsmen to seize Hypatios, not with the general crowd control that led to the immense loss of life. It is possible to imagine Belisarius actually urging Mundus, Mauricius, and Narses to lead a much more restrained attack, only killing those who actively resisted. Belisarius was, after all, praised by contemporaries as a champion of regular people. Pseudo-Zachariah describes him during his time as Duke of Mesopotamia as someone who "loved the peasants and did not allow the army to harm them." While fighting in Italy in the late 530s, Procopius noted that Belisarius "won the affection of peasants because he showed so much restraint and consideration for them that they never suffered any violence when he was general." If these feelings of consideration did affect Belisarius in January 532, however, he was unable to restrain either the other commanders or their soldiers, who must have taken hours to kill so many people. By his participation in the event, even if he did not personally cut down thousands of civilians, Belisarius' reputation is soaked in blood. The most positive thing that can be said about Belisarius' involvement in the Nika Riot is that he showed the virtue of constancy and loyalty by fighting for Justinian. Belisarius acted in the way a military retainer would have been expected to act. In fact, it is highly likely that the events of the Nika Riot served to draw Justinian and Belisarius even closer together, Belisarius in loyalty and Justinian in gratitude and trust. Their wives, Theodora and Antonina, might also be imagined to have bonded in this moment, seeing the power and destruction of the world of the entertainment factions from which they had come. The events of January 532 were then a crucible that forged these four people together in a way that would make possible their future collaborations. However, one cannot help but note that this would have been scanty consolation to the 30,000 citizens of Constantinople who lay dead and rotting in the hippodrome in the days after January 18, 532.[33]

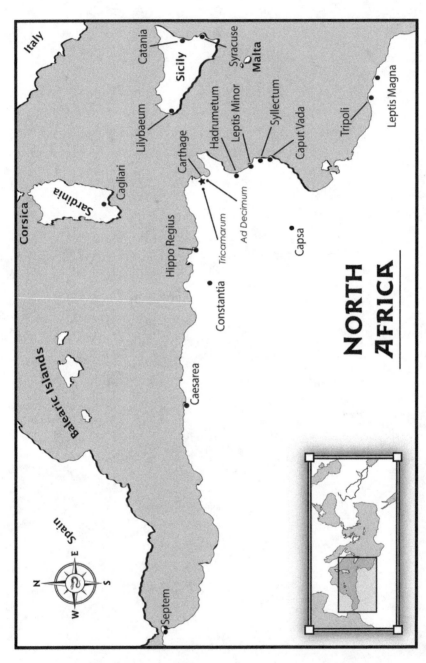

MAP 3 North Africa: an overview of important sites in the Vandal War. Created by John Wyatt Greenlee.

3

Victory in Africa

THE EVENTS OF the year 533 dramatically changed the fortunes of Belisarius and Antonina, catapulting them to heights of fame and success not enjoyed by a Roman general since perhaps Julius Caesar, more than 500 years before. Contemporaries would likely not have predicted this. Up to this point, Belisarius' career had been relatively typical for a Roman general of his era. He had won a battle handily (Dara), lost a battle (Callinicum), and been relieved of his duties for that loss. None of this was rare for the period. In fact, the most unusual thing about Belisarius' career so far was that he had played a direct role in suppressing the Nika Riot and in the slaughter of many civilians. Thus, Belisarius was probably little loved by the people of Constantinople by the end of 532. But in less than two years, they would cheer him to the echo. As for Antonina, she had not yet done anything particularly unusual. She was a military wife and mother who seems to have stayed home while her husband campaigned. She, thanks to Belisarius' salary, was wealthy, but that did not set her apart from other rich Constantinopolitan ladies. Yet within a couple years, Antonina would accompany Belisarius and his army to lands she had never seen and make a name for herself as arguably the second-most-famous woman of the century.[1]

For all the change that was about to take place in their lives, the process of this transformation began with the comfortable and familiar. Sometime between the Nika Riot in January 532 and February 533, Justinian reappointed Belisarius to his old position of General of the East. As far as we can tell, after his dismissal from this post in the summer of 531, Belisarius had held no official military command. But by February 1, 533, he was definitely General of the East again, as is attested by a mention in one of Justinian's laws. Why the change? The most likely explanation is that Justinian's trust in Belisarius was confirmed when the general stood by his side during the Nika Riot. The

Belisarius & Antonina. David Alan Parnell, Oxford University Press. © Oxford University Press 2023.
DOI: 10.1093/oso/9780197574706.003.0004

reappointment was perhaps even reward for Belisarius' part in the bloody affair. It cannot be determined when precisely Belisarius became General of the East for the second time, but if it was in fact a reward for service during the riot, then January 532 or shortly thereafter would make the most sense. It is not clear exactly what Belisarius did during the remainder of 532. Presumably he would have traveled to the eastern front to check on his army's dispositions there. However, it was not to reside in the East or to fight against the Persians that Justinian had reappointed Belisarius to this post. For in September 532, Justinian at last concluded a peace treaty with the new Persian King Khusro. Its terms stipulated that each side return the fortresses that they had captured from the other over the last few years, and that the Romans pay the Persians the enormous sum of 11,000 pounds of gold (or 792,000 *nomismata*). The treaty was known as the Endless Peace, for there was no fixed term of years that were to be covered by it. Belisarius thus came to command the Army of the East again at a time when its war was winding down. The emperor would use both general and army for a new purpose.[2]

Having secured peace with Persia to the East, Justinian turned his gaze to the West. His new focus was the Vandal Kingdom of North Africa. The Vandals were one of the Germanic peoples that invaded the Western Roman Empire in the fifth century. They worked their way through Gaul and Spain, eventually conquering and settling in Roman North Africa in the 430s under the leadership of their greatest king, Gaiseric. Since then, the Vandals had ruled over a multiethnic kingdom, with the majority of inhabitants being Roman natives of the region. This situation had remained more or less the same for a century. So why should it draw Justinian's attention now? Historians have long imagined that Justinian's interest in war with the Vandals was the product of a grand plan of reconquest. In other words, Justinian and his ministers felt it their responsibility to bring back to Roman control all the lands of the former Western Roman Empire that had been illegitimately seized by Germanic invaders. A law of Justinian, issued after the Romans had indeed recovered North Africa, does speak proudly of the emperor bringing freedom from Vandal oppression to the region. However, there is a certain amount of teleology involved in this argument, as it relies on the knowledge that Justinian's armies eventually did end up reconquering a significant portion of these lands, and on the way Justinian wrote about those wars after they had started. More recently, scholars have argued that Justinian's war with the Vandals was not related to any grand plan at all, but was instead a desperate attempt to earn a victory for propaganda purposes after the disaster of the Nika Riot. The historical precedents for the war and the immediate context of Justinian's decision to prosecute it suggest that the truth probably lies somewhere between these two extremes.[3]

Understanding Justinian's war with the Vandals requires knowing that the Eastern Roman Empire had a long and violent history with their kingdom. From the beginning of the Vandals' invasion of Africa, the Eastern Roman government had opposed them out of a desire to assist the reeling Western Roman Empire. In 431, Theodosius II had dispatched an expedition under his leading general, Aspar, which made an attempt to slow the progress of the Vandal army. Three years of desultory campaigning did nothing to prevent the ongoing Vandal conquest, which culminated with the capture of Carthage in 439. So in 441, Theodosius sent another expedition under the command of the general Areobindus. This force made it as far as Sicily, when it was recalled to the East because of an invasion by the Huns. The eastern Romans returned to the offensive in 468, when Leo I invested in a huge fleet and army to retake Africa from the Vandals. The emperor appointed his brother-in-law Basiliscus the leader of the expedition. This proved a poor choice, as Basiliscus was inexperienced and allowed his fleet to be ambushed and destroyed by Vandal ships before it even landed in Africa. Following this failure, the Romans gave up their hopes of dislodging the Vandals, and in 476 the Emperor Zeno concluded a treaty with them. So if Justinian envisaged war with the Vandals, this was nothing unusual in Roman history.[4]

There was also a significant religious component to the hostility. The Vandals, like many Germanic peoples of the time, subscribed to Christianity via an Arian creed. This version of Christianity stretched back to the fourth-century priest Arius, who had proposed that Christ was not coeternal with God the Father. Arianism was condemned at the Council of Nicaea in 325, and the coeternity of the Trinity was proclaimed, and by the sixth century most Romans were Nicene Christians. Germanic peoples like the Vandals, however, had been converted to Christianity by Arian missionaries, and they clung to this version of the faith. While other Arian conquerors, such as the Ostrogoths, came to a détente with their Nicene Christian subjects, the Vandals did not. They periodically but energetically persecuted the Nicene Roman natives of Africa, and this hostility did not go unnoticed in Constantinople. The conflict seemed to be resolved when Hilderic became king of the Vandals in 523. The new king suspended persecution, allowing the Nicene Christians to hold services and even a church council. But Hilderic's failure to defeat hostile groups of Berbers on the fringes of the Vandal Kingdom led to his ouster. In May 530, Gelimer, Hilderic's cousin, seized the throne, imprisoned his predecessor, and, among other things, reversed some of the more tolerant religious policies of the old king. When this news reached Justinian, he was not surprisingly displeased, as he saw Hilderic as protector of his co-religionists. Justinian and Gelimer exchanged angry letters, with the emperor urging the release of Hilderic, and Gelimer telling Justinian that it was not just for him "to meddle in another's affairs." So now Justinian had not just historical animosity and religious sentiment as reasons to think about war with the Vandals, but a more immediate and personal affront.[5]

Even still, Procopius makes clear that Justinian agonized over the decision to go to war with the Vandals. This was no easy choice dictated by a conviction of the moral righteousness of reconquest or by desperation to have a victory to prop up his popularity. His top generals and soldiers seemed uneasy with the idea, and with good reason. The previous expeditions from Constantinople to Africa had met with disaster, and many soldiers and sailors had been killed. John the Cappadocian, reappointed praetorian prefect after the Nika Riot, and the highest-ranking civilian official in the imperial government, also warned Justinian against war. The armada prepared by Leo I in 468 was so expensive that it had probably bankrupted the imperial government, so there was financial risk to consider as well. Procopius says that Justinian was persuaded by these arguments and seems to have given up on the idea of launching an expedition against Gelimer. Then, however, came more news. Sometime in late 532, Justinian received word of two revolts against Gelimer. In Tripoli, a local named Pudentius declared independence from the Vandals and sent to Justinian requesting soldiers to help him resist them. In Sardinia, the Vandal governor, Godas, also raised the banner of rebellion and requested assistance from the Romans. Surely Justinian saw these two revolts as a golden window of opportunity, and perhaps even as a sign that he was intended to go ahead with an expedition against the Vandals. On the other hand, Justinian might have made his own luck by instigating these revolts via imperial agents. Procopius also says that a bishop came to the emperor about this time and informed him that God had promised in a dream, "I will myself join with him in waging war and make him the master of Libya." This was all the encouragement Justinian needed. The weight of past hostility and conflict, the current resentment of Gelimer for his treatment of Hilderic and Nicene Christians, and the immediate context of two rebellions against Gelimer along with divine blessing was enough to convince the emperor of the rightness of war with the Vandals.[6]

FIGURE 6 The Lady of Carthage, a sixth-century mosaic from Carthage. Photo by the author.

The Expedition of Belisarius and Antonina

To lead the expedition against the Vandals, Justinian turned to Belisarius, his former and now reappointed General of the East. Procopius does not speculate as to why Justinian chose Belisarius for this role, but it is worth considering. He was perhaps not an obvious choice. As already mentioned, Belisarius so far had a rather average resume as far as generalship. He had in fact been dismissed from his position less than two years before. However, Belisarius did have one obvious appeal: he was unshakably loyal to Justinian. The general had been one of the few to stand with the emperor during the Nika Riot and had been willing to command his guardsmen to cut down rioting citizens to preserve Justinian's throne. It is likely that the emperor rated loyalty extremely highly when thinking about who to select to lead the Vandal expedition. After all, the general in charge of this force would be hundreds of miles away, in command of a combined army and fleet, and would have to make immediate decisions without time to refer questions back to the emperor. Procopius emphasizes the unique nature of this authority. He describes Belisarius as receiving "supreme authority over all." Justinian even wrote a letter that "gave him the authority of an emperor." Even without such grants of authority, Justinian must have realized that the long distances involved, the sole control of one general over army and fleet, and the mission of conquering a whole kingdom meant that there was considerable risk that this one general could turn the expedition into a chance to set up his own state. The emperor therefore needed a leader he could trust to make hard decisions and remain loyal to him. These are exactly the qualifications that Belisarius had demonstrated in the Nika Riot. It is perhaps not going too far to suggest that Belisarius received this job because of his service in the Nika Riot rather than because of his military career in the East. As with the choice of Belisarius, it is not immediately obvious that his army, the Army of the East, should supply the soldiers for a war in North Africa. Justinian could have just as easily made Belisarius General of Illyricum and drawn soldiers from there. It seems that Justinian deliberately chose to make use of the freedom granted him by the Endless Peace with Persia. The emperor expected Khusro to keep the peace and therefore felt he would need fewer soldiers on his border with Persia. So the Army of the East could be drawn upon to pull together an expeditionary army for the Vandal campaign.[7]

Justinian and Belisarius might have worked together to select units and maybe even individual soldiers to fill out the Vandal expedition. Planning probably began at the latest in late 532, since the expedition was ready to set sail by June 533. It took time to move around armies and to gather supplies. The force that the emperor and general assembled was about average size for a campaign army of the sixth century. Belisarius had at his command at least 18,000 soldiers. They included 10,000 infantry and 5,000 cavalry from the field armies and federates (*foederati*, who were something akin to elite soldiers). It is very likely that these soldiers were drawn from the Army of the East, which Belisarius commanded. The Army of the East at the time numbered about 20,000 soldiers, so some would have still been left to guard a substantially de-militarized border with Persia alongside the frontier forces there. In addition to these soldiers, Belisarius' African expedition included 2,000 marines, who both rowed ships and fought as infantry, 400 allied Herul soldiers, and 600 allied Massagetae Hun cavalry. The general also brought his own retinue of guardsmen, although Procopius does not number them. There might have been anywhere between a few hundred and a thousand of them at this time, but they would grow much more numerous in future campaigns. The overall size of the expeditionary army, then, somewhere between 18,000 and 19,000 soldiers, was about typical for a battle army of the time period—Belisarius had commanded 25,000 men at Dara in 530, and 20,000 at Callinicum in 531. It was, however, a notably smaller army than the last one dispatched to expel the Vandals from Africa. In 468, Leo I allegedly sent some 100,000 soldiers on his Vandal expedition. So Justinian's investment should be set in context: he was not exactly being cheap, but also not going all in, either. Belisarius would be expected to defeat the Vandals with a standard army, not a super-sized one.[8]

In addition to numbering the army, Procopius names its officers, many of whom he must have known personally, and some of whom had already served with Belisarius in the Army of the East. The commanders of the federates were Dorotheos and Solomon. Additional commanders (perhaps further officers of the federates) included Cyprian, Valerianos, Martinos, Althias, John, Markellos, and Cyril. Rufinus, Aigan, Barbatos, and Pappos commanded the cavalry, while John of Dyrrachium, Theodoros, Terentios, Zaidos, Markianos, and Sarapis commanded the infantry. Pharas, whom we have already met in Chapter 2, led the Herul contingent, while Sinnion and Balas led the Hun cavalry. Kalonymos of Alexandria commanded the fleet of transport ships, 500 in number with 30,000 sailors. Finally, the senator Archelaos was appointed as prefect of the army, to track expenditures. This list of officers is startling because it is so extensive. Even by Procopius' standards, this is an unusual amount of detail. Some of these names will appear again later in the narrative, but others are mentioned here and nowhere else. The author wanted to record their presence in a historic armada, regardless of whether it made literary or narrative sense.[9]

This was the largest, most significant amphibious assault force created by the Romans since the failed expedition of Leo I. When it assembled aboard 592 ships outside Constantinople in the waters of the Sea of Marmara, just off the coast from the Great Palace, in June of 533, it must have made quite a spectacle. In fact, this was a once-in-a-century event. Such an armada had last sailed in 468, and Constantinople would not see another one until Heraclius arrived to overthrow Phocas in 610. Exhibiting both a flair for the dramatic and anxiety over the safety of this expedition, Justinian arranged for a public blessing of the armada. The Patriarch of Constantinople, Epiphanios, prayed for the fleet and army, and then escorted onto one of the ships an unnamed soldier who had just been baptized into the Christian faith. This soldier has occasionally been identified with Theodosios, who was about this time adopted by Belisarius and Antonina, after they stood as godparents at his baptism. Belisarius himself raised Theodosios up from the baptismal font with his own hands, demonstrating his commitment to his Christian faith and formalizing the adoption of the boy. Theodosios might have been an orphan, but it is not clear why the pair decided to adopt him. Perhaps they did so because they had so far only had a daughter between them, and they wished to have a son. In the *Secret History*, Procopius describes Theodosios as a young man from Thrace and a member of Belisarius' household. He was probably a young teenager at the time of his adoption. Because Theodosios accompanied Belisarius on the campaign and Belisarius participated in his baptism, the young man has been linked to the newly baptized soldier brought aboard by Epiphanios at this time. The identification is, however, by no means certain, as the soldier escorted by Epiphanios is unnamed, and Theodosios is nowhere described as a soldier. Though the unnamed soldier and Theodosios were probably different people, they still might have been baptized around the same time as a part of religious preparation for this campaign. After boarding the final passengers and receiving the blessing of Epiphanios, the expedition made ready to set sail.[10]

Before following the fleet in its travels to Africa, it is worth pausing for a moment to consider one final passenger of this grand armada. Procopius explains that after the blessing, "the general Belisarius and Antonina, his wife, set sail." It is difficult to express the extremely remarkable nature of this single, short sentence. It is our first indication that Antonina was not a typical soldier's wife, and that the union of Antonina and Belisarius was not only a marriage but also a partnership. Nothing of their relationship so far had given a clue that Antonina might suddenly appear alongside her husband at the head of the greatest amphibious assault force the Roman Empire had launched in decades. Antonina and Belisarius had met and married, but as far as we know she had not been present with her husband during his prior military command in the East. She did not march with Belisarius' armies, talk to his officers, or witness his battles. But this single sentence changed all of that. She set sail with Belisarius on his way to Africa. She would stay with him through the entire African campaign. Although neither Procopius nor any other source explains why Antonina did this, it seems reasonable that she must have gone with Belisarius because she wanted to do so. To understand how unusual this was, it is necessary to put Antonina's presence with Belisarius' army into historical context. There are a few other situations in which wives of generals did indeed accompany their husbands to war in Roman history. For example, 500 years earlier, Agrippina the Elder accompanied her husband Germanicus during his campaign in Germania in 15–16 AD. The historian Tacitus reported, "In those days this great-hearted woman acted as a commander . . . Agrippina's position in the army already seemed to outshine generals and commanding officers." She later traveled with Germanicus in Syria and Armenia as well. Her contemporary, Munatia Plancina, accompanied her own husband Gnaeus Calpurnius Piso to Syria. Returning to the sixth century, Procopius describes one other general who took his wife to his posting: Areobindos, who was appointed General of Africa in 545, brought with him his wife Praiecta. So then it was not completely unprecedented for a Roman general to be accompanied by his wife during his service. Yet still, it seems to have been relatively rare. Areobindos and Praiecta are not really even a comparable example, because Areobindos was posted to a settled army in a Roman-controlled region, while Antonina joined Belisarius in an overseas campaign on enemy territory, which appears to have been much more unusual.[11]

Despite the rarity, the contemporary evidence suggests that some Romans thought Antonina's presence with Belisarius on campaign was quite normal, while others considered it to be highly inappropriate. As evidence of the latter, Procopius describes Antonina's presence with Belisarius in this way in the *Secret History*: "In order that the man should never be left by himself, at which time he might come to his senses, cast off her enchantments, and form a more realistic opinion of her, she made a point of accompanying him to the ends of the earth." By this criticism, Procopius is suggesting that a more appropriate marital relationship would have involved the opposite: Belisarius traveling to the ends of the earth in the execution of his military obligations on his own, without Antonina at his side. For bringing Antonina with him and allowing her to be involved in his public affairs, Procopius criticized Belisarius as "a confirmed fool." On the other hand, the way Procopius describes Antonina's presence with the army in the *Wars* suggests that some Romans found this quite natural. The brief sentence quoted above, in which Procopius describes Belisarius and Antonina setting sail on the African expedition, includes no indication that the reader should find her participation unusual. This casual reference to Antonina's presence in a military campaign at the side of her husband is really quite remarkable, especially when compared to Procopius' bitter complaint about her in the *Secret History*. Nor is this casual approach to the presence of a general's wife limited to Antonina. Procopius is equally casual about describing Praiecta's presence with Areobindos in 545: "With Areobindos were his sister and his wife, Praiecta, the daughter of Vigilantia, the sister of the emperor Justinian." The difference between the two takes on the presence of wives is a clue that in each of the two works Procopius is playing to a different audience, or catering to a different vision, about the appropriate role of military wives like Antonina. He evidently expected the audience for the *Wars* to be accepting of a wife campaigning with her husband, while he expected the readers of the *Secret History* to agree that Belisarius was ridiculous for involving his wife. All of this evidence suggests that Antonina's decision to join Belisarius on the African expedition in 533 was somewhat unusual, but not unexpected. It was also probably a divisive choice. It was accepted by some Romans, as evidenced by Belisarius and Justinian finding it reasonable and Procopius writing about it as if it were totally normal in the *Wars*, and also mocked by other Romans who found it inappropriate, as shown by Procopius' withering criticism in the *Secret History* and the fact that we know of few other wives who accompanied their husband generals on campaign in this period.[12]

Belisarius and Antonina, along with Procopius, Theodosios, and the army described above, sailed out of Constantinople in mid-June 533. The fastest a ship might have made the journey from Constantinople to Carthage in this period was around 19 days. However, the massive fleet moved slower than the fastest single ship of the era, and many stops were made en route. When combined with some bad luck with the wind, the fleet would end up spending about ten weeks on the trip. The fleet first put in at Herakleia (modern Marmara Ereğlisi), a mere 65 miles or so from Constantinople. For five days, the fleet loaded horses from the imperial pastures, presumably for the cavalry soldiers to ride in the upcoming campaign. The next stop was Abydos (near modern Çanakkale), at the southern entrance of the Sea of Marmara, about 100 miles away. Here the fleet was delayed for four days by a lack of wind. Apparently during this delay, some Hunnic soldiers got drunk and two of them murdered a third man who was mocking them for their intoxication. Belisarius announced he would not tolerate lawless behavior on the expedition, and he had the two murderers impaled on a hill overlooking Abydos. It is easy to imagine the general wanting to establish his authority over the expedition early, and this incident certainly provided the opportunity. From Abydos, the fleet sailed to Malea on the island of Lesbos, some 85 miles. The fleet then moved across the Aegean Sea to Greece, putting in first at Tainaron (modern Cape Matapan), and then at Methone (modern Methoni) in Messenia.[13]

Here the entire army disembarked, and Belisarius and the other commanders drew up the soldiers into ranks, probably to give them a chance to get off the ships and have some fresh air after the long journey across the Aegean. During this break, about 500 soldiers died from food poisoning. The bread provided by John the Cappadocian, the praetorian prefect, had not been properly baked, and so it had become quite moldy during the journey. Procopius bitterly blames John personally for this disaster, alleging that the prefect had ordered the bread baked on the "free" heat of a public bathhouse instead of paying for bread bakers to use their ovens, all to save some money. There was little that Belisarius could do about that now, so he ordered the remaining bread thrown out and replaced it with bread baked in Greece. After the soldiers reimbarked, the fleet sailed from Methone to the island of Zakinthos. There the ships took on fresh water in preparation for the long voyage across the Adriatic to Sicily (approximately 370 miles). With good wind, a fast ship might hope to make this trip in about 5 days, but the wind was gentle and so it took the expedition 16 days to reach the coast of Sicily just north of Catania. In the course of this journey, the fresh water taken on at Zakinthos spoiled on all the ships except Belisarius' flagship. Procopius credits Antonina for preserving the drinking water of Belisarius' household by putting it in glass jars and sinking those containers into sand piled up in the ship's hold. The glass jars would have been non-porous and impermeable, and the sand would have perhaps kept them out of the sunlight, thereby slowing the growth of algae and bacteria in the water. It is not clear where Antonina would have learned this neat trick, especially since we do not know of her ever traveling by ship before this, but it was doubtless appreciated by Belisarius and his household, which included Procopius, who thought this small detail important enough to record for posterity. Antonina was already proving her value to the expedition.[14]

With the fleet safely in Sicily, Belisarius made plans for the final leg of the journey and the landing in North Africa. He dispatched Procopius (and presumably others) to Syracuse, where the Ostrogothic Queen Amalasuntha had established a market so that the Roman expedition could buy food and supplies. The market was undoubtedly welcome and necessary, for the fleet probably needed at least bread and water. However, Belisarius also hoped to gain information at this stop. He ordered Procopius, perhaps rather unrealistically, to find out the location of the Vandal fleet and army, whether the Vandals suspected an attack, and whether they had prepared an ambush at any point along the coast. Procopius succeeded beyond the general's wildest dreams. He happened unexpectedly upon a childhood friend, who had a shipping business in Syracuse, and the friend told Procopius that one of his servants had been in Carthage just three days before. The Vandals did not suspect any attack from the Romans and had not set up an ambush. Moreover, not long before the Vandal fleet had taken a significant portion of the army to Sardinia, to put down the revolt of Godas there. Finally,

Gelimer, the Vandal king, was not even on the coast, but was in the interior of what is today Tunisia, a four-day journey from the sea. In other words, the timing for an amphibious assault on North Africa could not be better. Procopius could not believe the luck. In his exuberance, he abducted his friend's servant, eager to bring him before Belisarius to report this news in person. Procopius caught up with Belisarius and the fleet at Caucana in southern Sicily. The happiness of the moment was muted, however, for Procopius found an army in mourning. The General Dorotheos had just died. Belisarius was, however, overjoyed to hear the intelligence Procopius had discovered, and immediately ordered the expedition to set sail for Africa. The fleet moved quickly, first putting in at Malta, and then riding a strong east wind from Malta to the coast of Africa, where the Romans sighted land at Caput Vada (modern Chebba, Tunisia), about 150 miles south of Carthage.[15]

Belisarius now called together his commanders to discuss what to do. Archelaos, the prefect of the army, recommended sailing north to Carthage and making an immediate attempt upon the city. If successful, the capture of Carthage would dishearten the Vandals and provide a secure base for the army and fleet for the remainder of the war. However, this was also a risky maneuver, which had resulted in the destruction of the Roman expedition in 468. Belisarius accordingly pointed out that the Vandal fleet might return at any time. The Romans were already moored off the coast, the general reasoned, so better to land now in safety and have the army proceed up the coast by foot. Procopius reports that all the assembled commanders agreed with Belisarius' proposal. This is indicative of the way Belisarius would try to run his expeditionary armies. Although he had been endowed with supreme authority, he often endeavored to work collaboratively with the other officers of his army. Perhaps Belisarius realized he would have more success if the other commanders bought in to his plans than he would in simply issuing orders with which they disagreed. This might have also been a reaction to his failure to form consensus before the Battle of Callinicum in 531. After the meeting, the general gave the order for immediate disembarkation. And so, at the beginning of September 533, roughly ten weeks after they set off from Constantinople, Belisarius, Antonina, and the soldiers of the Roman expedition stepped onto African soil. The general immediately set them to work digging a trench and erecting a stockade around their camp. While digging the trench, the soldiers struck fresh water, which burst out from the earth in sufficient quantities for the whole army. Procopius rejoiced in this as a good omen and a sign of an easy victory to come.[16]

The Vandal War

The morning after the landing, some of the Roman soldiers ventured out of the camp and began to pick vegetables and fruit in the surrounding fields. Belisarius immediately put an end to this activity and delivered a speech to the army in which he forbade the soldiers to take the produce of others. The general emphasized that this prohibition was because such theft was an injustice, but also, more pragmatically, that such acts would push the Roman natives into the arms of the Vandals. Better to keep the locals well disposed to the army, and only have to fight the Vandals, than to have to fight both together, he reasoned. After lecturing his soldiers, Belisarius began preparations for the army to leave camp and march north. He sent a small force of his personal guardsmen ahead, where they secured the village of Syllectum (modern Salakta), about 14 miles north of Caput Vada. Here the overseer of the public post station in the village deserted to the Romans, and Belisarius took advantage of this to charge one of his couriers to carry a message to the Vandal magistrates. The message, purportedly a letter from Justinian himself, insisted that the Romans had not landed in Africa to make war on the Vandals, but instead to dethrone Gelimer, who had illegally seized the throne and imprisoned the true king, Hilderic. If the Vandals joined with Belisarius, the letter promised, they would "be able to enjoy both peace and freedom." It is difficult to know what to make of this message. It seems unlikely that Justinian risked an entire campaign army simply to restore Hilderic to the throne. Perhaps that was a backup goal if Belisarius was unable to completely defeat Gelimer and the Vandals in battle. Or perhaps the restoration of Hilderic was never considered a realistic option, and the letter was written only to stoke divisions among the Vandal elite that Belisarius could exploit in the war. Either way, the letter had no impact, for Procopius admits that the courier was too afraid to deliver it, so the message did not make its way to any prominent Vandals. Belisarius now ordered his army to break camp and to enter a marching formation for the trip to Carthage. As a vanguard, he sent ahead John the Armenian, a member of his domestic staff in charge of his household expenses, in command of 300 of his personal guardsmen. This unit was to stay a few miles ahead of the main army. The allied Hunnic soldiers, approximately 600 in number and under the leadership of Sinnion and Balas, were to travel a few miles to the west of the main army. The fleet of ships, off the coast to the east, was to travel alongside the main army at roughly the same speed, which Procopius specifies as about 10 miles a day. Procopius does not explain where Antonina was located, but likely she was in the main army with her husband's household personnel. Having thus arrayed his army, Belisarius gave the command, and the entire expeditionary force began the march up the coast. The army first passed Syllectum, then Leptis Minor and Hadrumetum, all cities along the Tunisian coast. As Belisarius and his forces neared Carthage, word finally reached Gelimer in the interior that the Romans had landed an army in Africa. The enraged king sent a message to his brother, Ammatas, in Carthage, with an order that he should kill Hilderic and prepare the Vandals there for war. Gelimer planned to wait until the Romans reached a place approximately ten miles south of Carthage (and thus known as Ad Decimum), and then he and Ammatas could attack from different sides, trapping the Roman army in between. Gelimer's orders were carried out. Ammatas immediately had Hilderic executed, along with all of his household. If the Romans had truly thought a restoration of Hilderic was a possibility before, it certainly was not now. Ammatas and Gelimer prepared their forces for the planned battle.[17]

Belisarius remained unaware of these plans. After a march of a little less than two weeks since leaving their camp at Caput Vada, the vanguard of the Roman army arrived at Ad Decimum. The date, Procopius informs us, was September 13, 533. The vanguard, 300 cavalry from Belisarius' personal guardsmen under the command of John the Armenian, ran right into Ammatas and his own men, and battle was joined. Fortunately for the guardsmen and John, Ammatas had been impatient and had not waited until the appointed hour to attack. The forces of Gelimer were still some distance away, so the pincer could not be closed, and more than this, Ammatas had raced ahead with only some of his forces, and the rest of his army was strung out along the road from Carthage to Ad Decimum. In a brief but furious battle, John's troops killed Ammatas, and the remaining Vandals fled, which allowed the Romans to ride all the way to the walls of Carthage, killing Vandal stragglers as they went. Several miles away, at roughly the same time, the west guard of the Roman army, 600 Hunnic allied soldiers, ran into elements of Gelimer's army. The Vandal king had divided his forces, sending 2,000 men under the command of his nephew, Gibamund, north of his position. It seems that Gelimer's idea was that the Romans would be trapped between Ammatas coming from Carthage in the north, Gibamund coming from the west, and Gelimer himself coming up behind them from the south. However, just as Belisarius' vanguard had foiled Ammatas' attack, so would his west guard foil the attack of Gibamund. The Huns ran into the Vandals of Gibamund at a place called the Field of Salt, approximately 5 miles west of Ad Decimum, and destroyed them utterly. Thus without the main army under Belisarius yet engaging in combat, the plans of Gelimer were already in tatters. However, neither Belisarius nor Gelimer was yet aware of these developments.[18]

Marching up from the south with his main force, Belisarius stopped about four miles shy of Ad Decimum and ordered his infantry to set up a fortified camp. He made a short speech, encouraging his soldiers to show valor, and offered a prayer. Leaving Antonina and the infantry there, Belisarius set out with only his cavalry (around 5,000 men), intending to do some reconnaissance in force and skirmishing with the Vandals, to gauge their strength before engaging in all-out battle. Even now, Belisarius was cautious. He sent ahead the units of federates from his cavalry, under Solomon and their other commanders, as a screen, while he followed with the remainder of the force. When these soldiers reached Ad Decimum, they discovered the bodies from John the Armenian's skirmish with Ammatas. Before any action could be taken, they saw a dust cloud to the southwest: Gelimer was arriving with the main Vandal army. Solomon and the other commanders were initially split on whether they should fight or flee back to Belisarius, but they decided to attempt to capture the highest hill at the spot and hold it. However, the Vandals of Gelimer were more numerous and easily captured the hill, forcing off the federates, who then fled in confusion back to Belisarius' force, sweeping up a unit of guardsmen 800 strong under Uliaris on the way. At this point, Procopius reports, the fortunes of the Romans were in perilous straits. The historian believes that if Gelimer had pursued the fleeing federates and guardsmen, he might have slaughtered them and ridden straight into Belisarius and routed his troops as well. Alternatively, Gelimer might have gone on to Carthage to make it secure and perhaps even captured the Roman fleet, which was still proceeding slowly up the coast around Cape Bon. The Vandal king chose neither option. Procopius claims, "I am unable to say what came over Gelimer that, with victory in his hands, he willingly gave it up to the enemy." However, the author offers an explanation: that Gelimer was so distraught at seeing Ammatas, his brother, dead on the plain of Ad Decimum, that he halted all military operations in order to lament and prepare his body for burial. There was likely also a tactical explanation to Gelimer's decision not to pursue, however. He did not have any additional intelligence since the armies under Ammatas and Gibamund had been defeated, and so he could not be sure of the location of the main Roman army. Pursuing the defeated federates would have been risky, especially if his was the only functioning Vandal army in the field, as he must have suspected after seeing Ammatas' body. So rather than pursue the defeated federates, or move immediately to Carthage, Gelimer lingered at Ad Decimum, and most likely conferred with his chief officers about what their next move should be. In the meantime, the fleeing federates and guardsmen reached the main body of Roman cavalry and Belisarius, who managed to restore them to order and placed them in line with his forces. At last Belisarius received a full report on everything that had happened at Ad Decimum, including the victory of John the Armenian and the death of Ammatas. This gave the general confidence, and he immediately ordered his cavalry to move at speed to Ad Decimum and engage the Vandals. Procopius claims the Vandals and Gelimer were unprepared for this, and they immediately fled when Belisarius and the Roman cavalry began their charge. The Romans pursued until nightfall, killing as many Vandals as they could. Gelimer and his remaining forces escaped west, toward Numidia (modern Algeria). At dusk, the west guard of the Huns and the vanguard of John the Armenian returned, and the Roman cavalry all camped overnight together at Ad Decimum. Belisarius had won the first battle of the Vandal War.[19]

The next day, September 14, Antonina and the infantry marched up from their camp and joined Belisarius and the cavalry forces at Ad Decimum, and then the unified army proceeded the last ten miles to Carthage, arriving late in the evening. The Carthaginians opened the gates willingly, and lit up the town to welcome the arriving Roman army, but Belisarius remained cautious. He feared that the surviving Vandals might have set up an ambush in the dark, and even if they had not, he was not certain he could guarantee a peaceful occupation of the metropolis at night. His soldiers might be emboldened by the cover of darkness to pillage as they marched in. So the general ordered his army to set up camp right next to the city, and there they spent the night. That same evening, the fleet under the command of Kalonymos arrived outside of Carthage as well. Although the city's harbor was open to them, the majority of the ship captains refused to enter it, as Belisarius had ordered the fleet to also avoid entering the city at night. So the fleet anchored at a harbor about 5 miles away from Carthage. However, Kalonymos in the flagship secretly snuck into the harbor of Carthage and plundered the property of the merchants along the coast, an action for which he would be required to make reparations by Belisarius later. On the morning of September 15, 533, Belisarius drew up his whole army and arrayed them for battle. He exhorted them to maintain good order, and to remember that they had come to restore freedom to the inhabitants of the city, not to harm them. The speech apparently served its purpose, for the Roman army entered Carthage unopposed and peacefully. Procopius was most impressed by this non-violent capture of the city, claiming that it gave Belisarius "such fame as no one of his contemporaries ever won nor indeed

FIGURE 7 The ruins of ancient Carthage. Wikimedia Commons.

any men of ancient times." Belisarius entered the palace and sat upon the throne of Gelimer. Then Belisarius and his officers all ate together the lunch which had been ordered before for the Vandal king and his chief officials. How satisfying that meal must have been! However, the war was certainly not over at this point. Gelimer was still in the field with the remnants of an army, and he could expect to be reinforced by the Vandal fleet and soldiers that had been sent to Sardinia. So Belisarius ordered his men to begin repairing the walls of Carthage, to make the city a safe refuge, and then considered what to do next.[20]

Belisarius decided to send out a small scouting party, to ascertain the location of Gelimer and the remnants of his army. So he appointed Diogenes, one of his personal guardsmen, to lead a small unit of 22 other guardsmen on a reconnaissance mission. They spent the night two days travel west of Carthage, having not yet discovered the Vandal army. However, Gelimer had spent the last few days bribing the farmers and rural inhabitants of the region to kill any Roman foragers they came across. So the local farmers informed Gelimer of Diogenes and his scout party. In the night, 300 Vandals sent by Gelimer surrounded the house where Diogenes and his men were sleeping. As the Vandals whispered about how they might take the house and capture Diogenes alive, one of the guardsmen woke up and noticed what was going on. He roused Diogenes and his fellow soldiers, and together they all put on their armor and weapons and stealthily mounted their horses. Then the guardsmen suddenly flung open the doors to the house and rode out at maximum speed. The mounted guardsmen ran the gauntlet of the Vandal soldiers, and although two were killed in the process, Diogenes and the remaining 20 soldiers escaped the ambush. This thrilling anecdote describes a mission that did not exactly change the course of the war, nor even provide Belisarius with accurate knowledge of the location of Gelimer and the Vandal army. It does, however, help us to understand just how important Belisarius' personal guardsmen were in the Vandal campaign. Belisarius chose men from his personal guard unit under John the Armenian to be the vanguard of his army leading up to the Battle of Ad Decimum, there was another unit of guards operating under Uliaris on the day of the battle, and now for the first operation after the capture of Carthage, he again turned to his guards. In an army of 18,000 soldiers, Belisarius frequently singled out his own personal guard unit to carry out important missions. Around the time of the mission of Diogenes, Belisarius dispatched Solomon, one of the commanders of the federates, to Justinian in Constantinople to report on progress thus far.[21]

While Belisarius was securing Carthage, Gelimer and his surviving soldiers reached the Plain of Bulla, about 100 miles west of the city and near the border between modern Tunisia and Algeria. There Gelimer sought to muster the remaining strength of his kingdom. He sent a message to Sardinia, to recall his brother Tzazo, and the fleet and army that he had under his command there. Tzazo had just successfully captured the city of Cagliari and slain the rebel Godas and all the men he had with him. Procopius was aware of the bitter irony that the Vandals had sent away a portion of their army and their fleet to enable them to keep hold of far-away Sardinia, but that this had cost them their capital of Carthage and indeed the richest part of the Vandal Kingdom. It was a poor trade. Procopius imagines a letter from Gelimer to Tzazo in which the king wrote, "It was not to recover the island for us that you sailed from here, but so that Justinian might be master of Libya." Indeed, Belisarius, Justinian, and the Roman Empire profited greatly from the rebellion of Godas and the Vandal determination to put down that revolt. Receiving this letter, Tzazo and the Vandals with him wept and then immediately boarded their ships and sailed back to Africa. Procopius informs us confidently that it took them three days to make landfall in Africa, and then they marched to the interior and joined Gelimer at the Plain of Bulla. It is not clear why the Vandals left their ships behind, but they are not mentioned again in the war, and all the remaining engagements were on land. Gelimer also attempted to woo to his side the groups of Berber people who lived in the region, on the border between the arable lands controlled by the Vandals and the desert farther inland. Few chose to join him, however, as most of these people shrewdly determined to make positive overtures to Belisarius and then wait on the sidelines to see whether Vandals or Romans would end up the victors in the coming conflict.[22]

It appears that many weeks passed in these activities, as Gelimer rallied his armies and Belisarius focused on rebuilding the fortifications of Carthage and secured control of the nearby region. In early December 533, Gelimer and Tzazo led their combined army out of the Plain of Bulla and began the trek east toward Carthage. It was the last march of the Vandals. They came near to Carthage and tore down its aqueduct, but this did not entice Belisarius to march out with his army, so they withdrew and placed guards along all the roads leading into the city. This was likely an ineffective siege, since the Roman fleet controlled the port and the entire coast. It is worth noting again that it is not clear why the Vandals did not make use of the fleet that had brought Tzazo's forces back from Sardinia. It seems to have been left aground at the coast when Tzazo returned. While maintaining this loose siege, Gelimer sent envoys to try to woo the Hunnic allied soldiers of Belisarius to betray the Romans. He had apparently been impressed by reports of their victory over Gibamund near Ad Decimum. Belisarius learned of this and countered by courting the Huns with gifts and banquets. The Huns therefore promised to remain loyal to the Romans if Belisarius would allow them to leave Africa after the war, but in secret they decided to hang back and avoid joining the coming battle until it was clear whether the Romans or Vandals were winning. Once the Romans finally finished repairing the wall around Carthage, Belisarius decided it was time to offer battle. He drew up his entire army, delivered a speech urging them to be brave and treat the Vandals with great contempt, and then divided the army in two. The first part, including all but 500 of the cavalry, left under the command of John the Armenian that day. The next day, Belisarius led out all the infantry and the remaining 500 cavalry. The two parts of the army marched west and came upon the Vandal army encamped at Tricamarum, the exact location of which is unknown but was some 20 miles west of Carthage. John and the cavalry camped nearby overnight, awaiting the arrival of Belisarius and the rest of the army. It is not clear where Antonina was at this time, because Procopius does not mention her at this point in the story. Perhaps she stayed in Carthage, seeing to the city's management.[23]

The next day was perhaps December 15, 533. Gelimer placed the women and children of the Vandal soldiers in the middle of his camp and drew up the army. He urged his soldiers to fight for children, wives, and land, and not to bring shame upon the name of Gaiseric, the Vandals' greatest king who had first led them to North Africa. Tzazo delivered a separate address to the Vandals who had come with him from Sardinia. Then the brothers led the Vandal army out of the camp and advanced on the Romans, lining up in battle order on one side of a small stream. The Roman cavalry, who were preparing lunch, quickly exited their camp and lined up in their own battle array on their side of the same stream. About this time, Belisarius arrived with his 500 cavalry, having sped up to join the battle. The infantry were several hours behind him, still marching. John the Armenian took the center of the Roman line with Belisarius and all the guardsmen of the general, while the commanders of the federates took the left wing, and the regular cavalry commanders took the right wing. For some time, the two armies stared at each other across the small stream, as though it were a raging river. Neither king nor general wanted to make the first step. At length, Belisarius decided to use his guardsmen to test the Vandal lines. He commanded John the Armenian to take some of the guards, cross the stream, and attack the center of the Vandal line, where Tzazo was in command. The Vandals pushed the Romans back and they retreated to their side of the stream, but the Vandals did not pursue. Then John repeated the process a second time, with the same results. Perhaps Belisarius was hoping to tempt the Vandals into committing to an assault. The third time, Belisarius had John take all of the general's personal guards, and this time the attack was not merely a quick probe. The fighting grew fierce, and Tzazo was killed. At this, Belisarius gave the command, and the rest of the Roman cavalry crossed the stream and attacked the Vandal lines. The Vandals almost immediately crumbled and began to retreat back to their camp. The Huns now joined the Romans in giving pursuit, but it was short lived because it was not a long run back to the Vandal camp. Procopius reports that 800 Vandals died in this engagement. Belisarius now held back his cavalry to await the arrival of the infantry. In late afternoon, these forces arrived, and Belisarius moved with them immediately against the Vandal camp. What should have been the dramatic last stand of the Vandals failed to materialize. Gelimer could see the writing on the wall, and rather than fight it out, he chose to flee, leaping on his horse without a word and galloping out of the camp, back west toward Numidia. Noticing his departure, the remaining Vandals lost heart and also fled, leaving behind their wives, children, and the camp treasure. The Roman army simultaneously captured the camp and pursued the fleeing Vandals. The men were ruthlessly cut down as they ran, and the women and children were captured and enslaved. This sounds harsh, but it was standard operating procedure in battle for ancient armies. The Battle of Tricamarum was over, and after a century Vandal power was broken forever. Belisarius had completed his signature victory.[24]

The Roman soldiers continued their pursuit and plundering of the defeated Vandals throughout the night, neither slowing down nor observing any discipline. Belisarius was unable to restore order until the morning, when he stood upon a nearby hill and brought the army to him, starting with his own personal guards. His first command was that his loyal man John the Armenian take 200 men and set off in immediate pursuit of Gelimer, for the war could not be considered truly over until he was dead or in captivity. John and this handpicked group, probably consisting again of Belisarius' personal guards, set off immediately and pursued the Vandal king for five days and nights. At dawn on the sixth day of the pursuit, the group was about to catch up to Gelimer when a tragic accident struck. Uliaris, one of Belisarius' guardsmen, was drunk and, upon seeing a bird perched in a tree, felt an uncontrollable urge to test his skill by shooting an arrow at it. He drew his bow and shot an arrow, which missed the bird, but landed in the neck of John the Armenian. He bled out and died not long after. This was a major blow, not just to the pursuit of Gelimer, but to Belisarius personally. We have seen throughout the preceding narrative how large of a role was played by John the Armenian, who although he was only the manager of Belisarius' personal household indeed seemed more important than the actual commanders and officers who accompanied the general. Procopius gives John a fitting epitaph: "For in manliness and every sort of virtue he was well-endowed, and he was gentle to those who came to him and equitable to a degree unsurpassed." He seems to have been genuinely loved. The pursuit of Gelimer was immediately halted. Uliaris fled to a nearby village and sat in its church in supplication, fearful for his life. Belisarius was called, and coming to the site he wept for John and honored his tomb. The general did not punish Uliaris, as John's dying wish had been that the man not be punished for what after all had been an accident. Belisarius now collected the soldiers and resumed the pursuit of Gelimer himself until he reached Hippo Regius (modern Annaba, Algeria), probably in January 534. Belisarius took the city by surrender, disarmed its Vandal defenders, and sent them on to Carthage. At Hippo, the general learned that Gelimer had ascended a steep nearby mountain named Papua, probably in the mountainous region of Kroumirie. The mountain was held by a group of Berbers who were loyal to Gelimer and would not be easy to take by assault, especially in the winter. So Belisarius selected a detachment of soldiers and put over them the redoubtable commander Pharas the Herul, with orders to guard the passes at the foot of the mountain so that nobody could leave the peak or bring supplies up to it. Having established this siege, and confident that Gelimer would surrender eventually, Belisarius returned to Carthage, signaling that he did not believe it necessary to be present personally at Gelimer's capture.[25]

Belisarius and Antonina, Triumphant

Back at Carthage in winter 534, Belisarius moved to secure the remainder of the Vandal Kingdom for Justinian by appointing commanders with small contingents of soldiers to move out and take important areas. To Sardinia and Corsica, he sent Cyril, and with him the head of Tzazo, to confirm to the islanders that he was really dead and would not come back and punish them again for joining the Roman cause. To Caesarea in Numidia (modern Cherchell, Algeria), he sent John, one of the infantry commanders. To Septem (modern Ceuta, Spain), he sent another John, one of his personal guardsmen. John was a distressingly common name in sixth-century Roman armies. To the Balearic Islands, he sent Apollinarius, who had once served the previous Vandal King Hilderic. Finally, he sent a unit of soldiers to reinforce Pudentius, who had raised a rebellion against the Vandals in Tripoli and was still holding out there. Plotting these locations on a map helps to paint a picture of the limits of Vandal power before the Roman restoration, which stretched from western Libya to the Straits of Gibraltar. It is worth noting that every place Belisarius moved to secure at this point was either an island or a port city. Initial Roman control of the region was very coastal in nature and perhaps focused on the economic advantages of controlling trading routes. In keeping with the coastal theme, Belisarius also sent some soldiers to attempt to take Lilybaeum in Sicily. Although the majority of the island was controlled by the Ostrogothic Kingdom of Italy, Lilybaeum had been granted as a dowry to Amalafrida, the daughter of the Ostrogothic King Theoderic the Great, when she had married the Vandal King Thrasamund, perhaps 30 years before. It had since been controlled by the Vandals. The Goths now argued that the city should return to them and not be considered Vandal territory that could be absorbed by Belisarius, and so rather than cause an incident, Belisarius referred the matter to Justinian.[26]

The only piece remaining in the Vandal War was now Gelimer himself. At Mount Papua, the siege dragged on. Pharas was unable to force an ascent, as the mountain passes were too steep and the Berbers defended them fiercely. So he was forced to wait until Gelimer and his defenders caved due to starvation.

Gelimer and Pharas exchanged letters during the siege, Pharas urging the king to submit and become a willing servant of Justinian, and Gelimer refusing to serve someone who had wronged him and reduced him to his present state. At one point, Gelimer requested a loaf of bread, a sponge, and a lyre. He had not seen bread since he ascended the mountain. His eye was infected and he needed to clean it. He had composed a lament and wished to sing it with musical accompaniment. Because these requests were reasonable and moving, and would not long delay Gelimer's surrender, Pharas agreed to them. By late March 534, Gelimer had been besieged for three months, and food was running low. One day he observed two children coming to blows over a small cake of grain, desperate to eat something, and this finally broke the king's will to resist. He requested reassurance from Pharas that if he surrendered he would be treated well by Belisarius and Justinian. Pharas sent to Belisarius for confirmation, and the general sent the commander Cyprian to give an oath concerning Gelimer's safety. Upon receiving this oath, Gelimer surrendered himself and those who were with him, and he was immediately escorted to Carthage. Coming into Belisarius' presence for the first time, Gelimer could not stop loudly cackling. The laughter seemed immoderate and inappropriate to the occasion. Procopius reasoned that either Gelimer had lost his mind, or that he was demonstrating that fate was so powerful that all people could do in response was laugh. Belisarius now sent another message to Justinian, informing him that the Vandal king was a captive in Carthage. The war now was well and truly over.[27]

It seems that Belisarius and Antonina had resided in Carthage throughout winter 534. With them was their adopted son, Theodosios. They might also have been accompanied by Photios, although no source mentions his presence. Perhaps the family was living in the former palace of the Vandal kings, where Belisarius had taken lunch on the day he captured Carthage in September of the previous year. Undoubtedly the members of Belisarius' household, including his personal guards and the historian Procopius, lived alongside them. The close quarters here, and indeed even before while on the march or in the ships, bred rumor and gossip. According to Procopius, during this time Belisarius and Antonina had an argument in one of the basement rooms of the palace. The general discovered his wife and Theodosios alone in the room, and he became angry and asked what they were doing. Antonina responded, "I came down here with the boy to hide the most precious spoils of war so that the emperor doesn't find out about them." Belisarius accepted the excuse, and the matter was dropped. If the incident was not completely fabricated by Procopius, or just the idle gossip of Belisarius' household in winter quarters, it is indication that a certain level of corruption was expected of higher Roman generals and officials in this period. After all, Belisarius became even wealthier than before as a result of the Vandal expedition, able to afford public celebrations in Constantinople and to maintain a large household of personal guardsmen in his subsequent campaign in Italy. This money had to come from somewhere, and so it is not unlikely that Belisarius and Antonina worked together to withhold some of the captured Vandal treasury from Justinian. So the idea of Theodosios helping Antonina to go through the treasure and select key portions of it to retain for themselves is not at all unbelievable.[28]

However, in the *Secret History* Procopius asserts that this was merely a cover story for a more salacious event. He charges that, in reality, Antonina had taken the teenage Theodosios down to the basement room to have sex with him, and that the two were carrying on an affair throughout the Vandal campaign. This is a serious accusation indeed. It has colored modern opinions of Antonina for centuries because scholars have almost uniformly accepted it as true. Antonina is therefore agreed to be not just an adulterer, but also a practitioner of incest, and perhaps even a pedophile. However, there is good reason to doubt the existence of an affair. The first cause of doubt is that the *Secret History* is an invective, in which Procopius is trying to make Belisarius and Antonina look as bad as possible. This story accomplishes that goal just a little too neatly, for the author is able to shame them both with it. Antonina is described as unable to restrain her passions, "smitten with desire and obviously driven by erotic passion, she did not see any further reason why she should refrain from the deed." Belisarius is described as being so under his wife's control that he could not believe her guilty of an affair: "He was so infatuated with this person, his wife, that he could not bring himself to believe the evidence of his own eyes." With this one anecdote, Procopius is able to smear Belisarius as the opposite of a strong husband, and Antonina as the opposite of a virtuous wife. If the historian wanted to invent a story that would easily accomplish a character assassination of both husband and wife simultaneously, he could scarcely come up with a better choice, which makes the entire story too neat to be true. The second cause of doubt is related to witnesses. Procopius does not suggest that he himself saw either an affair or the argument in the basement room. Nor does he name any other witnesses, although in Carthage at the time were hundreds of Belisarius' personal guards and other members of his household. Apparently, none of them saw any of this. In addition, this story is reported in no other ancient source, either in its particulars or in a more general sense. Of all the surviving written material from the sixth century, not a single other writer accuses Antonina of an affair.

There is simply no corroborating evidence of any kind for this charge. Finally, although Procopius provided the story about hiding wealth from the emperor as a cover for the alleged "real" reason Antonina and Theodosios were in the basement room, it is by far the more believable of the two options. It seems far more likely that Antonina and Theodosios were rifling through treasure, knowing how rich Belisarius was later in his career, than that Antonina was overcome with erotic passion for her teenage adopted son. So, when considering the story as a whole, and the fact that it appears only in an invective written to make Belisarius and Antonina look bad, it is likely that Antonina did not have an affair with Theodosios. The anecdote is, however, quite useful for understanding how Belisarius and Antonina began to accumulate the wealth that sustained them in future campaigns and made them some of the richest people in the Roman world.[29]

Soon after the arrival of the captive Gelimer in Carthage, Procopius charges that some of the officers in Belisarius' army were jealous of his success and so slandered him to the emperor. Perhaps they were also envious of the wealth that the general was pillaging from the Vandal treasury. They wrote a letter to Justinian, accusing Belisarius of seeking to set up a kingdom for himself in North Africa. This is an interesting accusation, and convenient in that it played on Justinian's worst fears about the result of a successful invasion. Yet, Justinian had probably selected Belisarius as the general of this expedition primarily because he felt that the latter was above reproach in this regard, particularly after his service in the Nika Riot. Beyond this, it is unclear whether the officers had any evidence for this charge, other than that Belisarius was sending detachments of soldiers to claim the major cities and islands of the Vandal domain in the emperor's name. So it is unlikely that Justinian was concerned that this accusation was true. Nevertheless, it would not have been prudent to leave Belisarius in charge of North Africa indefinitely, and someone did have to bring all the Vandal prisoners, including Gelimer, back to Constantinople. According to Procopius, Justinian sent Solomon back to Carthage, with a message to Belisarius. The general could choose whether to remain in North Africa directing affairs there, or to return to Constantinople with the Vandal captives. In the *Wars*, the historian says that Belisarius was eager to return, to report to Justinian and clear his name. In the *Secret History*, Procopius suggests that Belisarius was actually ordered to return. The law Justinian issued on April 13, 534, for the governing of the new African provinces also suggests Belisarius was required to return after he had established military defenses for the region. This evidence does not, however, indicate that Justinian believed Belisarius to be guilty of treason.

The general had been dispatched for a purpose and had accomplished that purpose. The fact that he retained the title General of the East throughout the Vandal War is also indication that Belisarius was not intended to remain permanently in North Africa. At any rate, Belisarius, after having established the requisite military commands in the region, prepared to return to Constantinople, perhaps in early summer 534. He loaded some of the ships with the Vandal prisoners, the Vandal treasure, and his own household. As he was about to set sail for the capital, the tone of his departure turned from triumphant to frustrated when Belisarius received word that some of the Berbers had begun launching attacks upon the freshly reclaimed Roman provinces. The Romans had supplanted the Vandals in ownership of these lands, but also had taken their place in a long series of wars with the neighboring Berbers, which stretched back to the accession of Huneric in 477 and would continue for years to come. Belisarius could do no more. He entrusted the defense of North Africa to Solomon, now appointed the new praetorian prefect of Africa, gave him most of his own guardsmen, and then set sail for Constantinople, Antonina again at his side.[30]

Belisarius and Antonina arrived in Constantinople in summer 534, only a year or so after they had sailed forth from the city. Justinian's actions leave little doubt that he was not suspicious of his general. In fact, the emperor was overjoyed. The calculated risk of the Vandal War had succeeded beyond his wildest dreams. Justinian, in his gratitude, heaped honor after honor upon Belisarius and Antonina. For the people of Constantinople, the most visible honor the general received was a triumph, a celebration of military victory common in the ancient Roman Republic, but exceedingly rare ever since. After Augustus took control of the Roman government, all triumphs had been reserved for emperors. The last traditional non-imperial triumph celebrated was in 19 BC. Belisarius' triumph took the form of a procession on foot from his house to the hippodrome, and then he marched around the hippodrome track from the starting gates until he reached the emperor's box. But the general did not walk alone. He was accompanied by servants and wagons bearing the gold, silver, and jewels he had seized from the Vandal treasury at Carthage and from Gelimer's camp. Procopius describes this as being worth an extremely great sum; he does not even attempt to quantify its value. Included among this treasure was spoils from the Temple in Jerusalem, which the emperor Titus had captured in 70 AD. From there it had come to Rome, and in Rome it had been pillaged by the Vandals in 455 AD. Beyond the wealth, Belisarius was accompanied by Gelimer, all his family, and the most attractive of the Vandal prisoners. This must have been an extraordinary sight for the people of Constantinople. Never in their lifetimes had they seen such a procession. It was evidence of the power and might of the Romans, but also, of course, of the success of Belisarius. The people cheered and shouted wildly. Belisarius, who two years before had been one of their butchers, was now their hero. By allowing this triumph and adulation for Belisarius, Justinian was demonstrating his continuing trust in his general. However, trust or not, the people were to be reminded that Belisarius had accomplished all of this on the emperor's behalf. At the end of the procession, Belisarius arrived in front of the emperor's box in the hippodrome, with some 100,000 Romans watching. The general forced Gelimer to throw himself on the ground before Justinian, formally submitting. The Vandal king was heard to whisper, over and over again, the words of Ecclesiastes, "Vanity of vanities, all is vanity." And then Belisarius himself was down on the ground, joining Gelimer in submitting to Justinian, illustrating to all his loyalty as a servant of the emperor. And thus ended the great triumph of Belisarius. Procopius gives no indication of the presence of Antonina in all of this. Perhaps she was allowed to march in the procession with Belisarius, or perhaps she observed it from a box in the hippodrome, but doubtless she was proud, for she had taken part with Belisarius in this adventure.[31]

Further rewards followed this grand event. Probably at this time Belisarius and Antonina were both granted patrician status, the highest senatorial rank that the emperor could directly bestow. In the Roman Senate of the time, the highest-ranked members were those who had held the ancient Roman office of consul, the next highest were the patricians, and below them were the illustrious, a group that automatically included generals like Belisarius. So this was a promotion of one rank for the conquering hero. For Antonina this was an exultation that most women from her circles would never see. She was now truly a lady on par with the leading, elite women of Constantinople. Finally, at the turn of the new year, Belisarius received promotion to the highest rank of the senate with one last reward for his great victory. Justinian granted his general the office of consul for the year 535. Belisarius enjoyed another procession, this time carried in a traditional Roman curule chair by some of the Vandal captives, and as he progressed through the streets of Constantinople, he flung Vandal jewelry and coins to the people. Like the triumph, it must have been a magnificent spectacle that deeply impressed the Constantinopolitans who witnessed it. Thus, as the year 534 drew to a close and 535 began, Belisarius and Antonina were without a doubt the most famous and powerful people in the entire Roman world with the exception of Justinian and Theodora themselves.[32]

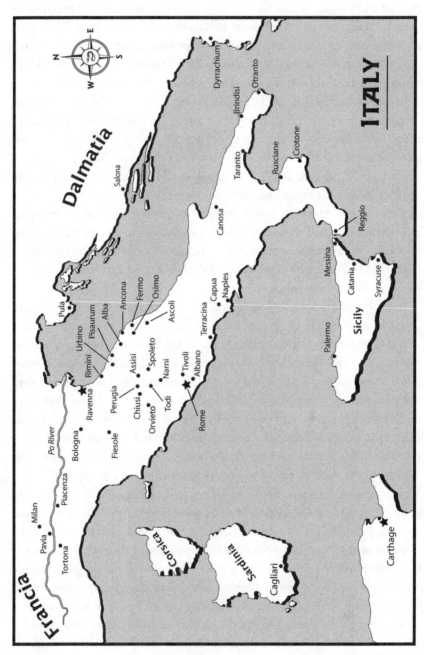

MAP 4 Italy: an overview of important sites in the Gothic War. Created by John Wyatt Greenlee.

4

The Eternal City

IN THE SUMMER of 535, Belisarius and Antonina embarked on their next audacious campaign. Justinian had appointed Belisarius to the supreme command of an expedition that was publicly bound merely for Carthage. This would not have been an unreasonable destination, as Africa had only just been taken from the Vandals in his previous campaign, and it would not have been surprising for the emperor to seek to reinforce the Roman position there. In fact, this even would have been sensible. A larger Roman army in North Africa would solidify imperial control and help the emperor's representatives there to negotiate from a position of strength with the neighboring Berbers, resulting in a safer and more prosperous region. However, the mission Justinian had tasked Belisarius with was not safe and sensible, but risky and daring. The general was instructed to sail to Sicily and make an attempt to capture the island, then to hold it and await further instructions. Sicily was at the time a dominion of the Ostrogothic Kingdom, which stretched from the island through the whole Italian peninsula and up into what the Romans called Dalmatia (today the western Balkans, encompassing Croatia, Albania, Bosnia and Herzegovina, and more).[1]

But why should Justinian send an army to invade the Ostrogothic Kingdom? As with the reclamation of North Africa from the Vandals, the emperor had many reasons. First, he took issue with the king of the Ostrogoths, as he had with Gelimer of the Vandals. The Ostrogoths were ruled by Theodoric from the moment he founded their kingdom in Italy (493 AD) until his death in 526. At this point, Theodoric's daughter Amalasuntha ruled as regent for her young son Athalaric. But when Athalaric died in 534, Amalasuntha turned to her cousin Theodahad for support. She crowned him king, but in return Theodahad first deposed her and then had her murdered in May 535. This provided Justinian's first reason, and primary justification, for an attack on the

Belisarius & Antonina. David Alan Parnell, Oxford University Press. © Oxford University Press 2023.
DOI: 10.1093/oso/9780197574706.003.0005

Ostrogothic Kingdom. Before her deposition and death, Amalasuntha had allegedly proposed to cede Italy to the emperor, to save herself from her polit-ical enemies, who were "the most notable Goths." This offer, combined with the seemingly easy victory of Belisarius in North Africa, seems to have stoked the emperor's ambition. He was now determined to recover Italy for his em-pire, as he had North Africa. This ambition, then, was his second reason to send Belisarius and an army to Sicily. As a third reason, it is important not to discount the possibility that Justinian now did see it as his duty as Roman em-peror to recover the empire's lost territories, particularly the ancient capital of Rome, and especially when recovery seemed like it might be relatively easy. The sixth-century *Chronicle* of Marcellinus Comes makes it clear that the occupation of Italy in particular rankled powerful people during Justinian's reign. He writes in his chronicle for the year 476, that "the Western empire of the Roman people perished" and that thereafter "Gothic kings" held Rome. Such opinions must have influenced the way Justinian looked at Ostrogothic Italy as he contemplated war to recover it for his empire.[2]

The makeup of Belisarius' army, the orders it was given, and the other initiatives undertaken by the emperor at the same time make it clear that he believed the war against the Ostrogothic Kingdom might be won without great difficulty. The army Belisarius commanded as he set sail in 535 was rela-tively small: Procopius reports that it numbered 7,500 soldiers, although this number does not seem to have counted the guardsmen of Belisarius and his subordinate commanders. As comparison, the general had 18,000 soldiers, not counting guardsmen, for his invasion of North Africa in 533. So Justinian was perhaps not expecting Belisarius to have to fight tooth and nail every step of the way in Italy: this was a force more appropriately sized to take control of lands ceded to it by an enemy. The orders again reiterate that Justinian did not expect a hard fight. Belisarius was to capture Sicily if it could be done "without any trouble," but if there was an obstacle, he was to sail on to Carthage in-stead. Finally, Justinian's other actions make clear that he still hoped for the easy acquisition of Italy. Even while dispatching Belisarius with this army and these orders, he sent Peter the Patrician as ambassador to Theodahad to put diplomatic pressure on him to cede his kingdom to the Romans, as Amalasuntha before him had proposed. Concurrent with this effort, the em-peror sent the General Mundus into Dalmatia with an army to seize Salona (modern Solin, Croatia) from the Ostrogoths. All of these initiatives add up to suggest that Justinian and his advisors thought that Theodahad could be cowed into ceding the entire Ostrogothic Kingdom to the Romans through a combination of military force on the fringes of that kingdom (Sicily and

Dalmatia) and diplomatic pressure. If this came to pass, Belisarius' relatively small army would be positioned well in Sicily to occupy Italy for the emperor. Even if that did not come to pass, control of prosperous Sicily was valuable in and of itself, so Belisarius' effort would not be wasted.[3]

So much then for the strategy of Justinian. Belisarius was tasked with carrying out these plans, and given the autonomy to make important decisions, such as whether it was possible to seize Sicily or not. For this reason, Justinian again invested Belisarius with the supreme command of the expedition. Procopius breaks Belisarius' army of 7,500 soldiers into different categories: 4,000 soldiers from the regular army units (probably from the Army of the East, of which Belisarius was still the general) and the federates, 3,000 soldiers from Isaurian units (meaning units that were originally, but perhaps not now exclusively recruited from Isauria in Anatolia), 200 allied Hunnic soldiers, and 300 allied Berber soldiers. Belisarius and his subordinate commanders would also have brought with them their own guardsmen, although Procopius does not number them. The guardsmen of Belisarius alone probably numbered somewhere between 500 and 1,000 at this point, but would grow much more numerous later. So perhaps the expedition, including guardsmen, might have approached 9,000 men. More interesting than this enumeration of the soldiers is that Procopius again names the commanders of the army, the officers that would serve under Belisarius. Named first, perhaps because they were Belisarius' top lieutenants, were Constantine, Bessas, and Peranios. The cavalry commanders were Valentinos, Magnos, and Innocentios, while the infantry commanders were Herodian, Paul, Demetrios, and Oursikinos, and the Isaurian commander was Ennes. Mentioned last is Photios, the son of Antonina, who was "a young man wearing his first beard, but possessed the greatest discretion and showed a strength of character beyond his years." This list of Belisarius' commanders is particularly important, because it foreshadows the characters that would play important roles in the years to follow. Most of the men listed here are mentioned multiple times in Procopius' account of the following campaign. The list also demonstrates that Belisarius did not work alone but relied heavily on trusted subordinate officers, which becomes quite clear later in the campaign.[4]

It is equally interesting to consider who is not mentioned in this passage: Antonina. Procopius has carefully listed all of Belisarius' prominent lieutenants and commanders of the army and has even named Photios, who does not appear to have had an official command position at the beginning of the campaign. But Antonina is not mentioned at all. She had also not been mentioned in the listing of officers for the campaign to Africa in 533, but then she had at least been described as accompanying Belisarius when he set sail. Here she is not mentioned as an individual, and her presence with the army at its departure is not recorded. And yet it is virtually certain that she was part of the original fleet that set sail in 535, at Belisarius' side yet again, because she appears with him later in Sicily. While it is tempting to infer that Procopius is slighting her by leaving her out of the narrative at this point, it is perhaps more likely that this omission is not a direct insult. For Procopius, the enumerating of soldiers and naming of commanders was a highly masculine, public matter. Antonina, even if she would later play an important role in the campaign, simply did not have a place in this listing in his eyes.[5]

Belisarius and Antonina, with 7,500 soldiers as well as Belisarius' own guardsmen, set sail sometime in summer 535. The voyage from Constantinople to Sicily would have taken between two and three weeks at the fastest, although with stops and a large fleet it likely took much longer. Upon arriving in Sicily, Belisarius was just as successful as Justinian could have hoped. He landed first at Catania, in the center of the island's eastern coastline, and the city immediately surrendered to him. This must have felt comfortably familiar, for it is the same spot where the fleet had made landfall on the way to North Africa in 533. From here, Belisarius moved south to Syracuse, which also submitted promptly. The other cities of Sicily followed rapidly. Palermo, with a Gothic garrison, was the only city to resist, but even it capitulated after a brief siege by the Roman fleet. With all of Sicily in submission, Belisarius returned to Syracuse to await further orders from Justinian. As luck would have it, the general entered Syracuse on the last day of the year, and so also the last day of his consulship: December 31, 535. His entry to Syracuse therefore became a general celebration. There was a parade and applause from his army and the local Syracusans, and Belisarius threw gold coins to all along the route (perhaps the main reason for the applause). Then he laid down the office of consul. Procopius describes the happenstance that led to this timely celebration as "good fortune beyond the power of words to describe," so this seems to have been a powerful moment. After the celebration, Belisarius and the army settled into winter quarters to await their next orders.[6]

Just as this was a time of good fortune and success for Belisarius, so it seems to have been for Justinian. The emperor received word not only of Belisarius' success, but also that the General Mundus had successfully captured Salona in Dalmatia. Consequently, Peter the Patrician ratcheted up the diplomatic pressure on Theodahad, who seems to have caved. According to Procopius, Theodahad offered to cede the Ostrogothic Kingdom to Justinian in exchange for a high title and extensive estates in the empire. If this is true, it means that the emperor had correctly measured up his opponent and all of Justinian's plans were coming to fruition. He sent word now to Belisarius to wait in Syracuse until he was summoned by Peter and Theodahad, and then to move quickly to take control of all of Italy upon their invitation. It seemed that Justinian had been right, and that the Romans were about to incorporate the remainder of the Ostrogothic Kingdom by cession rather than through war.[7]

Dreadful Portents

But the good fortune was not destined to last. Sometime in 536, a climate crisis began in the Northern Hemisphere. Procopius describes a "dreadful portent" in which the sun appeared to be only as bright as the moon. Modern historians and scientists believe that massive volcanic eruptions clogged the atmosphere, blocking the sunlight, and causing a Late Antique Little Ice Age. This cooling period would last for four or five decades and see average temperatures drop by about 1° C. Historians still debate the long-term environmental, social, and economic impacts of this climate change, but there is little indication that, in the short term, it had a significant impact on Belisarius and his campaign.[8]

Other dreadful portents of 536 hit Belisarius more directly on a professional and personal level. On Easter Sunday, the Roman soldiers garrisoning North Africa in the wake of Belisarius' annexation of the region mutinied. According to Procopius, they had three reasons: those soldiers who had married Vandal women at the end of the war wished to retain their wives' land, soldiers with Arian religious beliefs felt discriminated against in the Easter services, and finally 400 Vandal prisoners of war escaped a transport ship and their arrival further encouraged the mutiny. The mutineers attempted to kill their general, Solomon, but he escaped in the company of Procopius himself, who was apparently in Africa at the time. The author does not explain why he was present. Perhaps Belisarius had sent him there to inquire after the condition of the army. Solomon and Procopius sailed to Syracuse and begged Belisarius to come to Carthage to restore order. Belisarius, taking only 100 of his guardsmen and one ship, sailed straight to Carthage and rallied the soldiers that remained loyal. After a brief skirmish that saw the mutineers and their leader, Stotzas, flee, Belisarius received word of another mutiny, this one in his army in Syracuse, and was forced to return to Sicily, even though the mutiny in Africa was still ongoing. Leaving Ildiger, the husband of Antonina's unnamed daughter, in charge of Carthage, Belisarius hurried back to Sicily. Procopius tells us nothing about this second mutiny or how it was suppressed, in noted contrast to his detailed description of the revolt in Africa. It is possible that the mutiny in Sicily existed only in rumor, or in a vague feeling of discontent, and that the general was able to restore the situation quickly. Even still, these mutinies probably would have cast a pall over the rosy outlook Belisarius might have harbored after the successful end to 535. At roughly the same time as these events, a Gothic reinforcement army arrived in Dalmatia and attacked the Roman forces in the region. In a furious battle the Romans won, but the General Mundus died in the combat, and the Roman army then fell back. This success and reports of the apparent disorder of the Roman army in Sicily seem to have encouraged Theodahad to stiffen his spine and gamble his crown on war with the Romans. He refused to follow through on the promises he had made to Justinian, and arrested Peter and the other Roman envoys. At a stroke, all of Justinian's careful planning for an easy acquisition of Italy went up in smoke. Belisarius would now have to fight rather than just accept control, and he would have to do so with an army that was rather smaller than ideal for such a campaign. Justinian accordingly sent an order to Belisarius to invade Italy immediately.[9]

Sometime before embarking on this war, perhaps in early 536, Belisarius had to deal with another round of arguments with Antonina over their adopted son Theodosios. As with the situation in Carthage, related in the previous chapter, Procopius provides a lengthy and salacious description of this argument in Syracuse in the *Secret History*. The author writes that Antonina's "lust [for Theodosios] kept getting stronger until it was unspeakably disgusting." He claims that many people now saw what was happening between Antonina and her adopted son, but they kept quiet except for a slave named Makedonia. Now, in Syracuse, in early 536, Makedonia came to Belisarius and told him of Antonina's affair with Theodosios. She provided two young slaves to corroborate her testimony. According to Procopius, Belisarius believed what they said and ordered some of his men to kill Theodosios. The young man, however, was warned and fled all the way to Ephesus. Antonina then convinced Belisarius that the accusations of the slaves were false, so Belisarius sent to Ephesus to bring back Theodosios and turned over Makedonia and the other two slaves to his wife so that she could punish them as she saw fit. Procopius says that Antonina had their tongues cut out and then had them dismembered and cast into the sea.[10]

The story that Procopius has woven in this account certainly makes for entertaining reading, but there are indications that, as with the tale of Antonina and Theodosios in Carthage, this is more fiction than reality. It is worth noting that Procopius at no point says that he saw Antonina and Theodosios carrying on an affair. In fact, the author was absent for at least some of this time in Carthage checking in on Solomon and the army there, as he relates himself. Nor does Procopius name any influential figures, such as Belisarius' guardsmen or commanders, as witnesses. He slanders Belisarius and Antonina in the most disgusting way he can imagine, but despite the fact that he personally knows countless members of Belisarius' household and army, he names none of them. In fact, there are three witnesses to the alleged trysts: all three slaves, and two of them not even given names. This is a clue that Procopius is himself admitting that this story is less than trustworthy. The one officer named in this account is Constantine, one of Belisarius' chief lieutenants on the expedition. According to Procopius, the man announced to Belisarius that "I would sooner have done away with the wife than with the young man." On the surface this might suggest that Procopius was saying Constantine could corroborate the story of the affair, but actually here the commander is just made to respond to the reports of what had allegedly happened. And even then, Constantine is only included in this narrative so that later Procopius can slander Antonina with regards to Constantine's death in early 538.[11]

Yet it is unlikely that Procopius is fictionalizing the entire episode. There were enough people encamped in Syracuse at this point that if there was no argument between Belisarius and Antonina, and no immediate departure of Theodosios to Ephesus, this entire episode would have been completely unbelievable. Procopius was too clever with his invective to make it easily falsifiable. It seems likely that he was building up a more disgusting and sexually charged story out of a less salacious but also less fictional real argument that occurred in early 536. Fortunately, it is not necessary to guess what the real argument might have been, as Procopius himself hints at it in his account. He writes that "Theodosios was wielding power and amassing piles of money. It is said that Theodosios had plundered up to a hundred *kentenaria* (10,000 pounds of gold or 720,000 *nomismata*) from the palaces of Carthage and Ravenna." Although this statement is put forward rather imprecisely ("it is said . . .") and there are no witnesses that can testify to Theodosios' corruption, the suggestion does not seem implausible and is not offered to shame Belisarius, as the suggestion that Theodosios had a sexual affair with Antonina is meant to do. This makes it less suspect as an accusation. Instead, Procopius only brings this up to explain why Antonina's son Photios disliked Theodosios. Indeed, it would be less surprising and more expected for Photios to dislike Theodosios because of jealousy for his wealth than because he was sleeping with his mother, Antonina. The excuse that Procopius puts in Antonina's mouth for her alleged sexual tryst with Theodosios in Carthage also furthers the argument that the real cause of all this tension was money. At the time, Procopius had Antonina say, "I came down here with the boy to hide the most precious spoils of war so that the emperor doesn't find out about them." The fact that Procopius presents this as a banal excuse is a reminder of the expectation that powerful people like Belisarius and Antonina would engage in a certain level of corruption.[12]

And so both incidentally (to explain the anger of Photios) and accidentally (by pretending it was a false explanation), Procopius has revealed the real cause of the argument between Belisarius and Antonina over Theodosios in Syracuse. Antonina was helping Theodosios to embezzle money, first in Africa, and later to come in Italy, to enrich him. Evidently this was going on without Belisarius' approval. When he found out earlier in Carthage it had resulted in perhaps a warning, when he found out again in Syracuse it resulted in a huge argument and in Theodosios taking flight to avoid Belisarius' wrath. Incidentally, it is worth considering that Belisarius was not necessarily angry about this embezzlement because he was extremely virtuous and believed all the seized treasure should be turned over to Justinian. Perhaps Belisarius was simply angry that the embezzled money was going to Theodosios (and even Antonina?) instead of straight to him. The general himself had considerable need for money at this point, and he would need it even more as the war in Italy progressed. This, then, was most likely the real reason for the argument in Syracuse in early 536. Procopius' imagination, his hatred, and his desire to make Belisarius and Antonina look particularly bad led to the more salacious story of incestuous adultery and dismembered slaves.

Even if the true argument was less sexualized, it was probably not any less distressing for Belisarius and Antonina, so they likely received the order to leave Sicily behind and invade Italy as a welcome distraction from their domestic dispute. In summer 536, leaving small garrison forces in Syracuse and Palermo, Belisarius and Antonina sailed with the majority of the army from Syracuse to Messina, and from Messina across the strait to Reggio. The cities and towns of the southwestern region of Calabria surrendered immediately to Belisarius. At this point, the first major Gothic deserter also came over to the general. Ebrimuth, the son-in-law of Theodahad, was dispatched to Constantinople, where he received gifts and was promoted to the rank of patrician. The invasion of Italy was going extremely smoothly so far, but Belisarius was about to face his first significant test.[13]

The army marched north into Campania and came upon the great city of Naples. It would be the first city to offer substantial resistance to the Roman army. Belisarius suggested that the Neapolitans should submit immediately, and that the Gothic garrison in the city would be allowed to either depart

freely or serve with his army. A debate of the prominent citizens in the city revealed that some preferred to surrender to Belisarius, but the more convincing
party, perhaps buoyed by the presence of Gothic soldiers, argued for resistance. Belisarius therefore put the city under siege and cut the aqueduct that
provided it fresh water. As the weeks dragged by, however, Belisarius grew impatient. He hoped to be in Rome before the arrival of winter, and the longer he
besieged Naples, the more difficult it became to meet that goal. Fortunately,
Belisarius was saved by the curiosity of one of his soldiers. This man, sadly not
named by Procopius, climbed up into the aqueduct to see how it worked. He
found that the aqueduct provided an entrance through the walls into the city.
The entrance was not quite large enough for a person to squeeze through, but
could be widened with the appropriate tools. This man brought this suggestion to Paukaris, one of Belisarius' guardsmen, who then brought it to the
general. Belisarius commanded the men to undertake the mission, and they
widened the opening in the aqueduct. Now ready for an assault, Belisarius
again sent envoys to convince the Neopolitans to surrender, but they refused.
So he prepared to take Naples by storm. Belisarius placed 400 soldiers under
Magnos and Ennes and commanded them to enter through the aqueduct.
The commander Bessas was tasked with talking to the Goths on the walls in
their own language (Gothic) to distract them while the assault force snuck
through the aqueduct. The plan worked perfectly. Magnos and Ennes ended
up inside the city and led their 400 men to kill the guards in two towers on
the northern side of the city wall. The main army then climbed that stretch of
wall with ladders and Naples was taken by storm. The Roman army began to
rampage through the city, looting, killing Gothic soldiers, and seizing women
and children as captives, and only with difficulty was Belisarius able to restrain them and restore order. Naples was now subject to Justinian.[14]

In the meantime, Theodahad was encamped with the Gothic army at
Regata (inland from modern Terracina), roughly 40 miles south of Rome,
because the area provided enough grassland to pasture the army's horses. The
leading Goths were angry that Theodahad had not yet engaged Belisarius, and
perhaps embarrassed at the fall of Naples, so in November 536 they overthrew
him and raised up as king Vittigis, an experienced soldier. Theodahad fled
the camp, hoping to make it to Ravenna, but Vittigis sent a soldier after the
former king and Theodahad was quickly killed. He had gambled his crown on
war with the Romans, and had lost it along with his life less than a year later.
He would have been better off ceding Italy to Justinian and living in peaceful
retirement. Now under the leadership of Vittigis, the Goths marched into
Rome, probably in late November 536. The new Gothic king exhorted Pope

Silverius, who had just been selected by his predecessor Theodahad in June 536, to remain loyal to the Gothic cause, and bound him by oath. The senators and other leading citizens of Rome were likewise encouraged to remain loyal and required to swear oaths. The king took some of the senators with him as hostages for Rome's loyalty. Vittigis then left a garrison of 4,000 Gothic soldiers in Rome, and departed with the rest of the army to Ravenna. It seems that Vittigis planned to solidify his hold on power by marrying the grand-daughter of Theodoric, Matasuntha, end a war the Goths were waging with the Franks in the north, and prepare the rest of the Gothic army for war with the Romans before he engaged Belisarius.[15]

Rome Subject to the Romans

Belisarius now readied his army to march from Naples to Rome. He es-tablished a garrison of 300 infantry under the command of Herodianos in Naples. At this time, the general received an envoy from the inhabitants of Rome. The envoy, Fidelius, invited Belisarius to come to Rome, and prom-ised that the city would be surrendered. The people of Rome, and according to Procopius even Pope Silverius, had decided this was the best course of ac-tion after seeing what had happened to the people of Naples, notwithstanding the exhortations of Vittigis. This news must have cheered Belisarius, for it meant he would not have to fight to obtain entry into the ancestral capital. The Roman army departed Naples perhaps on the first of December, 536. They proceeded to Rome along the Latin Way, a journey that would have taken about eight days. As they approached, the Gothic garrison in Rome lost its nerve and decided to abandon the city and retreat to join Vittigis in Ravenna. And so it happened that on December 9, 536, Belisarius and his army peace-fully entered Rome through the Asinarian Gate on the southeastern side of the city, and at the same time the Gothic forces left Rome through the Flaminian Gate on the northwestern side of the city. Procopius saw this as a moment of significance, writing, "after a space of sixty years Rome again became subject to the Romans." It is not quite clear what Belisarius felt about the occupa-tion of Rome, but it is possible that this was a deeply emotional and satisfying moment for him. He would, over the rest of his career, return to Rome again and again, and would repeatedly refuse to surrender it even when facing the most daunting odds. These are not the actions of a general who thought of Rome as just any other city. Belisarius sent the keys of the city to Justinian and then began to repair the walls and collect supplies, a clear indication that he believed that the Goths would soon return and put the city under siege.[16]

FIGURE 8 The Porta Asinaria, through which Belisarius entered Rome in December 536. Photo by the author.

That the capture of Rome was seen as a critical turning point in the young war may be proved by the additional surrenders that followed. Pitzas, a Gothic commander, surrendered the southern region of Samnium to Belisarius, and the southeastern region of Apulia, having no Gothic garrisons, also submitted. Thus Belisarius now controlled most of Italy south of Rome. The general then decided to reach further afield, so he dispatched the commanders Constantine and Bessas into Tuscany. Constantine secured Spoleto and Perugia, while Bessas seized Narni. When a small army of Goths attempted to contest these victories, Constantine's forces defeated them in battle. This defeat apparently shamed Vittigis and drove him to hasten preparations to meet Belisarius in battle and to try to turn around the fortunes of the war. Procopius writes that Vittigis collected an army of 150,000 soldiers to attack Belisarius in Rome. This is an impossibly large figure, but was perhaps intentionally exaggerated by Procopius and Belisarius to provide rhetorical force to the general's later pleas to Justinian for reinforcements. Nevertheless, it is clear that Vittigis' army outnumbered that of Belisarius, which had started at 7,500 men plus the general's guardsmen, but had decreased as garrisons had been left behind in cities along the way. To maximize his army, Belisarius recalled Constantine and Bessas with the majority of their forces, ordering them to leave only small garrisons in the cities they had captured in Tuscany.[17]

As the Gothic army of Vittigis approached Rome, probably in early March 537, Belisarius tried to slow their arrival, to buy further time for supplies to be brought into the city and for reinforcements from Justinian to arrive. He ordered construction of a fortified tower at the Salarian Bridge over the Anio River, north of the city. This failed to hinder the progress of the Gothic army, because the small garrison of the tower panicked and fled as the Goths approached. Belisarius, unaware of this, marched to the bridge with 1,000 cavalry, to inspect the site and decide how he might further slow the Goths. To his surprise, he and his forces ran right into the Gothic army. The first battle of the siege began. In this battle, Belisarius fought in the front ranks of his men like a common soldier, reportedly with great valor, personally killing many Gothic soldiers. He came into greater danger than he had ever before as a general, but his guardsmen more than earned their pay, surrounding Belisarius with their shields and preventing any arrows from striking him. The battle swirled around the general, but by the dedication of his guards and sheer luck, Belisarius avoided injury, and he and his forces allegedly killed a thousand Gothic soldiers, forcing the Gothic army back in disarray. The Romans took advantage of this confusion to attempt to retreat back into the city via the Salarian Gate (now destroyed and replaced by the Piazza Fiume) on the northern side of the city. However, the men in charge of the gate refused to open it, not recognizing Belisarius and also terrified that the now-pursuing Goths would get in. So Belisarius and his forces turned and again charged the Gothic army, forcing them back by the shock of the charge. Now the Salarian Gate was opened, and Belisarius and his cavalry safely entered the city. The gate was then closed. The siege had begun in earnest. Belisarius cannot have known at this point, but it would last for more than a year.[18]

At this point, Procopius records a small contribution to the story by Antonina. Until now, the author had not mentioned Belisarius' wife being present in Italy at all in the *Wars*, and it is only from the scandalous account of the *Secret History* that we know Antonina was present in Sicily and thus had likely set sail with Belisarius from Constantinople in 535. But as the skirmish ended and Belisarius stabilized the defense of Rome for the night, Procopius explains that the general had been fasting all day. Antonina and his friends came to him in the night and persuaded him to eat something. This is a small glimpse into an Antonina quite different from the callous adulteress described in the *Secret History*. This is a supportive partner, a concerned spouse, who uses not only her own influence but also collects together Belisarius' friends to convince him to take care of himself even while he is worrying about his army and the city of Rome. This anecdote is also a strikingly casual reminder that Antonina has been present with the army through everything previously described: the siege of Naples, the march from Naples to Rome, the garrisoning of Rome, and the first skirmish with Vittigis' army. Perhaps Antonina even watched the skirmish from atop the Salarian Gate. Antonina's presence in an army on offensive campaign is unusual, and yet also presented as wholly natural. The brief mention of her presence in no way hints at it being out of the ordinary. Procopius simply writes, "Belisarius . . . was with difficulty compelled by his wife and friends who were present to taste a little bread." This is a small glimpse of domestic life, in something as mundane as a wife reminding her husband to eat, in the midst of war.[19]

Both armies now settled down and began dispositions for a protracted siege. Rome in the sixth century was still a large city, well fortified by the Aurelian Wall. The size of the city made it impossible for Vittigis to completely surround it with his army, so he instead cut the aqueducts that provided Rome with water and then established six fortified camps along the eastern and northern sides of the city. The Goths thus managed to cover about half the length of the walls. Belisarius for his part arranged his forces to defend the wall, not surprisingly paying special attention to those sections of the wall that faced the Gothic army camps. Belisarius stationed himself at the Salarian Gate and also assumed responsibility for the nearby Pincian Gate. He assigned the Praenestine Gate (now frequently called the Porta Maggiore) to Bessas and the Flaminian Gate (now destroyed and the site of the Piazza del Popolo) to Constantine. The selection of Constantine and Bessas for important roles here highlights their significance relative to Belisarius' other officers, foreshadowed earlier by Procopius listing them first in his description of the leading officers of the expedition at its departure in 535. The remaining gates of the city were distributed to the commanders of the infantry. The inhabitants of Rome, seeing preparations for a siege begin, turned their anxiety on Belisarius, reproaching him for taking their city when he did not have a large enough army to meet the Goths in pitched battle. They were clearly not looking forward to a long siege and the deprivations it would entail. Hoping to badger Belisarius into retreating, or at least further inflame the quarrel between the inhabitants and the general, Vittigis sent an envoy to Belisarius to upbraid him for taking Rome and promise him safe conduct if he departed. The speech that Belisarius gave in response, as recorded by Procopius, ended with a definitive promise to stay and fight: "For as long as Belisarius lives, it is impossible for him to relinquish this city." With this, both Romans and Goths settled down to begin constructing siege machines and

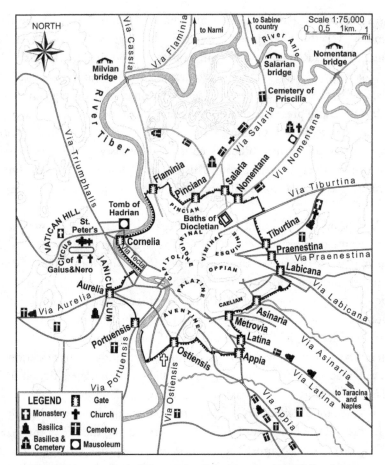

MAP 5 Rome in the Sixth Century: detail showing Aurelian Wall and its gates.
Researched by Christopher Lillington-Martin and drawn by Carlos García.
Originally appeared in Lillington-Martin 2013, 623.

stockpiling ammunition for the inevitable attempt by the Goths to storm the
city walls.[20]

On the 18th day of the siege, so perhaps in the third week of March 537,
the Goths assaulted the walls. The main thrust of their attack was aimed at
the Salarian Gate, where Belisarius was in command. Procopius records that
Belisarius simply laughed as the attack began. The Goths were attempting to
use oxen to drag their wooden siege towers from their camp up against the
city walls. When they had moved fairly close to the walls, Belisarius gave the
command for his archers to shoot at the oxen, who all died, leaving the siege
towers stranded some distance from the walls. It is interesting that Vittigis
would not have accounted for this kind of risk. With this prong of the attack

repulsed, Vittigis moved with some of his forces to attack the Praenestine Gate and ordered another assault upon the Cornelian Gate (now destroyed) on the northwest side of the city. Simultaneously, there was a brief, desultory Gothic attack on the Aurelian Gate on the west side of the city. Of all these assaults, Vittigis' personal attack on the Praenestine Gate was the most serious. Here, Belisarius' officers Bessas and Peranios were in command of the defense, and they sent a request for Belisarius to come personally to assist. When Belisarius arrived, he sent a small force of soldiers under Cyprian to distract some of the Goths attempting to breach the wall, and then he opened the gate and sent out the majority of his army in a sally against the Gothic forces. Whether by design or chance, the Roman soldiers still at the Salarian Gate also sallied forth at this time, and the result was a complete rout of the attacking Gothic army. The Goths turned their backs and fled, and the Romans chased them, slaughtering those whom they could reach and also burning their abandoned siege towers. Procopius writes that 30,000 Goths died in this battle, which is probably an exaggeration, just like his claim that the Gothic army consisted of 150,000 soldiers. However, if the total numbers are ignored and the ratio is instead examined, Procopius is claiming that the Goths lost a fifth of their army in this attack, which is not an impossible casualty rate. Such a defeat would have still left the Goths with an army comfortably larger than the Romans, but chastised enough to avoid further open battles, which is in fact exactly what happened. This was such a significant victory for Belisarius that Vittigis would not attempt another general assault of the city for the remainder of the long siege.[21]

After this battle, Belisarius wrote a letter to Justinian, reporting on the war and requesting reinforcements. Procopius provides the whole text of the letter. As Belisarius' personal secretary, composing such letters was one of the most important parts of the author's job. In the letter, Belisarius claimed that the Gothic army numbered 150,000 soldiers (an exaggeration, for reasons already discussed) and that his own army has dwindled to 5,000 soldiers (a reasonable estimate of the size of his army accounting for casualties and the losses of garrison forces between Sicily and Rome). Belisarius begs for reinforcements in order to continue the war and emphasizes that the inhabitants of Rome will grow less fond of the Roman cause if the siege is prolonged. According to Procopius, Justinian was distressed when he received this report and immediately began to make plans to gather soldiers and ships. He also makes clear that Justinian had already planned for at least some reinforcements: the Generals Valerianos and Martinos had already been dispatched in December 536 with an army, but they had been wintering in Greece. Justinian urged them to continue on to Italy with all speed.[22]

With the knowledge that the siege would stretch on, Belisarius had to prepare Rome for inevitable shortages of food. The day after the battle with Vittigis, Belisarius gave orders that all the inhabitants of Rome should transport their women and children to Naples. This would ensure fewer mouths to feed in besieged Rome. At the same time, he also ordered his own soldiers to send away their "male or female attendants." This is one of Procopius' few references in the *Wars* to the presence of females other than Antonina in the army of Belisarius. It is a casual reference, not judgmental in character, that suggests that both Belisarius and Procopius accepted and indeed expected the presence of women in the ranks of the army. The exact wording of the reference (*therápaina*) refers to female maids or slaves, but it is not hard to imagine that some of these "attendants" might have been concubines or otherwise sexual partners of the soldiers or officers. Probably Belisarius was not alone in having a female partner with him on campaign. One difference, of course, is that Antonina was not sent away at this time. The general retained the prerogative to keep his wife present even during this time of crisis.[23]

How to Depose a Pope

About this time, in late March 537, Antonina and Belisarius deposed Pope Silverius. This episode is worthy of detailed consideration, because it is one of the few acts of the professional partnership of husband and wife that is corroborated by multiple sources, not just Procopius. Each of the sources adds a new layer to the story. The description of this event in the *Wars* is minimalist: "A suspicion arose against Silverius, the chief priest of the city, that he was engaged in treasonable negotiations with the Goths, so Belisarius sent him immediately to Greece, and a little later appointed another man, Vigilius by name, to the office of chief priest." If this was the only account, it would be impossible to know that Antonina played a major role in this ecclesiastical coup. In the *Secret History*, Procopius charges in a similarly minimalist way that Antonina "disposed of Silverius" at the behest of Empress Theodora. In neither account does Procopius provide any additional explanation. It is likely that the author planned to provide further details in a future church history that he apparently never wrote.[24]

Fortunately, several contemporaries fill in the story with fascinating details. The fullest account is provided by the *Liber Pontificalis* (The Book of the Popes), an anonymous source compiled multiple times over the Middle Ages, although the description of the deposition of Silverius is probably nearly contemporary, dating to the mid-sixth century at latest. According to this account, Theodora was sympathetic to the recently deposed Patriarch of Constantinople, Anthimus, who had been removed from his position by Pope Agapetus in 536. This was a period in which popes and patriarchs commonly vied for authority over each other through the mediation of the emperors. The empress wanted Pope Silverius to reinstate Anthimus, and when he refused to do so, she decided that Silverius must be deposed so that a more compliant pope could be enthroned. Theodora then ordered Belisarius to depose Silverius and appoint in his place Vigilius, at that time the papal representative to Constantinople. The empress commanded, "Look for some pretexts to deal with Pope Silverius and depose him from the bishopric." At this point the *Liber* makes Belisarius appear both humble and pious, and he says, "For my part I will carry out the mandate, but if anyone gets involved in killing Pope Silverius he will have to account for his actions to our Lord Jesus Christ." Belisarius then called Silverius into his presence in what the author described as the "Pincian Palace," which was perhaps a villa on the Pincian Hill or a confused reference to Belisarius' defensive position at the Pincian Gate. When he arrived, the pope found a most unusual scene: "the patrician Antonina was lying on a couch with the patrician Belisarius sitting at her feet." This is an extraordinary description of Belisarius and Antonina. It portrays Antonina in the dominant position, with Belisarius sitting at her feet indicating his subservience to her and placing her firmly in the role of the active individual in these proceedings. It is all the more interesting because the *Liber* has up to now not even mentioned Antonina! That she first appears here in this fashion is most likely meant to shock the reader. The surprise is continued by the fact that Belisarius remains silent while it is Antonina who accosts Silverius: "Tell us, lord Pope Silverius, what have we done to you and the Romans to make you want to betray us into the hands of the Goths?" She makes no mention of Theodora, or Patriarch Anthimus, and instead focuses on Silverius' loyalty in the ongoing siege of the city, a reasonable concern at the time. The *Liber* does not allow Silverius any reply to this question, but goes on to describe how subdeacons immediately stripped the pallium (an ecclesiastical vestment worn by the pope) from Silverius and announced to the rest of the Roman clergy that the pope had been deposed. This account is at once full confirmation of the effective working partnership between Belisarius and Antonina and of the hostility with which this partnership was viewed by some of their contemporaries. It shows Antonina fully engaged in the task, but takes it to the extreme of also showing Belisarius essentially emasculated, relinquishing authority to his wife to do his dirty work. In this the author of the *Liber* reflects some of the attitudes demonstrated by

Procopius in the *Secret History*: he is aware of the partnership of general and wife, but, because he disapproves of it, he makes Belisarius appear as unmanly and his relationship with Antonina as perverse as he can in the situation.[25]

The *Breviarium* of Liberatus of Carthage and *Chronicle* of Victor of Tunnuna, both likely written in the 560s, offer further confirmation of Antonina's significant role in the deposition of Silverius and the elevation of Vigilius. Liberatus agrees with the *Liber* that the initiating force behind the deposition of Silverius was the machinations of Theodora. The empress allegedly extracted from Vigilius a promise to write a letter espousing her own theological views after his elevation to the papacy. It is in the context of this letter that Antonina appears most actively involved in these events. Liberatus writes that after his elevation, "Vigilius fulfilled the promise he had made to the Augusta through the intermediary of Antonina, wife of Belisarius." It is fascinating that the letter that Vigilius purportedly wrote under this pressure actually named Antonina: "Because today my glorious daughter, the most Christian patrician Antonina, has been able to obtain the fulfillment of my desires to send these letters to your Fraternity, I greet you in the grace that unites us to Christ the Savior our God." Victor of Tunnuna confirms both the power of Antonina in compelling this letter and the mention of her by Vigilius. He writes, "Pope Vigilius was compelled by the patrician Antonina, wife of the patrician Belisarius, to write to Theodosios of Alexandria, Anthimus of Constantinople, and Severus of Antioch . . ." The letter, according to Victor, reads in part, "since the glorious lady and my daughter the most Christian patrician Antonina desires me to implore you, and to present letters to you brothers . . ." The two accounts are remarkably close to identical in giving Antonina credit for pressuring Vigilius to write a letter, and in maintaining that Vigilius named Antonina in the letter. They even use the same language to describe Antonina, labeling her glorious, Christian, and patrician. Although they refer to a different portion of the story than the *Liber*, they work with it to confirm Antonina's involvement in this delicate operation.[26]

At the same time, other sources maintain the involvement of Belisarius in the deposition. Procopius in the *Wars* had of course laid the responsibility on the general, but his role is also affirmed by the *Chronicle* of Marcellinus Comes, which states, "Belisarius removed from his see Pope Silverius who was at that time favorable to Vittigis, and ordained the deacon Vigilius in his place." The collective impression given by these six sources is that Antonina and Belisarius were both involved in the deposition of Pope Silverius and the elevation of Pope Vigilius. The differences in the individual accounts and the possibility that hostility toward Antonina's involvement warped some of those descriptions mean it is probably impossible to determine exactly what role each spouse played in these events. It is unlikely that Belisarius literally sat at Antonina's feet and said nothing, as the *Liber* suggests, but given the number of sources corroborating her involvement, it is also unlikely that Belisarius acted without her, as Marcellinus suggests. Some sort of cooperative effort, with Belisarius and Antonina sitting side-by-side, is more likely. In fact, the two might even have been intentionally aping their imperial counterparts, as Justinian and Theodora often sat side-by-side to dispense justice and worked together to come to decisions in general. Theodora herself, alongside Justinian, was playing a major role in religious matters in Constantinople at this time, so it would not be surprising if Antonina was following her lead.[27]

There is one more question to ask about this change in popes before returning to the siege of Rome. Why did this swap take place? The *Liber* makes the deposition of Silverius about Theodora and Patriarch Anthimus, and both Liberatus and Victor make it about Theodora's opinion on the major Christian doctrinal disagreement of the day, an ongoing dispute over the number of natures contained within the person of Christ. The Council of Chalcedon in 451 had proclaimed that Christ had two natures, one truly God and one truly human. However, fervent dissenters to this council maintained that Christ had only one nature (*physis*) that was truly God. Because of this, these dissenters became known as Monophysites. More moderate Monophysites argued that Christ had one nature that was both God and human at the same time, but even this was not seen as compatible with the two-nature believers of Chalcedon. Far from getting better over time, the dispute between Chalcedonians and Monophysites grew more bitter in the sixth century. Liberatus and Victor, who were Chalcedonian, charge that Theodora, who supported the Monophysites, wanted to install a pope that would be sympathetic to that doctrine. However, it is likely that this explanation is ahistorical window dressing added by authors who were influenced by the later struggle over the Three Chapters controversy: in the 540s, Justinian tried to anathematize the writings of three Christian authors, a move seen as a shot at the decisions of Chalcedon that was intended to please Monophysite Christians. That move by Justinian did inflame the doctrinal dispute. But the deposition of Silverius occurred years before the Three Chapters became an issue, and in the midst of a perilous position for Belisarius and the Roman army under siege. It is far more likely that the change in popes was therefore related to that siege than to doctrinal concerns. And this is in fact what is suggested by Marcellinus, who says that Silverius favored Vittigis. This explanation is also clear from the placement of the story in the *Wars*, in which Procopius charged Silverius of treasonous communication with the Goths. And not just Silverius: Procopius says that Belisarius banished from Rome on the same charge some of the senators, and he says this right after his description of Silverius' deposition. So the order of events in the narrative makes it clear that Silverius was deposed as part of a general eviction of Gothic sympathizers from Rome. Finally, even the *Liber* has a hint that political reasons lay at the heart of this episode: it explains that Silverius was appointed pope by Theodahad in 536, and that he was not confirmed in the usual way by the priests of Rome. The picture painted by this evidence suggests that Silverius was a Gothic appointee, not approved by the clergy of Rome, who might reasonably be suspected of loyalty to the Gothic cause, and he was deposed at the same time other Gothic sympathizers were expelled from Rome during a tense and dangerous siege of the city by the Gothic army. Some of the authors who wrote in the coming years took advantage of this event to allege other causes for this deposition to advance their theological agendas, but in March 537 what probably mattered most to Belisarius and Antonina was the loyalty of the pope and the security of the city of Rome.[28]

Perhaps to confirm his relationship with the new pope, Belisarius made a donation to the See of St. Peter at about this time. The *Liber* reports that Belisarius, from the spoils of the Vandals, "presented to St. Peter by the hands of Pope Vigilius a gold cross with jewels, weighing 100 pounds, with an inscription of his victories," as well as two silver-gilt candlesticks, which Vigilius placed before St. Peter's tomb. These gifts must have been given during the siege of Rome, because this was to be the last time that Belisarius and Vigilius would be in the Eternal City together at the same time. Having made friends with the new pope and ensured the loyalty of the other inhabitants of Rome, Belisarius and Antonina were as prepared as they could be to brave a long Gothic siege.[29]

FIGURE 9 The Porta Pinciana, which Belisarius defended during the siege of Rome, 537–538. Photo by the author.

5

From Rome to Ravenna

THE WISDOM OF Belisarius and Antonina's actions in securing the loyalty of those within Rome may be contrasted with the actions of Vittigis outside the city. While his forces settled in for a siege, the Gothic king busied himself with revenge against the people of Rome whom he could reach, and whom he thought of as betrayers. He sent word to Ravenna that all senators of Rome being held hostage there should be killed. Some learned of this beforehand and managed to escape, including the brother of the new pope, Vigilius. This act of murderous rage does not make sense either tactically or strategically, and therefore it can probably be chocked up to Vittigis' anger at his failure to dislodge Belisarius and the Roman army from the city. Once his fury was spent, Vittigis returned to strategy. Realizing that his frontal assault had failed, he accepted that he must deny the Romans food and supplies if he wanted to force their surrender. On the 21st day of the siege, he sent a force of Gothic soldiers to seize Portus, Rome's active port city on the mouth of the Tiber at the Tyrrhenian Sea. This they accomplished easily. Now for Belisarius and the city of Rome to safely receive supplies by sea, the ships had to dock at Anzio, a day's journey south, and then route through Ostia, Rome's older port, a perilous process. This made it much more difficult to get food and supplies into the besieged city.[1]

At last, on the 41st day of the siege (so perhaps in the middle of April 537), the first reinforcements arrived from Justinian when the Generals Valerianos and Martinos landed at Ostia with 1,600 cavalry. If Belisarius' army in Rome truly did consist of only 5,000 soldiers at the time, this represented an increase in his fighting capacity of nearly one-third. Belisarius was pleased with their arrival and immediately began to think about offensive operations against the besieging Gothic army. From this point, the siege of Rome would take on a different character. The day after the arrival of the reinforcements,

Belisarius & Antonina. David Alan Parnell, Oxford University Press. © Oxford University Press 2023.
DOI: 10.1093/oso/9780197574706.003.0006

Belisarius tested the waters with a small offensive sally. He selected one of his guardsmen, Traïanos, and ordered him to ride out against the Goths with 200 cavalry from among his fellow guards. This small force succeeded in killing nearly 1,000 Gothic soldiers and then retreated back into the city unharmed. A few days later, Belisarius repeated the experiment with another 300 mounted guards under the command of Mundilas and Diogenes, and their sortie was similarly successful. Then he sent another 300 cavalry under the guardsman Oïlas, who was also victorious. Procopius says that these three sallies killed about 4,000 Goths, although this is probably an exaggeration. The great success of these attacks was due to the training and equipment of the soldiers Belisarius selected for them: they were all mounted archers. They galloped up to the enemy army, fired their arrows until their quivers were empty, and then immediately turned around and galloped back to the safety of the walls before the enemy could counterattack. This sort of attack proved devastating against the Goths, who did not equip themselves in this way and did not have the same mobility and range as the Roman mounted archers. It is also interesting that in these first three sallies, the only soldiers Belisarius utilized were his own guardsmen. Although he had just received 1,600 fresh cavalry reinforcements, he instead turned to his own men who had been with him in this campaign since the beginning. Perhaps he trusted them more to have the discipline to unleash arrows and then flee before hand-to-hand combat began. It is also possible that they were simply better marksmen and horsemen than the regular soldiers of the Roman army. After all, Belisarius would presumably only select the best soldiers to be in his personal guard unit. On the other side of the siege, Vittigis apparently did not understand the reason for his losses in these small skirmishes and decided to emulate the Romans, sending out small units of 500 cavalry each to engage the Romans in battle. Twice the Goths rode out, and twice the Romans sallied forth and defeated them.[2]

The successes of these Roman sorties apparently encouraged both the inhabitants of Rome and the soldiers of the Roman army, who began to agitate and urge Belisarius to plan a large-scale, general battle against the Goths. Although Belisarius was reluctant to change his plans because the small-scale sallies were going so well, he allowed himself to be carried away by the ardor of his troops, in an eerie repeat of the arguments before the Battle of Callinicum. After giving a brief speech of encouragement, he divided his army by sending the commander Valentinos with a small force of cavalry to the Plain of Nero, north of the Vatican Hill and just outside the Cornelian Gate, to distract the Gothic soldiers encamped there and prevent them from joining the battle.

He also stationed an infantry unit under the command of the guardsmen Prinkipios and Tarmoutos outside the Pincian Gate, to provide cover for the cavalry to retreat to if necessary. Finally, Belisarius led the main body of the Roman army out through the Salarian Gate and the nearby Pincian Gate. He planned to engage in a primarily cavalry battle, and the combat began as the sorties had begun, with the mounted archers raining down arrows upon the Gothic army. Once the battle turned hand-to-hand however and the Romans began to sustain casualties, they began to notice how much they were outnumbered by the Goths, and when the Goths launched a counterattack with their own cavalry, the Romans were routed and began fleeing back toward the walls and the infantry. This caused the Roman infantry to also retreat, and all began running to the gates, desperate to escape. At this point Prinkipios and Tarmoutos rallied some of the infantry to stand and guard the withdrawal. Prinkipios died in the fighting, and Tarmoutos was carried injured through the Pincian Gate only to die two days later, but their sacrifice enabled the Roman army to escape back into the city. The battle had ended in a clear loss for the Roman army, but Procopius does not provide a tally of the casualties, perhaps to avoid embarrassing Belisarius.[3]

Following this battle, Belisarius returned to the strategy that had been working for him before it. He kept the majority of his army within the walls of Rome and sent out small offensive sallies of mounted archers. Procopius describes numerous sorties, explaining that altogether during the siege of Rome there were 67 engagements of this type between Roman and Gothic forces. Thus the majority of the spring and probably summer of 537 was taken up with this kind of warfare. But by the early fall of 537, the army and inhabitants of Rome were beginning to suffer from hunger from the protracted siege. The people of Rome begged Belisarius to stake everything on a major engagement to break the siege, but Belisarius refused to be rash and promised the people that reinforcements and supplies would come soon. Despite Belisarius' dismissal of the people's concerns, their complaint does seem to have inspired additional action. The general commanded Procopius to go to Naples, there to collect food, supplies, and any additional troops that might have arrived from Constantinople, and bring them back by ship to Rome via the port at Ostia. Belisarius also decided that he would make the Gothic army feel the pressure of hunger during the siege. Accordingly, he dispatched three small forces, each numbering between 500 and 1,000 men, to various strongholds outside Rome: Martinos and Traïanos took a unit to Terracina (47 miles southeast of Rome), Magnos and Sinduit were sent with a small army to Tivoli (19 miles northeast of Rome), and Gontharis took soldiers to Albano (16 miles south of Rome). These divisions of the army were ordered to make camps in these locations and then harass Gothic foragers and supply trains, in order to deny the Gothic army the food it needed to maintain the siege. Belisarius' army in Rome was still not large, so there was some risk in this strategy. The general himself stayed in Rome to supervise defense of the walls in case the Goths attempted to storm the city again.[4]

At about the same time, Antonina also set out from Rome. As far as can be determined, she had not left Belisarius' side for this entire campaign up to this point, and she had shared in the deprivations of the siege of Rome since the beginning. And yet now she and Belisarius decided she could be of more use elsewhere. Procopius attempts to paint Antonina's departure as an issue of safety. He states that Antonina went with Martinos and Traïanos to Terracina, and from there went on to Naples, "to await in safety the fortune that would befall the Romans." Try as he might to make Antonina a damsel in distress, awaiting the outcome of manly wars, Procopius cannot hide that she was in fact nothing of the sort. In fact, Antonina had set out with a purpose, and she ended up crashing the author's big moment. He, Procopius, had been sent by Belisarius to Naples to secure supplies and reinforcements. He proudly relates that in Naples he had collected 500 soldiers and a great amount of grain for the army in Rome. And yet the author is forced to admit that not long afterward, he was joined by Antonina, "who immediately assisted him in making arrangements for the fleet." How this must have vexed Procopius! Here had been his big moment to contribute to the conduct of the war in some way other than writing Belisarius' correspondence, and he found himself upstaged by Antonina. Because although Procopius writes that Antonina assisted him, it is not improbable that in reality Antonina assumed direction of the operation and Procopius assisted *her*. After all, this was a woman who had recently played a significant role in deposing a pope. She was unlikely to play the part of assistant to her husband's secretary. Perhaps a bitter memory of this moment contributed to the nasty tone Procopius took about Antonina when he later wrote the *Secret History*.[5]

As Antonina and Procopius prepared to leave Naples, significant reinforcements from the emperor, requested by Belisarius back in March, at last began to arrive. Altogether, these reinforcements totaled some 5,000 soldiers. They came divided into smaller units. The largest group was 3,000 under the command of Paul and Konon, who sailed into Naples while Antonina and Procopius were there. Much farther south, at Otranto, Alexander and Markentios arrived with 1,000 cavalry, along with John, the nephew of Vitalian, commanding 800 cavalry. Of all of these men, John would play the largest role in the Gothic war, serving in Italy longer than even Belisarius. Finally, the commander Zeno appeared with 300 cavalry at Rome itself. With these arrivals, the job of Antonina and Procopius perhaps became more difficult. Now they had many more thousands of men and ships to coordinate. The army of Paul and Konon, which had arrived at Naples by sea, was ordered to proceed by sea to Ostia. The armies of Alexander, Markentios, and John marched from Otranto up to Naples, where they were joined by the 500 soldiers raised by Procopius, and then were ordered to march from there directly to Rome. While the soldiers were marching, Procopius and Antonina apparently boarded the ships filled with food and supplies and sailed from Naples to Ostia. Apprised of the incoming reinforcements and supplies, Belisarius planned an engagement with the Gothic army to distract them and provide cover for the traveling soldiers and fleet. Diogenes and Traïanos, since recalled from Terracina, took 1,000 cavalry through the Pincian Gate and began shooting arrows at the Gothic forces encamped there. When the Goths emerged from their camps to counterattack, Belisarius sent a larger force through the Flaminian Gate, and the Goths were trapped between the two forces, and many were slaughtered.[6]

Shortly after this engagement, and even before the Roman supplies and reinforcements arrived in Rome, Vittigis and the Goths began to consider diplomatic negotiations. They had lost most of the small battles and other engagements with Belisarius' army, and beyond that, disease was running rampant in the Gothic army camps. Finally, Procopius says that the Goths were suffering from famine, an indication that Belisarius' strategy of harassing their supply trains was working. So in December 537, Vittigis sent three envoys to Rome to treat with Belisarius. The general and the envoys had a debate over the merits of the Roman invasion of Italy and the Goths made several offers: first that they would give the Romans Sicily, second that they would give the Romans Naples, and third that they would also pay the Romans tribute each year. Only the last offer represented anything new, of course, as Belisarius already controlled both Sicily and Naples. In recognition of the absurdity of these offers, Belisarius bemusedly replied that he would give the Goths Britain, a fair trade since the Romans did not currently control it any more than the Goths currently controlled Sicily. The meeting ended with both sides agreeing that the Gothic envoys should be sent on to Justinian to negotiate with him, and that an armistice would be arranged between the Roman and Gothic armies in the meantime for the duration of three months.[7]

During these negotiations, the fleets, armies, and supplies arrived in Ostia. Under the cover of darkness, Belisarius went to Ostia to meet them and assured them that he would keep the road between Ostia and Rome clear as the soldiers and supplies moved toward the city. He then returned to Rome. Procopius reports at this point that "Antonina with the commanders began to consider means of transporting the cargo." This is itself an extraordinary admission of the role played by Antonina in these events. Before, of course, it had been Antonina and Procopius who had been responsible for the supplies, but now the author disappears and Antonina works directly with commanders of the army, apparently on a basis of equality. Perhaps Procopius had returned to Rome with Belisarius. But that Antonina would still be involved in this process and perhaps even in charge of it, even with plenty of commanders present (we know that the army of reinforcements included at least Paul, Konon, Alexander, Markentios, and John among its high-ranking commanders), is fascinating and speaks to the authority that her status as wife and partner of Belisarius gave her. Antonina and the commanders apparently decided that the best way to transport the supplies from Ostia to Rome was via small boats, which were rowed up the Tiber. Because there were many supplies and not enough boats, the process was repeated many times. The Goths did not interfere, perhaps because of the recent armistice agreed between Belisarius and the envoys. And so by late December 537, the army of Belisarius was swelled by substantial reinforcements, and both the army and the inhabitants of Rome were once again well fed thanks to the arrival of Antonina's supply train.[8]

Not long after this, perhaps in the new year, additional reinforcements in the form of cavalry commanded by Ildiger, the son-in-law of Antonina, arrived in Rome from North Africa. Feeling that his army in Rome was now larger than necessary for winter during an armistice, Belisarius decided to send some of his soldiers out of the city. He gave overall command of this expedition to John, the nephew of Vitalian. This force consisted of the 800 cavalry that had arrived with John, 400 guardsmen of the General Valerianos, and 800 of Belisarius' personal guards. This is the first indication that we have of what must have been an ongoing process of Belisarius' guard unit increasing in size. Prior to this, the largest unit of Belisarius' guards in Italy mentioned was 300 soldiers. Now it is clear that his guards numbered at least 800, and probably much more than that, for it is unlikely that he would send all or even the majority of them away. Belisarius had money, and he needed soldiers to defend Rome, so it would only be logical for him to be hiring more soldiers whenever he could during the siege. Once this force was assembled, Belisarius ordered John to take this army to Alba, in Picenum (modern Morro d'Alba in Marche). There John was to remain quiet through the winter, and if the Goths breached the armistice, he was to overrun the land and seize control of any fortified places he could. This accomplished two goals—getting some soldiers out of Rome to spread out the burden of supply in winter, and preparing for the next phase of the war if necessary.[9]

The End of the Siege of Rome

During the winter of early 538, Belisarius had a deadly quarrel with one of his top officers, Constantine, who had already featured prominently in the siege of Rome. The dispute is recorded by multiple sources in a variety of detail. The fullest account comes, as it often does, from Procopius. In the *Wars*, the author describes the quarrel as the result of a theft. He charges Constantine with seizing a pair of daggers, valuable because they were sheathed in scabbards adorned with gold and jewels. The daggers belonged to a distinguished Roman civilian named Presidius, who had originally lived in Ravenna but fled when Vittigis marched from there to Rome with his army. Presidius now, seeing that the fortunes of the Roman army were turning and expecting Belisarius to be victorious, approached the general and requested his aid in getting his property returned to him. Although Belisarius urged Constantine to return the daggers to Presidius, he refused. According to Procopius, the cycle of appeal by Presidius, request by Belisarius, and refusal by Constantine occurred multiple times. Finally, after Presidius had publicly accosted Belisarius in the forum of Rome, the general called Constantine along with the other commanders into his presence. Belisarius again ordered Constantine to restore the daggers, and the latter said that he would obey the general in all other matters, but he would never obey this order. Belisarius then ordered his guardsmen to enter the room, so that they could force Constantine to comply. Constantine believed the guards were coming in to kill him, so in a moment of desperation he drew a dagger and thrust it at Belisarius. The general stepped behind his officer Bessas, avoiding the strike, and Ildiger and Valerianos stepped forward and restrained Constantine. The whole room erupted in an uproar. At that moment the guardsmen of Belisarius entered, seized Constantine, and removed him from the room. Procopius claims that Belisarius had Constantine put to death "at a later time."[10]

In the *Secret History*, Procopius provides more background on this event, pinning the blame for Constantine's death on Antonina. As has been previously described, Procopius claimed that in early 536, Constantine had given advice to Belisarius to do away with Antonina over her alleged affair with Theodosios. The author argued that Antonina had learned of Constantine's advice, and hated him for it, but bided her time. Now, two years later in 538, Procopius claims that Antonina saw her chance. He wrote that Constantine "would surely have been acquitted" even after his attempt to stab Belisarius, but that "Antonina did not relent until he had been punished for the remark that I just mentioned." This is an interesting claim, to say the least. Procopius is asking us to believe that Antonina nursed a grudge for two years, patiently waiting until Constantine was involved in some sort of crime because of which she could nudge her husband into executing him. This is not impossible, but it seems to fit in a bit too neatly with the caricature that Procopius also painted of Theodora, whom he said held grudges for a long time and was "an implacable enemy once roused." In other words, the claim that Antonina hated Constantine for years, patiently waiting for a chance to strike at him, is a literary trope. Perhaps it contains some truth, or perhaps it is just a way for Procopius to paint Antonina as a typical anti-heroine in the *Secret History*. The chronicler Marcellinus Comes also mentions this argument between Belisarius and Constantine, but leaves Antonina out of it, saying Belisarius "did away with the patrician Constantine, an opponent of his."[11]

It is difficult to know what to make of the role played by Antonina in the execution of Constantine. As we have seen in numerous other instances, Antonina and Belisarius were partners, so it would not be surprising at all if Belisarius had talked with Antonina before deciding to execute his subordinate officer. That does not necessarily mean that Constantine only died because Antonina disliked him, as Procopius suggests. The general could have easily found other reasons to have Constantine executed. Belisarius had a fraternity, a social network, with his officers, and his successes depended on the strength of this network. He could hardly afford to let Constantine go unpunished for refusing to obey orders and then making an attempt on his life, not even secretly but in a room full of his peers. Doing so would have undermined respect for the general, potentially weakening his social network and therefore his authority over the army. Surely this would have weighed just as heavily on Belisarius' mind as any dislike Antonina may or may not have had for the man. However, it is also possible that Belisarius and Antonina underestimated the negative reaction that might result from a perceived overly harsh punishment of Constantine. Procopius says that because of Constantine's death, "Belisarius earned the hatred of both the emperor and all the best men among the Romans." The use of the phrase "best men" is interesting, as it indicates that not everyone hated Belisarius for this. Perhaps only one faction of officers resented this punishment, or the comment was aimed at readers of the *Secret History* whom Procopius believed were opposed to Belisarius. If Belisarius and Antonina decided to execute Constantine to preserve Belisarius' reputation among his social network and his authority in the army, it seems to have had mixed results, if Procopius is to be believed.[12]

Throughout early 538, the Goths made furtive attempts to break into Rome, perhaps hoping that the Roman soldiers would have let their guard down because of the armistice. They first planned to attack the walls of Rome through one of the broken aqueducts, then hoped to launch a surprise attack on the Pincian Gate, and finally even attempted to drug some of the Roman guards to allow Gothic forces to sneak past. All of these attempts were foiled by Belisarius' troops. Either in response to these attacks, or because he planned to all along, or because the three-month truce was nearly expired, Belisarius now sent to John, the nephew of Vitalian, ordering him to begin operations in Picenum. John immediately rode out with his 2,000 cavalry and began plundering the region. The only resistance John's forces faced came from Ulitheus, the uncle of Vittigis, who met him in battle with an unspecified number of Gothic soldiers. John won an overwhelming victory, slaying Ulitheus and scattering his army. After this victory, John led his forces to the major cities and fortresses of the region, considering which one he might easily capture. Procopius makes it possible for us to track his movements: he first visited Osimo, but deemed it nearly impossible to capture with his force, then came to Urbino, about which he made the same conclusion, and finally he moved on to Rimini, which opened its gates to his forces willingly. Thus John and his cavalry secured Rimini, which was only one day's travel from Ravenna, the capital of the Ostrogothic Kingdom. Procopius explains that John reasoned if Rimini was captured and Ravenna threatened, the Gothic army at Rome would finally lift its siege and move toward Rimini and Ravenna. This is exactly what happened.[13]

In March 538, around the time of the spring equinox, the Gothic army burned its camps outside Rome and began to retreat northward. The siege of Rome had finally ended. Procopius records that it had lasted for one year and nine days. Belisarius had kept his promise, made a year before, that as long as he lived he would not surrender the city. Though he must have cherished this moment and felt vindicated in his defense of Rome, Belisarius immediately began thinking about how to gain an additional advantage from the Gothic retreat. He waited until more than half the Gothic army had already marched away, and then opened the Pincian Gate and sent out his forces to attack the remaining Gothic soldiers. The Romans succeeded in killing many Goths and turned their retreat into a rout. Vittigis led the surviving Gothic forces north, placing some soldiers in the cities and strongholds of Tuscany and Picenum

along the way. His force slowly marched toward Rimini, which he intended
to recapture from John. Belisarius was aware of the danger, so he dispatched
Ildiger and Martinos with 1,000 cavalry to race ahead of the Gothic army.
The men were to pick up infantry in Ancona, take the infantry to Rimini, and
order John with his 2,000 cavalry to evacuate the city and leave the infantry
there to garrison it. The reason for this order is not hard to divine: infantry
tend to make a better garrison force for manning city walls, while cavalry tend
to be more useful harassing the enemy army in the open country. Although
the order made sense in this way, John was completely unwilling to obey it.
When Ildiger and Martinos arrived, John refused to comply, and insisted on
remaining in Rimini. Ildiger and Martinos evacuated the 800 cavalry that
were part of Belisarius' personal guardsmen, over whom John had no authority, but were forced to leave the remaining forces with John in Rimini.
Procopius provides no explanation or reason for John's insubordination.
Perhaps he was ambitious, or simply thought he knew better. Either way, it
would not be the last time John refused an order from Belisarius. To no one's
surprise, Vittigis and the Gothic army arrived not long after John's act of insubordination, surrounded the walls of Rimini, and commenced a siege. In
the meantime, Belisarius was preparing to move out from Rome. To ensure
Rome was restored before his departure, he ordered repairs to the aqueducts
that Vittigis had cut the year before: Belisarius is named in an inscription
on an arch of the aqueduct of Trajan, in what is today Vicarello (on Lake
Bracciano) near Rome. Belisarius was also now thinking about the entire theater of Italy, and he dispatched 1,000 soldiers to the northwestern region of
Lombardy, to take Milan and the surrounding territory. Their commanders
were Mundilas, Ennes, and Paul. However, when Vittigis caught word of this,
he also sent an army to the region, and by the end of 538, Milan was under
siege by the Goths as well.[14]

The March to Ravenna

The war had clearly now entered a different, more fluid phase. Instead of both
armies concentrated at Rome, they were now both dispersed throughout
northern Italy. Belisarius needed to move his main army from Rome quickly,
choose a target, and hope that further reinforcements arrived soon from
Constantinople. In June 538, Belisarius took his army, leaving only a small
garrison in Rome, and marched north into Tuscany, capturing Todi and
Chiusi. Procopius does not say whether Antonina marched with Belisarius
in this phase of the war, but given her previous history of staying by his side,

it is likely that she did. The general was considering his next move when he received word that further reinforcements from Constantinople had arrived in Picenum. This was a substantial army, totaling some 7,000 soldiers. There were 2,000 allied Herul soldiers and 5,000 Roman soldiers under the command of Justin and two brothers named Aratios and Narses. But in overall command of this force was another Narses, commonly known as Narses the eunuch, a chamberlain and steward of Justinian, whom we last saw during the Nika Riot of 532. This was the first military command given to Narses, who would later have a resplendent military career. It is possible that Narses had been ordered to spy on Belisarius and Antonina and ensure they were remaining loyal. This would go some way to explaining the conflicts that would later emerge between the two generals. Belisarius and Narses the eunuch arranged to meet with their respective armies at Fermo, on the coast of the Adriatic Sea. There, in the summer of 538, they held a conference of war with all the high-ranking commanders and officers to decide where they should next attack the Goths. In the meeting, the majority of the assembled officers expressed hostility to John, still besieged in Rimini. They accused him of irrational daring, avarice, and insubordination. Narses, however, gave a speech in favor of marching immediately to Rimini to rescue John. Apparently during the conference a messenger arrived from John saying that he would be compelled by hunger to surrender within a week if he did not receive rescue. Belisarius decided therefore to bring the army to Rimini to lift the siege and save John and his forces.[15]

Belisarius devised a complicated rescue operation. He divided the army into thirds, sending the first third under the command of Ildiger by sea to Rimini, the second third under the command of Martinos to march along the coast, and bringing the final third himself via the interior. All three armies converged on Rimini. As they approached, the Goths believed that they were about to be attacked by three great armies, instead of one army divided in three, and thus panicked and fled. Rimini was saved. When Belisarius arrived, he informed John that he owed a debt of gratitude to Ildiger and the other officers for coming to his rescue. That Belisarius did not name himself here is either humility or perhaps an attempt to give credit to his social network of supporting officers. John replied that the only debt he owed was to Narses. This began a great rivalry between Narses and Belisarius. John, who had already defied Belisarius, had now publicly declared his loyalty to Narses. Factions were clearly beginning to develop in the Roman army. The rift was emphasized when Belisarius gave orders that the army should be divided, part to go to Osimo next and part to go to Milan to rescue those besieged there.

Narses flatly refused the order, matching John's earlier insubordination. At this, Belisarius struck camp and led the army to Urbino to besiege the city. Narses and John and their forces initially followed, but then decided that it would be better to invade the region of Emilia. So they marched from Urbino to Rimini, and from there Narses dispatched John into the northern region of Emilia, which he overrun. In the meantime, Belisarius and his army captured Urbino in December 538.[16]

Belisarius and his forces then proceeded to Orvieto and placed it under siege, which lasted through the winter of 538/539. During this period, Belisarius received word that his forces in Milan were themselves being besieged by a Gothic army under Uraias. So the general sent Martinos and Uliaris with a unit of soldiers to chase off Uraias and relieve Milan. Arriving in the region, Martinos and Uliaris felt that their force was too small to defeat the Goths, so they sent to Belisarius, requesting that he order John, nearby in Emilia, to come to their aid. Belisarius agreed and sent an order to John to proceed to Milan to relieve the city. But John, still in a spirit of insubordination, refused him, stating he would only move if Narses ordered it. So Belisarius was then compelled to write a letter to Narses, urging Narses to order John to move to Milan, to support Martinos and Uliaris in defeating the Goths and rescuing the city. Narses did so, and then John agreed to go to Milan. However, too much time elapsed in the sending of all these orders, and the Roman garrison in Milan surrendered the city to Uraias and the Goths in February or perhaps March 539. The Goths took the soldiers alive, but razed the city to the ground, killing all the men and enslaving the women. After witnessing this savagery, Martinos and Uliaris retreated to Rome. This was a disaster for the Roman cause, as it was an obvious victory for the Goths and an equally obvious failure of the Roman army to defend Italian civilians. One good thing did emerge from this situation, however. Justinian learned that Milan had fallen because some in the army were following Narses rather than Belisarius, so the emperor recalled Narses to Constantinople and confirmed Belisarius' role as commander-in-chief.[17]

By this time Orvieto had fallen, and Belisarius prepared to lead his army on to Osimo. He detached some soldiers under Cyprian and Justin to go to Fiesole to lay siege to it, dispatched another force under Martinos and John to Tortona to guard against interference from the Goths in Lombardy, and then marched with 11,000 soldiers to Osimo. Thus Fiesole and Osimo were both under siege by April 539. The sieges would last some time, as both places were well fortified. Vittigis, knowing that his army in Ravenna was already suffering want because of a famine in the area, was unwilling to send reinforcements to either town. Uraias and the Goths in Milan attempted to intervene, but were swept up in Lombardy by a sudden invasion of the Franks, who had crossed the Alps to take advantage of the situation. This might have spelled bad news for both Goths and Romans, but the Frankish army began to suffer from dysentery and had trouble finding enough food due to the famine, so they returned to Francia by the end of summer. Throughout the summer and into the fall, the Roman forces maintained their sieges of both Fiesole and Osimo. They were rewarded in October or November 539, when both cities surrendered. The way to Ravenna now lay open.[18]

Belisarius marshalled his forces and marched directly to Ravenna, no doubt hoping to bring about an end to the war by capturing the capital and Vittigis within it. The Roman army arrived before Ravenna in late 539, or very early 540. To ensure that Ravenna was completely cut off, Belisarius sent some units north to the Po River, to make sure that the Goths would not be able to float supplies or food down river and then eventually along the coast to the city. With Ravenna suitably isolated, Belisarius began to negotiate with Vittigis. The substance of these early negotiations is unclear, and they were interrupted in early 540 by the arrival of two envoys sent directly by Justinian. Domnikos and Maximinos, both senators, came armed with a specific proposal that Justinian believed would bring about an immediate end to the war. The emperor offered to allow Vittigis and the Goths to rule over Italy north of the Po, while Justinian and the Romans ruled Italy south of that river. Moreover, the royal treasury of the Goths was to be divided between the two governments. Given that Belisarius had repeatedly defeated the Gothic army, captured cities throughout Italy, and currently had Vittigis locked up in Ravenna, this was a remarkably generous offer. This generosity was the fruit of a plan that Vittigis had launched in 539. Sensing the walls closing in, Vittigis had cast about for an alliance. He had sent two envoys to Khusro, king of Persia, to urge him to make war on the Roman Empire. Whether because of these envoys or because of his own plans, Khusro did intend to break the Endless Peace and invade Roman territory. It is likely that knowledge of Khusro's military preparations induced Justinian to offer such generous conditions to Vittigis, in order to end the Gothic war and prepare for a new Persian war. Vittigis was thrilled with the offer, and was more than willing to make a treaty on these terms. And why not? It offered a chance for the Goths to get breathing room, reorganize, and then consider renewing the war later when the Romans were distracted by war with the Persians.[19]

But neither Justinian, in his generosity, nor Vittigis, in his exultation at his fortune, had reckoned with what Belisarius would think of this treaty. The general had waged war for five years, had survived being besieged in Rome for a year, had painstakingly taken fortified cities on the way from Rome to Ravenna, and was in no mood to be denied the victory that he believed was in his grasp. He was reportedly frustrated at the proposed treaty and refused to ratify it. Procopius gives no justification for Belisarius' refusal. It seems unlikely that Justinian had intended that his general should be able to scuttle the peace plan that he had personally approved. So in refusing to ratify the treaty, Belisarius was sailing into dangerous waters and opening himself up to accusations of dereliction or even treason. His refusal made Vittigis and the Goths suspicious that the offer was not genuine and was part of some Roman ruse. Belisarius loomed so large in their eyes that no treaty could be legitimate if Belisarius did not approve, even if the offer came from the emperor himself. The leading Goths then took matters into their own hands: they sent to Belisarius, proposing to surrender to him if he would assume imperial power. In effect, they seem to have envisaged a rebirth of the Western Roman Empire, with Belisarius ruling over Italy and commanding a Romano-Gothic army. This is of course further indication of the respect with which his opponents regarded Belisarius. However, to accept this proposal would have meant open rebellion against Justinian, and this is something that Belisarius was not prepared to do. Procopius reports that Belisarius loathed the label "rebel" and had sworn to Justinian to never plan a rebellion during the emperor's lifetime. However, Belisarius did see this offer as his chance to capture Ravenna, Vittigis, and the Gothic treasury. So the general pretended to go along with the Gothic suggestion and said he would swear to assume imperial office once inside Ravenna. It is unlikely that Belisarius had time to get this plan approved by Justinian, although perhaps he notified the emperor that this was the course of action he was taking. The Goths, delighted at Belisarius' apparent acceptance of their proposal, invited the general to enter Ravenna. Belisarius was acutely aware that some of his officers might disapprove of his methods, so he sent away a handful of them just before this moment. Bessas, John, and the brothers Aratios and Narses (not to be confused with Narses the eunuch, who had already been recalled) were dispatched with their forces to areas farther afield, allegedly to forage for food and supplies. These were however the men that Belisarius believed at that moment were most opposed to him, so the real reason was to get them away so they would not divine how exactly Belisarius had gained access to Ravenna. It is interesting that Bessas, one of the top officers of Belisarius in the early part of the war, was now considered one of the general's enemies among his officer corps. Then, perhaps in May 540, Belisarius and the remainder of his army marched into Ravenna unopposed and peacefully occupied the city. It is worth noting that this was the third metropolis (following Carthage and Rome) that Belisarius had captured peacefully, in stark contrast to the Goths' violent seizure of Milan the year before. In Ravenna, the general held Vittigis under guard and gave permission for the Gothic soldiers who lived in regions already held by the Romans to leave the city and return to their homes. Belisarius then took possession of the entire palace treasury of the Goths. Of course, up to this point the Goths still expected Belisarius to declare himself emperor.[20]

When the summer of 540 began, those expectations would be dashed. As the weeks passed by, the Goths must surely have realized that Belisarius had no intention to follow through with the plan. Then Belisarius began to make preparations to leave Italy. With Vittigis under lock and key, the Goths outside Ravenna banded together and acclaimed Hildebad as their new king. Hildebad immediately sent envoys to Belisarius, urging him to take up imperial power as he had agreed to do, and saying that even now the Goths would follow him. But Belisarius flatly refused, saying that "never, while the Emperor Justinian lived, would Belisarius usurp the imperial title." The emperor had recalled him to Constantinople, for Khusro had invaded Roman lands in the east, and the General of the East now had another war to prosecute. So sometime in summer 540, Belisarius and Antonina set sail from Ravenna, bringing with them some of Belisarius' officers (including Ildiger), Vittigis, the Gothic nobles, and the treasury of the Goths. Belisarius' role in the Ostrogothic War came to a close for now, although the situation was far from settled, and the presence of a King Hildebad suggested that the war would be continuing. It is not clear if Belisarius' improvisational capture of

Vittigis and Ravenna improved the position of the Roman army in Italy vis-à-vis simply following through with Justinian's peace offer. On the one hand, Vittigis and many Gothic nobles were removed from the war, along with the entire Gothic treasury, so the remaining Goths had less money and leadership than before. On the other hand, the leadership of Vittigis had not been particularly effective up to this point anyway, and now there was no peace. If Belisarius had just ratified the treaty, he would have received Ravenna (as it is south of the Po) without violence and have left behind a Roman and Gothic Italy that was ostensibly at peace. Perhaps this would have been better for Italy in the very short term, but in the long term it is hard to imagine either the Goths or Romans maintaining that peace through the Romans' renewed war with the Persians.[21]

Sailing from Ravenna to Constantinople would have taken perhaps a month, so Belisarius and his fleet may have arrived in Constantinople in very late summer or early fall of 540. Justinian marveled at Vittigis and the other captive Goths, and he arranged to display the Gothic treasury privately in the Great Palace to the members of the senate. Belisarius was not granted a public triumph or the consulship, both of which he had received after the capture of the Vandal kingdom. This is not particularly surprising given the strained circumstances surrounding the seizure of Vittigis and Ravenna. Doubtless Justinian was well aware by now that Belisarius had only captured the city by feigning usurpation, and the emperor probably felt that he could not be too cautious about heaping additional public honors on Belisarius, who was popular enough as it was. Procopius explains that the people of Constantinople were in love with Belisarius, who was at the apex of his power, wealth, and prestige. Nevertheless, Justinian did not seek to deny that Belisarius was directly responsible for some of the greatest achievements of his reign. The emperor saw to it that Belisarius was immortalized in mosaic. In the grand entrance to the Great Palace in Constantinople, known as the Chalke, the general featured prominently in the ceiling decoration. Procopius provides a breathless description of the mosaics: "On either side is war and battle, and many cities are being captured, some in Italy, some in Libya; and the emperor Justinian is winning victories through his general, Belisarius, and the general is returning to the emperor, with his whole army intact, and he gives him spoils, both kings and kingdoms and all things that are most prized among men." These mosaics do not survive today, but must have made quite an impression on visitors to the palace in the sixth century and beyond. Victorious in war, immortalized in art, Belisarius now spent several months in Constantinople, living the life of a wealthy elite. He walked about the city with an enormous entourage, called on Justinian and Theodora, and advised them on matters of interest. Antonina, Photios, Theodosios, and Ioannina all presumably resided with Belisarius in Constantinople at this time. Doubtless this was a happy time—after years of hard campaigning, the prosperous family could enjoy a season of plenty before Belisarius set out for his next campaign. Further tests were, however, not far off.[22]

FIGURE 11 Portrait of a sixth-century woman, probably Antonina, detail from the imperial panel of Theodora in San Vitale, Ravenna. Photo by Steven Zucker.

6

Trying Times

BELISARIUS AND ANTONINA stayed in Constantinople for some months, through the remainder of 540 and into the new year. It seems likely that this was a celebratory and restorative period for the couple, who had been campaigning hard in Italy for five years straight. Little is known about their activities during these months. Procopius does indicate that Belisarius' popularity was at a high: "everyone was talking about Belisarius . . . the people took delight in watching Belisarius as he came out of his house every day and went to the forum or as he returned to his house, and none of them could get enough of this sight." The author paints a vivid picture of Belisarius' entourage at this moment, the height of his power. "His movements resembled a crowded festival procession, as he was always escorted by a large number of Vandals, Goths, and Berbers. Furthermore, he had a fine figure and was tall and remarkably handsome." In addition to processing around the city to the marvel of its inhabitants, it is quite likely that Belisarius used this time to catch up on the events that had been occurring in the East in the previous summer. In spring 540, perhaps in April, Khusro, king of the Persians, had invaded the Roman Empire by marching into Syria with the Euphrates on his army's right, a replay of Azarethes' invasion in 531. In quick succession, the Persian king sacked Sura, extracted ransom money from Hierapolis, sacked Beroia, and then sacked the great city of Antioch. From here, the Persian army marched to Seleukeia, where Khusro bathed in the waters of the Mediterranean. Having received a promise from Justinian that he would be paid 5,000 pounds of gold (or 360,000 *nomismata*) the Persian king decamped for his own lands, stopping along the way to plunder Apamea as well. The invasion had been a resounding success for Khusro, who had marched throughout Roman Syria at will, enslaved tens of thousands of Roman citizens, and seized money and treasures in all the cities he had sacked. Belisarius must have grieved to learn

Belisarius & Antonina. David Alan Parnell, Oxford University Press. © Oxford University Press 2023.
DOI: 10.1093/oso/9780197574706.003.0007

of the extent of the destruction. And where was the Roman army during this crisis? Belisarius himself was still General of the East, and he was obviously in Italy when Khusro's invasion began. The Army of the East, which he commanded on paper, had been stripped of many of its soldiers for the invasion of Africa, and perhaps again for the invasion of Italy, and it is not clear how many of those soldiers had been replaced with new recruits. Just before Khusro's invasion, and probably to try to oppose it, Justinian had given temporary command of the Army of the East to Bouzes, Belisarius' old colleague, until the latter could arrive. This general however did nothing to arrest Khusro's advance, perhaps having insufficient forces to bring him to battle. Justinian's cousin Germanos also arrived in Antioch shortly before its capture, but had brought too few soldiers to safely defend it, and retired from the area before Khusro arrived. So if the invasion was a success for Khusro, it was equally an embarrassment for the Roman army, which was caught undermanned and unprepared.[1]

For these reasons, Belisarius' idyll in Constantinople in the last third of 540 could not be of long duration. As General of the East, the responsibility fell on him to restore order in Syria and Mesopotamia and to put the pieces of Roman defenses in the region back together again. So as soon as the winter ended, perhaps in March 541, Belisarius was on the road across Anatolia, moving quickly to get to the eastern front before Khusro could launch a new invasion. With him he brought his officers from the war in Italy, including his stepson Photios and his ally Valerianos, who was now appointed General of Armenia. Those Goths who had surrendered to Belisarius and been transported to Constantinople also marched with Belisarius, an interesting instance of military manpower transfer from West to East, just as captured Vandals had been shipped east for military service a few years before. However, one significant figure from the previous campaign did not march to the east with Belisarius: Antonina stayed in Constantinople, and the couple were separated for the first time since the early 530s.[2]

Antonina the Operative

The separation of Belisarius and Antonina was unusual enough by their previous standards that it occasioned comment from Procopius, their constant historian. In the *Secret History*, he charges that Antonina stayed behind in Constantinople in 541 "in order for Theodosios to have easy access to her." He conjures up an image of Antonina preferring to stay in the city to have sex with her adopted son rather than travel with her husband on campaign as she had been doing faithfully for more than seven years by this point. This is quite simply slander, and even by the usual standards of the *Secret History* it is not particularly thoughtful or believable slander. This accusation holds no water because in the *Wars* the historian provides the real reason that Antonina remained in Constantinople at this time, and that explanation is good enough that it is not necessary to imagine any additional, incestual reasons. Procopius says that Antonina was busy with a scheme to organize the downfall of the Praetorian Prefect John the Cappadocian in order to ingratiate herself with the Empress Theodora, who considered John a political enemy. This was not a small or trivial operation, as John was the most senior civil official of the entire Roman Empire and was well ensconced in his position by 541, having held it continuously since his restoration after the Nika Riot in 532. Therefore, completing this scheme was more than enough of a reason for Antonina to have stayed behind in Constantinople when Belisarius marched for the eastern front, without having to posit the continuation of an incestuous affair.[3]

The downfall of John the Cappadocian shows Antonina operating on her own as a political operative of considerable skill, indeed enough skill to perhaps match the military capabilities of her husband, so it is worth examining the episode in some detail. Even Procopius praises her abilities, writing with regard to this incident that Antonina "was the most competent of all people when it came to devising means by which to accomplish the impossible." About the time that Belisarius was preparing to march to the East, Antonina was crafting the scheme that would ensure John's fall from grace. Procopius suggests that the initiative belonged entirely to Antonina, who did this to "ingratiate" herself with Theodora. While this is possible, it seems more likely that Antonina would have gone to Theodora first to be assured of her support. After all, taking on the most senior civil magistrate of the empire was not something to be done without the backing of someone powerful. And it is likely that Antonina and Theodora were already at the very least acquainted by this time, and perhaps even friends. The two had probably met in Constantinople in the 520s, but even if that was not the case, they must surely have met in 534, when Belisarius and Antonina were honored for the conquest of Vandal Africa. The idea that in 541 Antonina needed to ingratiate herself with Theodora is based upon Procopius' fiction that Antonina was engaged in a long affair with Theodosios and needed to appease Theodora, who judged the general's wife for the alleged affair. Therefore we can dispense with the idea that Antonina came up with the idea of removing John the Cappadocian entirely on her own. In all likelihood, Theodora and Antonina conspired together to cause John's downfall, although it is certainly possible that it was Antonina who came up with the specific plan for how to achieve this goal.[4]

That plan required Antonina to make a new friend. Sometime in early 541, or perhaps even as early as late 540, Antonina began to cultivate the friendship of a young, impressionable woman named Euphemia. Procopius describes Euphemia as discrete, but because of her young age quite vulnerable. Over a long period of time, Antonina and Euphemia became fast friends, and the latter developed an absolute trust of the former. This friendship was the first step in the downfall of John the Cappadocian, for Euphemia was his cherished daughter and only child. Antonina used her relationship with Euphemia to skillfully lay a trap for the praetorian prefect. One day in the late spring of 541, Antonina complained to Euphemia that Justinian was ungrateful to Belisarius despite the general having captured two kings and enormous wealth for the emperor. With delightful naivete at the danger she was placing herself in, young Euphemia enthusiastically replied, "But for all this, dearest friend, you yourselves are responsible, given that you are not willing to use the power that you currently have at your disposal!" Antonina must have smiled inwardly at this, for the conversation had taken the exact turn that she had desired. Her next sentence would be the riskiest in the history of this new friendship, but also the most important. Antonina, very seriously, said to Euphemia, "But we are not able, my daughter, to attempt a rebellion in the armies unless someone inside the administration joins in our attempt. Now if your father were willing, then we could easily put it into motion and accomplish all that God wants." This exchange was the beginning of a classic entrapment scheme. It is interesting that out of this entire episode, these two lines are the only direct quotes of the conversations that Procopius provides. It is tempting to suspect that Antonina reported them for the official record of the inquiry that followed, and that the historian was able to get access to the report. However, it is equally possible that Procopius creatively invented the lines as being the kind of thing that was likely said in this clandestine conversation. At any rate, poor Euphemia, convinced of Antonina's friendship and earnestness, responded to the older woman's statement by promising to bring this matter to her father's attention. The trap was laid.[5]

Procopius reports that Euphemia went immediately to John the Cappadocian and told him of her conversation with Antonina. John was pleased and agreed to meet with Antonina so that the two could discuss a possible rebellion against Justinian. Antonina demurred on an immediate meeting and suggested that meeting in Constantinople was too risky, and that they should wait until Antonina had departed the city on the way to the eastern front to meet up with Belisarius. At that point, Antonina reasoned, John could come to meet her in a suburb of Constantinople under the pretense of bidding her farewell. In all of these negotiations, Euphemia must have served as the go-between for Antonina and John, perhaps a thrilling job for a young, impressionable woman. No doubt she thought she was laying the groundwork for her beloved father and new best friend to make a new world. It is impossible to contemplate this story without feeling regret at the way Euphemia was manipulated. As for Antonina, she was constantly calculating how to proceed in such a way that maximized the success of her mission and minimized the risk to her. And there was risk for her and, by extension, Belisarius as well. She had to make it look as if she and Belisarius were truly willing to plot rebellion in order to entrap John, and if John reported her, what defense could she have? To ensure her safety, Antonina continued to report to Theodora throughout the process, letting the empress know of the entrapment scheme, and no doubt assuring her that the alleged resentment of Belisarius for Justinian's ingratitude was fictional. This probably partly explains the delay in the meeting between Antonina and John—the former needed time to report to Theodora and make arrangements. Theodora was reportedly very pleased with Antonina's progress and urged her to continue with the meeting with John. The empress then began her own contribution to the plot. She went straight to Justinian and reported to him that John was having treasonous communications with Antonina, who was acting as her agent. Theodora then, presumably with Justinian's approval, dispatched Narses the eunuch and Markellos, commander of the palace guard unit the Excubitors, with a detachment of his guards. Their orders were to investigate the accusation by concealing themselves and listening to the meeting between Antonina and John. Justinian allegedly also sent a secret message through one of John's friends, urging John not to meet with Antonina under any circumstances. If the emperor truly believed that John was being entrapped and was not really his enemy, this is certainly possible. However, it is also possible that this is simply a fiction introduced by Procopius to add another layer of drama. The historian distances himself from this element of the story by prefacing it with "they say," which suggests he had no firm source for it. If there was a warning, John ignored it.[6]

One evening in May 541, Antonina crossed the Sea of Marmara and lodged at the suburban home she and Belisarius shared in the Asiatic suburb of Constantinople known as Rouphinianai. Thence also came Narses, Markellos, and the guards, who concealed themselves behind a wall in the home. Finally, by agreement through the intermediation of Euphemia, John the Cappadocian came as well. He and Antonina met around midnight, and John talked at length about the plot to rebel against Justinian and began swearing oaths that he would participate fully. Procopius provides no quotations of this discussion, so it is not possible to track how it unfolded, but given the way Antonina expertly handled Euphemia, we can imagine that here also Antonina carefully guided the conversation. Given her evident skill at manipulation, it is possible that Antonina managed John in such a way that she avoided herself mentioning rebellion or implicating Belisarius while still leading John into incriminating himself. However the discussion unfolded, it was enough to convince Narses and Markellos, who rushed in with the guards to attempt to arrest John on the spot. Antonina perhaps immediately withdrew. John had not come unprepared, but was escorted by his own personal guards, and a brawl ensued between John and his men and Markellos and his men. In the confusion, John managed to escape and quickly returned to Constantinople. However, instead of going straight to Justinian to report the matter and blame Antonina for entrapping him, John sought refuge in a church, where he perhaps clung to the altar and requested sanctuary. This was an admission of guilt. Between the testimony of Antonina, Narses, and Markellos, and the flight to sanctuary, Justinian had all that he needed. He could not allow such plotting to go unpunished. John was stripped of his position as praetorian prefect, shipped to Cyzicus on the southern shore of the Sea of Marmara, and forcibly ordained as a priest. The imperial treasury confiscated John's property, although a portion of it was set aside to provide for him in his new life. This was a rapid collapse in fortunes for a man who had been the most important civilian official in the empire for almost a decade. Antonina had outwitted John at every turn.[7]

Before moving on, it is worth taking a moment to consider why Antonina and Theodora would have wanted to do all of this to John. According to multiple sources, Theodora and John had long been enemies. In the *Wars*, Procopius wrote quite openly that "Theodora hated John more than any other person," and explains that John set himself up as Theodora's enemy and slandered her to Justinian. In the *Secret History*, Procopius elaborates that John's slanders to Justinian about Theodora almost caused the emperor and empress to wage war upon each other. The civil servant John Lydus, seeking to bolster his own complaints about John the Cappadocian, relates that Theodora actually assembled a list of grievances against the praetorian prefect and presented it to Justinian in an attempt to get him fired. Although both authors confirm serious antipathy between Theodora and John the

Cappadocian, neither exactly explains the source of it. Perhaps John was not sufficiently deferential to Theodora and thought his position secure enough to get away with that. If so, he was seriously mistaken. The impression that these two sources give is that the rift between Theodora and John was of considerable duration, and that Theodora had been pressuring Justinian to get rid of John for some time. The fact that Justinian had not already done so by 541 indicates that John was actually quite good at his job and that Justinian felt he was nearly indispensable.[8]

It is important to note that Antonina also had good reason for wanting to take down John the Cappadocian. As explained above, it is unlikely that she undertook this mission solely to ingratiate herself to Theodora. Rather, she worked as Theodora's agent in this matter because it was in her and Belisarius' best interests as well. Procopius claims that everyone in Constantinople admired Belisarius except for John, who resented the general and even plotted against him because he was jealous that Belisarius was more popular. There is some obvious hyperbole in this argument, as it is extremely unlikely that John was the only person who resented Belisarius for his success, but otherwise this is not implausible. John and Belisarius had both toiled for Justinian for long periods of time by 540, but Belisarius had indisputably earned the better rewards and more popularity. However, we should be slightly skeptical that John was openly plotting against Belisarius. If that were the case, why would he have trusted Antonina and met with her to discuss rebellion? If John was an enemy of Belisarius and Antonina, he probably did not broadcast it. Even beyond current events in 541, Antonina would have had reason to want to take revenge on John and see him taken down a peg. In 532, John had tried to convince Justinian not to declare war on Vandal Africa. If he had succeeded, Belisarius and Antonina would not have earned their signature victory there. In 533, John had provided the bread for the Vandal expeditionary army, but had taken the cheap route in baking the bread, with the result that it grew moldy along the way and killed 500 soldiers. Perhaps this incident, above all else, was the catalyst that drove Antonina to want to take down the praetorian prefect. In the two campaigns, Antonina had been frequently concerned with issues of supply. She had taken charge of water supplies on the voyage to Africa in summer 533, urged Belisarius to eat some food in Rome in early 537, and personally directed the delivery of supplies to Rome in late 537. If she was so attentive to supply chain issues, John's malfeasance with the bread in 533 must have rankled. And it might have been more personal than simple professional disgust. Perhaps Antonina believed John's recklessness with supply could have killed someone she cared for, and she harbored resentment about that. With this history in mind, it is not hard to see why Antonina would have had her own reasons to undertake a scheme to bring down John the Cappadocian. So both Theodora and Antonina had their own reasons to disgrace John, and the two friends worked together to make it happen. Both also enjoyed rewards for their effort. Theodora was rid of a powerful enemy and perhaps took some of John's property that had been absorbed by the imperial treasury. Antonina and Belisarius received John's mansion in Constantinople, perhaps as a sort of payment for Antonina's services. By the end of May 541, Antonina, flush with triumph, was ready to travel to the eastern front and join Belisarius, who was in the midst of preparing for a new campaign against the Persians.[9]

In the East Again

While Antonina was expertly manipulating Euphemia in Constantinople, Belisarius was attempting to restore stability to the shattered Roman East. The journey from Constantinople to the frontier in Mesopotamia, a distance of some 900 miles, probably would have taken about a month assuming that Belisarius and his officers were mounted. The general bypassed stricken Antioch and made straight for his old headquarters, the great Roman fortress of Dara, hard by the frontier with the Persian Empire. Here, Belisarius began to gather together the scattered elements of the Army of the East, trying to reforge it into a fighting unit that could oppose a potential second Persian invasion. This must have involved painstaking work reviewing unit rosters, gathering arms and armor, and arranging for supply caches to be created. This is exactly the sort of work Belisarius would have needed secretaries and other administrative figures to assist with, so it is interesting to note that he had lost his chief man of letters, Procopius. Although Procopius does not himself confirm his departure from Belisarius' service, it is highly likely that the historian resigned his post in 540 after the capture of Ravenna and return to Constantinople. Procopius likely settled down in Constantinople at this time to begin writing the histories that would eventually ensure his fame. Perhaps the historian's absence explains why he describes this campaign as a whole and Belisarius' efforts to reforge the Army of the East in particular in vague generalities. He writes that Belisarius "was organizing on the spot and equipping the soldiers, who were for the most part without either arms or armor and in terror of the name of the Persians." This work probably occupied more than a month, because Belisarius and the reformed army did not move out from Dara until June 541. While putting the army back together again, and presumably drilling it and preparing it for battle, Belisarius sent out spies to determine the location of the Persian army. When the spies returned, they reported that the Persian army was nowhere to be seen and there was no danger of the Persians invading Roman Mesopotamia or Syria again this year, for they had moved north to defend their territory from the Huns. This was actually disinformation intentionally spread by Khusro to mask his true objective, which was an invasion of Roman Lazica (modern Georgia in the Caucasus). So Khusro and the Persians had in fact invaded Roman lands, but the disinformation in this case did not harm Belisarius or his army because either way the Persian army was still far away and would not in fact be an impediment to Roman operations in Mesopotamia.[10]

Upon hearing this news, Belisarius decided that the time had come for an invasion of Persian Mesopotamia. If the Persian army was nowhere to be found, this made strategic sense and could also have been perceived as a first step to getting revenge for the Persian invasion of the previous year. At roughly the same time, the general also received an order from Justinian that he was to immediately invade the Persian Empire, so it seems Belisarius and Justinian were thinking the same. Belisarius then called together a meeting of his officers to seek their opinion, humbly noting that he had only recently returned from the west after a long absence, and that he desired their judgment on a potential invasion. In this action we can again see Belisarius trying to preempt the kind of discord he had faced before the Battle of Callinicum in 531. Most of the assembled officers agreed that the army should immediately invade Persian territory, although two commanders of frontier troops stationed in Syria voiced concern that the Persians' Arab allies might raid their lands while they were gone. Belisarius pointed out that it was the time of the summer solstice (June), and the Arabs would be participating in a religious festival. Having settled this objection, Belisarius led out his army, the size of which is unknown, from Dara and marched across the frontier toward the great Persian fortress of Nisibis. He encamped about five miles away, hoping to draw out the garrison of the city into a pitched battle there. However, one of his commanders named Peter thought the camp was too far away, and against orders he led his detachment to a spot only one mile from Nisibis. The Persian forces noticed this smaller unit, sallied forth and defeated them, but retreated back to the city when Belisarius brought the main army up to support Peter's troops. At this, Belisarius gave up hopes of capturing Nisibis and led the army some 25 miles east to a smaller Persian fortress named Sisauranon, on the border between today's southeastern Turkey and northeastern Syria. An initial assault on its fortifications failed, so Belisarius arranged the army to besiege the place. At the same time, he sent a large raiding party south across the Tigris River into modern-day Iraq, with instructions to plunder the undefended region. The raiding party consisted of the Romans' Arab allies, led by Al-Harith, and 1,200 of Belisarius' personal guardsmen, led by Traïanos and John the Glutton. Sometime after the departure of the raiders, Belisarius learned that the defenders of Sisauranon were short on food, so he sent an envoy to persuade them to surrender, and they agreed. The date of the surrender is unknown, with Procopius simply saying that "much time" was consumed in the siege, so it might have been in July or early August. When the fort surrendered, Belisarius released the Christian inhabitants of Roman origin unharmed, but all the Persian inhabitants including the garrison force were taken into captivity and sent to Constantinople. Justinian later formed a cavalry unit of the captured Persian warriors and sent it to Italy to fight against the Goths, just as captured Goths had accompanied Belisarius to the East to fight the Persians. Not wanting to hold Sisauranon, Belisarius razed its walls to the ground, and then considered his next move.[11]

Belisarius and his officers began to grow nervous, because the large raiding party had neither returned from the south nor sent a messenger to report on progress. In fact, the raid had been an unqualified success, with the Arabs and Belisarius' guardsmen seizing huge amounts of booty and facing no opposition whatsoever. But the general had no idea. Procopius blames Al-Harith, saying that the Arab leader was afraid that Belisarius would seize his plunder, and therefore decided to make up a rumor that a Persian army was approaching to give him an excuse to flee and not return to the main Roman army. Using this rumor as an excuse, Al-Harith and his followers disappeared, presumably returning to their homes. Traïanos and John the Glutton, at a loss, led Belisarius' guardsmen in a westward retreat along the Euphrates River toward Roman territory, not returning to the main army either. The disappearance of the raiding party created consternation among Belisarius and the officers at Sisauranon, who feared that an additional Persian army must have appeared and wiped it out. Added to this fear was a practical concern about health. Procopius said that a third of the Roman army at Sisauranon was ill and blamed the dry heat of the region. Perhaps the soldiers were suffering from heat stroke. Finally, the two commanders of Syrian troops were concerned because the time of the Arab religious festivals had ended, and they feared Arab raids on the lands they were supposed to be protecting. These three reasons were more than enough to suggest a retreat to Roman territory might be in order, and in fact Procopius says that Belisarius' subordinate officers demanded a retreat. The general gave in to the request and ordered a retreat back to Roman territory, with the sick of the army transported in carts. Procopius does not say where they went, but presumably the army returned to Dara. As with the date of the capture of Sisauranon, the date of the retreat is unknown. Perhaps it was mid-August, since Belisarius had promised the Syrian commanders that the invasion would last only two months.[12]

So goes the public explanation for the end of Belisarius' invasion of the Persian Empire in 541. In the *Secret History*, Procopius offers, as often, a more scandalous explanation for the general's retreat back to Roman territory. Procopius accuses Belisarius of being unwilling to march more than one day from Roman territory, so that he could return swiftly when he heard news of Antonina's arrival. Allegedly, Belisarius had been tarrying near Sisauranon after its capture waiting to hear news that Antonina was on her way to join him. And so, when he learned that she was in fact en route and would arrive soon, he immediately ordered the retreat and marched the army back to Roman territory so that he could meet her. The reason for Belisarius' haste to confront Antonina was allegedly, again, the accusation of her affair with Theodosios, to which we shall return shortly. Before doing so, however, it is worth exploring the accusation that Belisarius failed in his duty, cutting short his promising military campaign to satisfy his personal need to see his wife. This is one of the most serious allegations Procopius makes against Belisarius in the *Secret History*. Most of the other accusations touch on Belisarius' character and the alleged nature of his relationship with his wife, but this one is nothing short of a dereliction of duty charge. Procopius makes this clear by explaining that because of the reason for his retreat "Belisarius was reviled by all the Romans for sacrificing the most critical needs of the state to his paltry domestic affairs." The author suggests that if Belisarius had only remained in Persian territory, he might have advanced through Mesopotamia all the way up to the walls of Ctesiphon, the Persian capital (just southeast of modern Baghdad). Despite the gravity of this charge, there is every reason to believe that Procopius is at the least exaggerating substantially, and perhaps even simply making this up. Why? Procopius already gave three good reasons for the retreat of the Roman army in late summer 541 in his account of the events in the *Wars*, namely the disappearance of the raiding party and fear of a new Persian army operating in the area, the emergence of disease and incapacitation of a third of the army, and the concern that the Persians' Arab allies might be raiding Syria. This would already be enough of a reason to retreat. Belisarius had only just finished putting the Army of the East back together again after at least a month of work. It would have been irresponsible to risk that army in a headlong further invasion of Persia when the enemy's

strength was unknown and the army itself was partially incapacitated. There
is no reason to propose alternative explanations for the retreat of the Roman
army. Now, if Procopius was to admit that he falsified the reasons for the
retreat he gave in the *Wars*, it might be necessary to consider an alternative
explanation. But the historian cannot and does not suggest he falsified any
of those reasons. In the *Secret History*, he admits to them, saying that there
were "certain other things that occurred in this campaign . . . which had
predisposed him to retreat . . . but this caused him to implement it all the
sooner." This is transparently churlish reasoning on the part of Procopius.
He essentially agrees that Belisarius had legitimate military reasons to retreat
from Sisauranon back to Roman territory, but then complains that he went
sooner than necessary. But who was Procopius to say it was sooner than necessary? He himself had admitted that one third of Belisarius' troops had been
rendered incapacitated by illness, which would have made further offensive
operations difficult at best. The claim that Belisarius could have marched
his army to the walls of Ctesiphon is also fanciful at best if Procopius is
admitting Belisarius should have retreated but did so too soon. If Procopius
agreed Belisarius needed to retreat, why should he think the general should
precede that retreat with a major advance to Ctesiphon, some 350 miles
deeper into Persian territory? In short, Procopius' suggestion that Belisarius
and the Roman army should have advanced deeper into Mesopotamia up to
Ctesiphon is ludicrous when examined in context of what Procopius said
in the *Wars* (and does not deny in the *Secret History*). By extension, then,
the idea that Belisarius hurried the retreat to Roman territory in order to
meet with Antonina is unnecessary given the other reasons he had to retreat.
This does not necessarily mean that Belisarius was not eager to return to
Roman territory and meet with Antonina, but it does suggest that any
accusations that Belisarius was derelict in his duty in this instance can be
dismissed as slander.[13]

The Family Implodes

And so sometime in the late summer of 541, perhaps in late August, Belisarius
and Antonina were reunited at an undisclosed location on the eastern front,
probably Dara. The lack of specificity in the location is interesting and another indicator that Procopius was not present for this meeting. According to
Procopius, it was not a happy reunion. In the *Secret History*, the embittered
author weaves together a complicated drama involving Belisarius, Antonina,
Theodosios, and Photios that we must now untangle to try to discover what

happened in this difficult period. As mentioned above, Procopius alleges that Antonina remained in Constantinople in spring 541 to continue an affair with her adopted son Theodosios. However, there was a fly in the ointment: Photios. As we have already seen in Chapter 4, Procopius says that Photios and Theodosios did not get along. It is not particularly clear why this mattered in 541, since Photios was in the East with Belisarius and according to the story Theodosios was in Constantinople with Antonina. At any rate, the author says that Antonina began slandering Photios and harassing him, allegedly to make her adopted son-turned-lover Theodosios feel more comfortable. This angered Photios enough that he went to Belisarius in summer 541, possibly while the army was besieging Sisauranon, and informed him that Antonina and Theodosios were carrying on an affair in Constantinople. Belisarius was enraged. He begged Photios to help him revenge himself upon Theodosios, called Photios his "dearest boy," and insisted that he was Photios' father, mother, and entire family. Convinced, Photios agreed to help Belisarius, and the two exchanged oaths that they would never betray each other. They formed a plan: Belisarius would confront Antonina when she arrived in the East, and Photios would set out across Anatolia to Ephesus, where they believed Theodosios was now residing, and take him into custody there. And so when Antonina arrived at Dara in late summer 541, Procopius says that Belisarius "placed her under guard and in disgrace." The general allegedly tried to murder her many times, but each time he shrank back from the deed, "overcome by a burning erotic passion." Meanwhile, Photios seized Antonina's eunuch Kalligonos and dragged him to Ephesus, torturing him for information along the way. At Ephesus, Photios captured and bound Theodosios, and confiscated the young man's considerable wealth. According to Procopius, the Empress Theodora now intervened on behalf of her friend Antonina. She recalled both Belisarius and Antonina to Constantinople. Inexplicably, Photios chose to return to Constantinople as well, after sending Theodosios to be held by Belisarius' personal guardsmen, who were quartered for the winter in Cilicia (southeastern Anatolia). In Constantinople, Theodora allegedly arrested or exiled many men who belonged to the social circles of Belisarius and Photios and had Photios tortured to try to uncover where Theodosios was hidden. Theodosios was eventually discovered and restored to Antonina, and Photios was kept imprisoned in the palace for three years. Finally, Theodora forced Belisarius against his will to reconcile with Antonina.[14]

This is an extraordinary story, both complex and absurd, and, of course, carefully woven together to make Belisarius and Antonina look extremely bad. Belisarius comes off as weak and faithless, the opposite of his portrayal in the *Wars*. He is unable to revenge himself on his wife for her adultery and he is forced by the empress to reconcile with his wife, thus emphasizing his subjugation to two powerful women. He swears oaths to not betray Photios, but then stands by passively while the young man is tortured and then imprisoned. Meanwhile, Antonina is presented not only of course as an incestuous adulterer, but also as a hateful mother, who chooses her lover over her son. In fact, the story is so carefully engineered to make Belisarius and Antonina appear as absurd and evil as possible that it is hard to take it seriously as a description of events that actually happened. And yet, historians have for centuries done exactly that—they have accepted this story uncritically, swallowing whole the events it describes and assuming it to be a true part of the biography of Belisarius and Antonina. A better approach to this story is to accept that Procopius presents it as invective, not history. The author here is not looking to present an honest biography of the married couple, but instead to make them look bad. A clue that this is the case is that Procopius names no sources for this information and names no witnesses to this titanic argument between Belisarius and Antonina or its aftermath. Procopius himself was not present for any of these events either, having left Belisarius' service in 540. In addition, inconsistencies within the story suggest that this was not true history, or at the very least is history that has been substantially modified. The chronology of the story is disjointed compared to what Procopius presents in the *Wars*. Procopius claims that Belisarius and Photios swore to take revenge on Theodosios while the Roman army was in Persian territory, but also says this was at the same time that Antonina was arranging for the downfall of John the Cappadocian. However, those two events did not occur simultaneously. As explained above, John the Cappadocian was removed from office sometime in May and was certainly gone by June 1. Belisarius and the Roman army did not even begin the invasion of Persian territory until later in June (at the time of the summer solstice). So Procopius errs by suggesting that the two events occurred at the same time. Similarly, the flow of the story makes it seem that Theodora intervened and recalled Belisarius and Antonina as soon as she learned that the former had turned on the latter. Yet this should have taken place at the end of summer. The other evidence of the story, however, suggests Belisarius and Antonina did not arrive in Constantinople until winter. The *Wars* refers to them being in Constantinople in winter, and in the *Secret History* story Procopius says that Photios sent Theodosios to the winter quarters of the guards in Cilicia before he proceeded to Constantinople. Even accounting for travel time for messengers, there seems to be a gap of several months between when Theodora should have recalled Belisarius and Antonina if the story is accurate and when they actually returned to Constantinople. However, just because there are inconsistencies in the story and it is patently designed to make Belisarius and Antonina look bad does not mean that every aspect of the story is fictive. Dismissing the entire account as a creation of Procopius' imagination would be almost as irresponsible as accepting the entire account as historical fact. As with the argument between Belisarius and Antonina at Syracuse, discussed in Chapter 4, there would have been enough high-ranking people present first at Dara, where the couple met in summer 541, and later at Constantinople, where they were allegedly reconciled, that if there was no dramatic argument this story would have been roundly rejected by those in the know as complete fiction. In addition, it would have been obvious that Photios had disappeared from Belisarius' side in 541 and was not present when the general resumed his campaign in 542, so this part of the story cannot have been entirely fictionalized. In writing the *Secret History*, Procopius wanted to distance himself from Belisarius and Antonina, and that was best done by building on as much real history as possible to make his claims believable. Because of this, it seems likely that the author took a real argument that occurred in 541 between the husband and wife, and that resulted in the disappearance of Photios, which was witnessed by many people, and used it as the basis of a fictional story of adultery and humiliation.[15]

If this is the case, then it is necessary to try to untangle this hypothetical real argument from the invective window-dressing in order to understand what really happened between Belisarius and Antonina in 541. Fortuitously, Procopius leaves plenty of clues in the text of the *Secret History* that suggest the real cause of the argument. In his long speech to Photios in which he asks him to help him revenge himself upon Theodosios, Belisarius twice refers to wealth. First, he praises Photios for attaining the rank of honorary consul and amassing vast wealth, and then he complains that because of Antonina and Theodosios' affair, he himself has lost vast amounts of wealth. Later in the story, after Photios has captured Theodosios in Ephesus, he comes to Constantinople bringing with him the money of Theodosios, described as a substantial sum. When this is combined with the earlier mention of Theodosios amassing "piles of money" from the palaces of Carthage and Ravenna, described in Chapter 4, and of Antonina in Carthage hiding spoils of war with Theodosios in a basement room, described in Chapter 3, the consistency of the messaging is striking. Throughout the whole story

he has woven together, which is ostensibly about an incestuous affair between Antonina and Theodosios, Procopius retained a central thread about
disputes over the family's wealth. The money argument is clearly not his
main focus, which makes it all the more plausible as the true historical root
from which Procopius grew the slanderous tree of adultery. This gets us
closer to understanding what actually happened in 541, but to really uncover the true disagreement we have to shift our focus for a moment from
Belisarius and Antonina to Photios and Theodosios, because it seems highly
probable that the argument between the former pair sprang from a dispute
between the latter. As with the theme of contention over money, Procopius
does not hide this in his narrative. While Belisarius and Antonina were on
campaign in Italy in 536, Theodosios refused to return from Ephesus and
join them as long as Photios was with them. The reason given is that Photios
hated Theodosios and made life difficult for him: "For Photios was by nature quick to turn against those who had more influence than he with any
person. Of course, in this business with Theodosios he had a good reason to
choke with rage insofar as he, who was after all a biological son, had been
marginalized, while Theodosios was wielding power and amassing piles of
money." The division of labor in Belisarius and Photios' plot to revenge themselves on Theodosios also speaks to a serious conflict between Photios and
Theodosios. While Belisarius was to confront Antonina, Photios was given
the task of capturing Theodosios, allegedly to stop the affair, but as we saw
the practical result of this move was that Photios confiscated Theodosios'
money. All of this points to a major disagreement bordering on open warfare between Photios and Theodosios. What could they have been fighting
about? It is possible that the two young men were engaged in a titanic
struggle over which of them would be Belisarius and Antonina's principal
heir. By 541, it must have been obvious that Belisarius and Antonina were
not expecting any additional children. Antonina was in her mid-forties, and
had last given birth (to Ioannina) a decade earlier. Indeed, the couple might
have given up on having additional biological children as early as 533, when
they adopted Theodosios before the Vandal campaign. Thus, by 541, both
Photios and Theodosios were probably in their early twenties, were more
than aware that their parents were fabulously rich, and were likely in an
epic fight about which of them would inherit. While this might seem crass
and inappropriate, given that Belisarius was probably only around 40 years
old himself, the two young men would have known that Belisarius had a
hazardous career and could in theory be killed in combat in the very next
campaign. This might have lent a sense of urgency to their rivalry.[16]

If Belisarius and Antonina had been united in their response to the two children over this struggle, all might have ended well. Unfortunately, it seems that the husband and wife, who were such good partners in other areas of their marriage and careers, were not on the same page with regard to their own children. It is clear that Antonina's favorite was Theodosios, and that Belisarius' favorite was Photios. These pairings are most obviously apparent in the career paths of the two young men. Photios served with Belisarius in his army on multiple occasions, showing up in Sicily in 535, at the siege of Naples in 536, and during the siege of Rome in 537, and finally, of course, serving during the campaign into Persian territory and the capture of Sisauranon in 541. Theodosios, perhaps slightly younger than Photios, did accompany Belisarius and Antonina to Africa, Sicily, and later Italy, but there is no indication that he had a commission in the army or even served as a member of Belisarius' personal guardsmen. Of the two young men, Photios was clearly the one following in Belisarius' footsteps. The hyperbolic and slanderous story that Procopius wove in the *Secret History* also serves as evidence of these parent/child pairings, even when the incestuous elements of the story are removed. Procopius reveals that Belisarius considered himself Photios' father and expressed his pride in what Photios had accomplished, which is what we would expect if the general considered Photios his favorite. Meanwhile, the story reveals that Antonina sided with Theodosios, as it accuses her of plotting against Photios in favor of Theodosios, and had previously paired Theodosios with Antonina in both Carthage and Syracuse. With this, the pieces of the argument fall into place. Instead of a sordid tale involving incestuous adultery, we find that Photios and Theodosios were arguing over the family money and who would be the heir, and that Belisarius supported Photios while Antonina supported Theodosios.[17]

Now that the source of their argument has been unraveled, we can return to that moment in late summer 541 when Antonina arrived on the eastern front, possibly at Dara, and met with Belisarius. Procopius alleges there was a volcanic argument and that Belisarius even put Antonina under guard in his immense anger. Yet it seems fairly clear that the dispute between Photios and Theodosios was at least several years old at this point, and that Belisarius and Antonina had already known they were on opposite sides of this issue, so why should the long-simmering argument explode now? It is possible that Photios, determined to settle the argument once and for all, decided to accuse Theodosios of something particularly horrible just before Antonina arrived. Jealous of Theodosios and concerned that Antonina was enriching him with the money that should have been his as an eventual inheritance, Photios might have unscrupulously accused Antonina of having an affair with Theodosios. This is an attractive possibility, because it would both account for the huge argument Belisarius and Antonina had when they met at Dara, and also at the same time explain the source of the complicated story Procopius later wove about the alleged affair. Thus, without there being an actual affair, Photios could have prompted a blowout argument between Belisarius and Antonina, and he succeeded in temporarily winning the dispute with Theodosios when Belisarius gave him permission to go to Ephesus and take Theodosios with his money into custody. Of course, once Belisarius and Antonina actually began talking it through after the initial anger faded, it would have been quite obvious that Antonina was not having an affair and that this was a slander created by Photios to try to win the long-standing feud. In that case, we should expect some sort of punishment of Photios for this outrageous step. And in fact that is exactly what happened. Photios disappears for several years, before eventually emerging as a monk in Jerusalem. Although Belisarius and Antonina were still alive, and Belisarius was still campaigning, Photios never rejoins them, which is exactly the kind of retribution that might be expected if Photios had slandered them and nearly destroyed their marriage to try to gain the upper hand against Theodosios.[18]

In this reconstruction of events, it seems likely that Belisarius and Antonina would have reconciled their personal argument fairly quickly, once Antonina convinced Belisarius she was not having an affair. Therefore they were not recalled to Constantinople in winter 541 in order for Theodora to force them to reconcile, as Procopius alleges in the *Secret History*. And yet, that Belisarius went to Constantinople in winter 541 cannot be explained away or discounted as fictitious, since Procopius mentions this travel in both the *Secret History* and the *Wars*. If Belisarius and Antonina were already reconciled to each other by the time they went to Constantinople, then they might have traveled there to finally settle the business of the longstanding dispute between Photios and Theodosios. This would help to explain why Photios willingly came to Constantinople after capturing Theodosios. Belisarius and Antonina probably sent a message to come to the city so that the family could settle the issue once and for all. This would have been more incentive for Photios to come than a summons by a vengeful Theodora who planned to torture Photios on Antonina's behalf. However, it is not impossible that Theodora was involved in these events somehow. As Antonina's friend and patron, she might have offered to help mediate the family drama. And so in winter 541/542, the entire family assembled in Constantinople: Belisarius, Antonina, Photios, Theodosios, and maybe also Ioannina. Perhaps prodded by Theodora, Antonina and Belisarius agreed that Photios had to be rebuked for escalating the dispute with his outrageous accusation that Theodosios and Antonina were sleeping together. His punishment was complete. Procopius alleges that Theodora had Photios tortured, and then imprisoned in a small room in the palace for three years, and that finally after three years Photios escaped and fled to Jerusalem, where he became a monk. It is not necessary to believe every aspect of this tale, but the basic fact of Photios' downfall is unavoidable, as he never appears with Belisarius again or serves again in the army until after Belisarius' death. And yet, despite the removal of Photios, Theodosios did not exactly come out of this disagreement a winner. He did not join Belisarius on campaign in the coming spring, a sign that his adopted father had not warmed to him even with the downfall of Photios, and within a year Theodosios was dead of dysentery.[19]

FIGURE 12 Floor mosaic from the Great Palace, Constantinople. Photo by the author.

The inescapable conclusion is that late 541 was an awful, heart-wrenching, and tragic period for the family of Belisarius and Antonina. There was no incestuous affair, so it was probably not nearly as bad as Procopius paints it in the *Secret History*, but while less salacious, the argument nevertheless still detonated the family. The prosperous, successful nuclear family of the 530s was gone and never to be retrieved. Toward the end of his active career in the late 540s, Belisarius had only one heir, his daughter Ioannina, a situation that would present its own problems then. On the one hand, one cannot help but feel bad for Belisarius, who while at the apex of his military glory and financial power saw his personal life wrecked. On the other hand, the careful observer cannot avoid the conclusion that Belisarius and Antonina nurtured this problem by supporting different children as their favorites, and stoking their ambitions about which of them would become the principal heir of a vast fortune. Belisarius and Antonina spent the 530s distracted by constant military campaigning in Africa and Italy, and while this was advantageous for their careers and finances, and for their patron Justinian, it seems to have meant they neglected some of their family dynamics. If the couple had made a decision about which child would be their heir in 536, when the rivalry between Photios and Theodosios first became apparent, they might have stopped this long-standing feud before it had a chance to blossom. Belisarius and Antonina cannot be blamed for Photios' decision to radically escalate the argument by fabricating a slander about an incestuous affair, but they certainly bear a portion of the blame for allowing the situation to fester long enough that such an escalation became possible. As 541 came to a close, Belisarius and Antonina must have been keenly aware of their part in this and regretted it. They spent the winter in Constantinople, waiting until the approach of spring to return to Belisarius' command on the eastern front.

The Arrival of the Plague

In late 541, while the family of Belisarius and Antonina was coming apart at the seams, the Roman Empire was experiencing the first shocks of what would become known as the Justinianic Plague. This pandemic was an outbreak of bubonic plague, which is caused by infection with the bacterium *Yersinia Pestis*. Centuries later, this same microbe would cause the more famous pandemic known as the Black Death (starting ca. 1346), and the disease still exists in the world today in routine, smaller-scale outbreaks. Modern historians have identified the Justinianic Plague with infection by this bacterium thanks to both historical descriptions of the symptoms and, more recently, DNA examination of human remains from the time period. The bacterium resides in rodent populations, but can be transmitted to humans by the bite of fleas who have previously bitten infected rats. Infection by *Yersinia Pestis* results in fever, general weakness, and (typically) swollen lymph nodes. The swellings are known as buboes, hence the name of the bubonic plague. Today, this infection is treated with antibiotics, but such treatment and even knowledge of microorganisms did not exist in the ancient world. The plague therefore killed perhaps 70% of those it infected.[20]

The plague first appeared in Justinian's Roman Empire in southern Egypt in 541, leading to speculation that the outbreak originated in central Africa. From there, the plague traveled up the Nile all the way to Alexandria, and then in spring 542, with the return of the shipping season, the plague moved from Alexandria to other major ports in the Eastern Mediterranean, including Constantinople. Inland cities were not spared either. One historian records the plague in Jerusalem, and it likely reached most cities of the empire by summer 542. In this case, the interconnectedness of the Roman world, with its web of shipping routes and crisscrossing roads, proved a dangerous liability. According to our best sources of the period, the immediate death toll of the plague was very high. Procopius says that 10,000 people died per day at the height of the pandemic in Constantinople. John of Ephesus ratchets the death toll up further, suggesting that 16,000 people died in a single day. It is not necessary to give full credence to these estimates, but that many people died in Constantinople seems indisputable. The number of dead was not the only immediate impact of the plague. As a reaction to the spread of the disease, people stayed in their homes and all work in the city ceased. We have the fullest information about the impact in Constantinople, but the plague is mentioned by many contemporary writers, and it seems plausible that it caused death and chaos throughout the empire and beyond. Procopius states, ominously, that this pandemic "embraced the entire earth and wrecked the lives of all people."[21]

Modern historians continue to debate the casualties and long-term impact of the Justinianic Plague. There are a range of positions on the death toll of the outbreak, from an extremely small 0.1% of the total population of the empire to a very large 60% of it. Some historians argue from the qualitative evidence of the literary sources, and some from quantitative evidence of number of bodies discovered or coins and laws issued. Much of the argument revolves around what the death toll meant for the long-term evolution of the Roman Empire and the Mediterranean world more broadly. From the perspective of Belisarius and Antonina, however, the short-term impact of the plague was more important. The immediate military impact of the Justinianic Plague in the 540s is rarely discussed by modern historians of Belisarius' campaigns. Admittedly, the lack of direct evidence for this impact in contemporary sources makes it difficult to form definitive conclusions. It is hard to imagine, though, that a pandemic that ravaged the empire's cities and spread like wildfire in areas where people lived in close proximity did not also have an impact on Roman armies. After all, what are encamped armies but places where people live in close proximity to each other and to rats? It is likely that outbreaks of the plague therefore played an outsized role in the military campaigns of the next few years by killing soldiers. These soldiers would eventually be replaced through recruitment among the surviving population, but that would take time, time in which Belisarius would struggle with a lack of available, experienced soldiers.[22]

As the plague hit Constantinople at the beginning of spring 542, Khusro and the Persian army invaded the Roman East for the third year in a row. He followed the same route as his first invasion in 540, marching into Syria with the Euphrates on his army's right. According to Procopius, however, his intended target was Palestine in general and Jerusalem in particular. Perhaps caught off guard by an attack in early spring, Belisarius was still in Constantinople dealing with the aftermath of his family's explosion. He returned to the eastern front with as much rapidity as possible, by using the government's post system, in which stables dotted the main roads of the empire to facilitate quick transport. Riding from stable to stable on the road from Constantinople to the East, Belisarius would have stopped at each stable long enough to switch to a fresh horse. This would have enabled the general to make the trip in around eight days, about four times faster than if he rode a single horse the entire way, which would have required frequent stops for the horse to rest. Unusually, neither Procopius nor any other source informs us of Antonina's location in spring and summer 542. It is possible that she rode with Belisarius and stayed with him throughout the coming campaign. However, it is equally possible that she stayed behind in Constantinople to supervise the couple's property or even to securely settle Theodosios with his own estate as a result of decisions made at the family conference in the winter. Alternatively, perhaps at this point, after the downfall of Photios, the couple thought of Theodosios as their principal heir, and therefore it would make sense for Antonina to be going over finances with Theodosios at this time. It is also possible that Antonina even planned to follow Belisarius to the East at a later time (and at a more leisurely pace), just as she had in 541. Ultimately, however, this is all speculation, and there is no evidence to suggest any of these options is more likely than the others. Antonina's location in the first half of 542 must remain a mystery.[23]

As Belisarius neared the eastern front, he received a report from his subordinate officers of the Army of the East, including the redoubtable Bouzes, and Justus, the emperor's nephew, who were ensconced at Hierapolis (modern Manbij in northern Syria). They urged Belisarius to join them there to help guard the city. But Belisarius rejected the suggestion, concerned that Khusro's ultimate destination was unknown and therefore feeling that the army should not bunker down in that location. Instead, Belisarius called for these officers and the whole Army of the East to muster about 20 miles farther north at Europos (known in earlier times as Carchemish and near modern Jarabulus in northern Syria). Following this mustering came the strangest conclusion to any of Khusro's invasions so far. Procopius says that Khusro, hearing that Belisarius had mustered the army, decided not to continue his advance toward Palestine. Instead, the Persians turned back, and Khusro dispatched a secretary named Abandanes to Belisarius to argue with him about why Justinian had not sent ambassadors to follow up on his offer of gold and to negotiate a peace. Belisarius decided to put on a show for this envoy, and selected the best looking 6,000 of his soldiers. They moved away from the main army camp and set up a tent on the plain in which Belisarius met Abandanes. During the meeting, the select soldiers milled here and there around the tent, as if they were eager to go hunting their enemy. Procopius describes these picked soldiers as a representative slice of Belisarius' achievements: they consisted of Thracians and Illyrians, from Belisarius' homeland; Goths, Vandals, and Berbers, from Belisarius' conquests; and Heruls, who had fought as his allied soldiers in both East and West. Abandanes, according to Procopius, was suitably impressed by this display and advised Khusro to avoid combat and depart Roman territory, because Belisarius was manly and wise, and his soldiers were admirable. Khusro accepted this advice, led his army across the Euphrates, and began to head back to Persian territory. The Persian king did sack and raze Callinicum (modern Ar Raqqah, in north central Syria), site of Belisarius' defeat in 531, along the way, but otherwise avoided combat and Roman fortresses before returning to his own kingdom.[24]

Procopius writes that this largely peaceful end to Khusro's invasion impressed Belisarius' contemporaries: "The Romans praised Belisarius and he seemed to have achieved greater glory in their eyes by this feat than when he brought Gelimer or Vittigis captive to Byzantium." However, in the *Secret History*, the author faults Belisarius for the fall of Callinicum, arguing that the general either "willfully neglected his duty or that he was too afraid" to engage Khusro's army. This had been a strange campaign. Belisarius had rushed to the eastern front as fast as he could get there and had mobilized his army, but had never fought. Khusro had rushed to invade as soon as he could at the beginning of spring, but had not progressed very far into Roman territory before turning back and contented himself with sacking a single city, a far cry from his previous campaign into Syria in 540. Perhaps all of these unusual events can be explained by an explosion of the plague in the region. The plague was in Egypt in 541 and was ravaging Constantinople by summer 542, so there is no reason to suspect it had failed to penetrate into Syria and probably even Mesopotamia by the time this campaign was going on. Perhaps both Belisarius and Khusro's armies were experiencing their first outbreaks of the plague. This would explain both why Khusro failed to press his invasion and why Belisarius seemed reluctant to engage Khusro's army in combat. Procopius was in Constantinople and well aware of the devastation of the plague there, so it is a little surprising that the historian could not have imagined the impact the plague might have on the armies operating in the East at the same time. But the plague spread well in cities, where many people were gathered together, and there is every reason to suspect that it spread well in army camps also. It would be a recurring problem in the armies of the 540s.[25]

Belisarius in Disgrace

Thus ended the summer campaign season of 542. As the campaign wound down, Belisarius and his officers received word from Constantinople that there the Emperor Justinian had contracted the plague and was grievously ill. If Antonina was still in Constantinople, perhaps the message even came from her. Even if it was not her, the news was likely passed along through unofficial channels, because it is hard to imagine Justinian or Theodora wanting to advertise this situation. The rumor suggested Justinian was so ill that he would die or indeed had already died. In the *Secret History*, Procopius records the alleged response of the officers of the Army of the East to this news: "some of the officers there began to declare that if the Romans in Byzantium foisted another emperor like that upon them all, they would never allow it." The implication here is that if Justinian were to die, these officers would not accept a new emperor chosen by Theodora, but would insist on one of their number being declared emperor. The logical choice of course would have been Belisarius himself. Procopius was not present in the East at this time and cannot have had direct knowledge of which officers made this statement or even if it was made at all. However, once Justinian recovered, some of the officers began to accuse others of plotting. In particular, the commander Peter, Belisarius' rival at Nisibis in 541, and the guardsman John the Glutton, accused Belisarius and Bouzes of making the quoted statement. Their accusation is therefore the likely source for Procopius' story. Perhaps Belisarius and Bouzes really did make this statement. It is not unreasonable that Belisarius would have felt himself to be the most qualified person to take the throne if Justinian were to die. On the other hand, Belisarius might never have said this at all, and this accusation could have simply been an opportunistic attack by one of his rivals and an ambitious guardsman.[26]

For what happened next, Procopius provides two different stories. In a detailed account in the *Secret History*, he explains that Theodora was personally offended by the statement and, convinced that the accusation was true and that Belisarius and Bouzes had certainly plotted for the throne, she punished them. Theodora would indeed have had reason to be uneasy, for if Justinian died, she as empress would be in a vulnerable position and likely would be pushed out of power if the army raised up an emperor such as Belisarius. The empress summoned both generals to Constantinople and into her presence. Theodora ordered Bouzes imprisoned under the Great Palace, and he was not seen for two years and four months. As for Belisarius, Procopius says that Theodora convinced Justinian to strip the general of his command, take away all of his personal guards who had served him so well in multiple wars, and finally confiscate the vast majority of his wealth. If true, the downfall of Belisarius was swift and complete. Procopius writes affectingly, "what a bitter spectacle and incredible sight it was to see Belisarius going about in Byzantium as a private citizen: virtually alone, always gloomy and sullen, in constant terror of a murderer's knife." The version presented by Procopius in the *Wars* is much briefer and omits mention of any kind of fall from grace for Belisarius. In this narrative, the historian simply records: "Belisarius came to Byzantium at the summons of the emperor, in order to be sent again to Italy, as the situation there was already full of difficulties for the Romans." This is one of the few occasions when the version of the *Secret History* is to be preferred. The brief description of Belisarius' recall in the *Wars* is clearly meant to hide something, as illustrated most clearly in the timing of these events. Belisarius finished the summer campaign season of 542, which means he probably did not receive word of Justinian's illness until late summer. Allowing for travel time back and forth of the various messages (the notice of Justinian's illness, the notice of the alleged conspiratorial chatter, and the summons to Constantinople), it is likely that Belisarius and Bouzes were not recalled to Constantinople until fall 542. If Belisarius had been summoned to take command of the war in Italy, one would expect him to set out for Italy in spring 543. However, he did not receive the new appointment or begin traveling to the peninsula until spring 544. This means that there was about an 18-month gap between Belisarius' recall from the East and him setting out for his new command in Italy. The best explanation for this gap is the disgrace that Procopius describes in the *Secret History*, which means that at least some portion of Procopius' account in that text is accurate. That Belisarius faced difficulty during this period is confirmed by the *Chronicle* of Marcellinus Comes, which explains, "Belisarius was summoned from the East and, although running into enmity and serious danger and being exposed to envy, he was again sent back to Italy."[27]

The available evidence is convincing: Belisarius was definitely disgraced for a time and certainly lost his position as General of the East. The other punishments enumerated by Procopius are also not unlikely. Belisarius and Antonina had long been extremely rich, so that Justinian and Theodora would confiscate their wealth as punishment is not surprising. A good portion of Belisarius' military might was tied to his army of personal guardsmen, which numbered in the thousands. If Justinian and Theodora were worried about Belisarius' loyalty, of course they needed to deprive the general of his personal army. It is tempting to look at this story and feel sympathy for Belisarius. Even Procopius, not kind to the general overall in the *Secret History*, insists that he was not convicted of a single charge, and seems to suggest that this punishment was more due to Theodora overreacting than to Belisarius being a threat. However, it is important to keep in mind how Justinian and Theodora must have felt, and the long history they had with Belisarius and Antonina. As we have already seen, the monarchs owed their thrones to Belisarius' intervention in the Nika Riot (Chapter 2). During his conquest of the Vandals, they learned that Belisarius was accused of plotting to establish his own kingdom in Africa, and they then watched Belisarius become the most popular man in Constantinople after his triumph (Chapter 3). More than that, they knew that Belisarius had feigned interest in imperial power to bring about the surrender of the Ostrogoths at Ravenna in 540 (Chapter 5) and that Antonina had feigned resentment of Justinian to ensnare John the Cappadocian. Is it at all surprising that, given all of this, Justinian and Theodora might have been nervous about their relationship to Belisarius and uncertain about Belisarius' ambitions? When added to this history, the monarchs learned that Belisarius was perhaps considering himself the next emperor while Justinian was lying ill with the plague—it must have seemed too much at a vulnerable time. Perhaps

Justinian and Theodora thought that failure to respond to this provocation would have been fatal to them. For Belisarius and Antonina, this was a disaster. They plummeted from the summit of society, losing their power and wealth, and fell out with their emperor and empress, with whom they had been on good terms, and perhaps even friends. Coming hard on the heels of the implosion of their nuclear family the year before, this might have seemed too much to bear. How the two spent their months of disgrace is unclear. Belisarius was a private citizen and had nowhere to go, so presumably he and Antonina lived together in one of their residences in Constantinople. At some point during this period, their adopted son Theodosios died of dysentery. What a gloomy time this must have been! Belisarius and Theodosios do not seem to have been close, as the general had sided with Photios before his slanderous accusation of an affair, but Antonina had been close to him, if not as close as Procopius charges. The two must have mourned together, comforted by their surviving child, their daughter Ioannina. Hanging over all of this would have been the fear that one of them or even the whole family might suddenly contract the plague and die. Stripped of position, supporters, and wealth, while grieving through the betrayal of Photios and the death of Theodosios and fearing illness or death themselves, Belisarius and Antonina were certainly at the nadir of their fortunes.[28]

And yet, there was light at the end of this dark tunnel. At some point between the disgrace in fall 542 and spring 544, Justinian and Theodora forgave Belisarius and restored him to favor. Our only source for this reconciliation is the *Secret History*, and in it Procopius predictably crafts a slanderous and gendered account of this moment. According to the author, Theodora decided to forgive Belisarius, and to make him think it was happening only because she was friends with Antonina. Belisarius is presented as lying on his bed, paralyzed by fear, completely lacking in manliness. When a messenger from Theodora arrives, he offers himself up to be slaughtered, only to discover that the messenger brings not death but a letter stating that Belisarius has been reinstated because the empress owes much to Antonina. Belisarius was so thrilled that he jumped from the bed, fell on his face before his wife, and "began to lick the soles of his wife's feet with his tongue, one after the other, calling her the Cause of his Life and Salvation, promising that henceforth he would be her devoted slave and not her husband." There is some reason to doubt this sequence of events. Procopius, having left Belisarius' service several years earlier, was not present for this, and it is unlikely he knew what happened in the bedroom of Belisarius and Antonina. The story is also clearly written to assert that Belisarius was subordinate to his wife, in keeping with the author's accusations of his being enslaved by his passions for her elsewhere in the text. Procopius believed that the husband should have more influence than the wife in a marriage, and that it was the husband's job to save the wife, not vice versa. About this situation, Procopius writes, "The empress therefore contrived to gratify Antonina by doing everything to create the impression that it was the *wife* who had interceded on the *husband's* behalf and had delivered him from this crushing adversity." So as with previous accusations of Belisarius' subordination to Antonina, the goal here is to present a perfect invective in the form of an inversion of the accepted social order. Procopius wants to make Belisarius look subservient to Antonina, so he does so in the most extreme way possible by not just suggesting that Antonina's friendship with Theodora proved useful, but by claiming that the general literally licked his wife's feet and called himself her slave. In short, we can discard as fictive insult much of the detail of this reconciliation, while still accepting that a reconciliation occurred and that Antonina probably played a part in it. Antonina and Theodora seem to have been friends, and Antonina had done Theodora an important service in helping to get rid of John the Cappadocian, so why should Antonina not intervene on behalf of her husband?[29]

However, it also seems likely that both Belisarius and Justinian were far more involved in this reconciliation than Procopius pretends in the *Secret History*. In fact, the author's story does not mention Justinian as an active agent in this process at all. But it seems rather impossible that Justinian would have been a disinterested party in Belisarius' restoration. Justinian had the most to lose if he did believe Belisarius to be a potential usurper. Moreover, Justinian had a long tendency, perhaps even policy, toward mercy, which is evident in a broad array of sources from the time period. Procopius himself trumpets this virtue loudly in his panegyric to Justinian, *On Buildings*: "Those who treacherously formed the plot against him, going so far even as to plan his assassination, are not only living up to the present moment, and in possession of their own property, even though their guilt was proved with absolute certainty, but are actually still serving as generals of the Romans, and are holding the consular rank to which they had been appointed." In addition to forgiving Belisarius, Justinian forgave the general Artabanes, who had conspired against him, and to whom this passage in *On Buildings* probably refers. Artabanes was only forgiven and restored to military service after a disgrace of more than a year, which comes close to matching the time that Belisarius spent out of favor before his forgiveness. Perhaps Justinian made a habit of offering clemency to conspirators only after a period of penance. In the preface to one of his new laws, known as novels, written in the year

551, Justinian wrote, "No offense on the part of any of our subjects is so great as to be deemed unworthy of our clemency. Even though our abhorrence of what they have done rouses us to punish them for it, still, *having regard for time*, we soothe our righteous indignation by considerations of clemency." In Belisarius' case, Justinian's clemency certainly did happen only after what the emperor must have considered a due regard for time passed. The available evidence therefore suggests that Justinian would have had a role in Belisarius' pardon, and that it was not just a matter resolved between the general and Theodora.[30]

Thanks to the way Procopius shrouds the story of the restoration of Belisarius in gendered language, it is impossible to know exactly what role each party actually played in this process. Antonina probably beseeched Theodora for her help, relying on their friendship and the service she had rendered the empress. Belisarius possibly went to Justinian directly, perhaps abasing himself before the emperor and renewing his previous oath never to rebel against him or seek the throne while he still lived. Theodora might have recommended forgiveness to her husband. Justinian might have felt inclined to offer forgiveness based on his previous acts of clemency. It is possible, maybe even likely, that all of these factors were at play. However these elements came together, at some point Belisarius was forgiven and restored. It is not clear when exactly this restoration occurred. In spring 544, Belisarius was appointed Count of the Sacred Stables (*comes sacri stabuli*) and given the command of the ongoing war in Italy against the Ostrogoths. But he might have been forgiven sooner than that and kept as a private citizen for a time before the military appointment. According to Procopius, Belisarius' restoration included the return of most of his wealth, although a portion of it, said to be the enormous sum of 3,000 pounds of gold (or 216,000 *nomismata*), was kept by the emperor, perhaps as a sort of fine for his behavior.[31]

It is possible that a marriage alliance formed about this time was also part of the financial settlement. Belisarius and Antonina's daughter, Ioannina, was betrothed to Anastasios, the grandson of Theodora (through a probably illegitimate daughter she had before meeting Justinian). With Theodosios now dead, and Photios disgraced and probably disowned, Ioannina was the sole heir of Belisarius and Antonina. Thus Procopius sees this marriage alliance as a naked ploy by Theodora to bring Belisarius and Antonina's wealth into her family. While this is possible, it seems more likely the betrothal was politically motivated and intended to seal the rapprochement between the imperial couple and Belisarius and Antonina. Since Ioannina was perhaps only 11 years old at the time, this engagement was a promise for the future rather than a plan for immediate action. Beyond the disposition of his fortune, there were other ways in which Belisarius' restoration to favor was incomplete. The general was not given back his army of personal guards, who were being used on the eastern front against the Persians. Belisarius was also not restored to his position as General of the East. Procopius slanderously alleges that this is because Antonina refused to go back to the eastern front, where she and Belisarius had such a terrible argument. It is more likely that Justinian and Theodora were uneasy about Belisarius returning to the East, where his personal guards were located along with a large Roman army. Italy, as we shall see, had a far smaller army, fewer resources, and the war against the Ostrogoths there was going poorly. In other words, if Belisarius were somehow still plotting to rebel, Italy would be a far less optimal place for such a plan. More charitably, perhaps Justinian remembered Belisarius' great successes in the West and, weighing them against his relatively average record in the East, decided his old general's skills were best to be used pulling off another miraculous victory in Italy.[32]

FIGURE 13 Portrait of a sixth-century man, probably
Belisarius, detail from the imperial panel of Justinian in
San Vitale, Ravenna. Photo by Steven Zucker.

7

Italy Redux

IN THE SPRING of 544, Belisarius and Antonina made ready to travel to Italy for the second time, nine years after they first set out with hopes of subduing the Ostrogothic Kingdom. An entirely different situation awaited them. Although Belisarius had captured Ravenna, Vittigis, and the Ostrogothic treasury in 540, his victory had not been complete. Too many Gothic soldiers remained at large, and they had simply acclaimed a new king, Hildebad, who gathered them together at Pavia in Lombardy. Hildebad however failed to win universal support, and after some political maneuvering and a couple of assassinations, his nephew Totila became king in fall 541. The Ostrogoths united behind Totila and this proved disastrous to Roman fortunes in Italy. While the Goths were unified, the Roman army had no single commander. It seems that Justinian declined to appoint a commander-in-chief for the Italian theatre after Belisarius left, so the remaining generals did as each thought was best. In two battles in 542, Totila's forces defeated the best armies the Romans could muster. This won Totila freedom of movement in Italy, which he used to besiege and capture many inland cities. Though the Romans still held Rome, Ravenna, and most of the coastal cities, Totila captured Naples in 543, which threatened the Romans' ability to resupply Rome. The momentum of the war in Italy had clearly swung in the favor of Totila and the Goths. No doubt Belisarius learned of this news with dismay as he prepared to depart Constantinople in 544.[1]

Just as the circumstances in Italy were different, so were the circumstances of Belisarius' army. In fact, it appears that he was not provided an army at all. While Belisarius had received 18,000 soldiers for the Vandal campaign in 533, and 7,500 soldiers for the first Ostrogothic campaign in 535, now in 544 Procopius records that Belisarius, the Count of the Sacred Stables, had "an extremely small number of soldiers." That Procopius does not enumerate the soldiers could be due to the fact that he was no longer on Belisarius' staff and

Belisarius & Antonina. David Alan Parnell, Oxford University Press. © Oxford University Press 2023.
DOI: 10.1093/oso/9780197574706.003.0008

did not have access to the records, but it probably also indicates that Belisarius set out literally with only a handful of personal guardsmen and household staff. Procopius makes clear that Belisarius was not allowed to bring any soldiers from the Army of the East, which he had formerly commanded, and that he also no longer had his original, large unit of guardsmen, which had been stripped from him in his disgrace in 542. That Belisarius would not be given significant resources to bring to Italy is noteworthy. Justinian and Belisarius knew the situation there had grown grim, that Totila was in the ascendant, and that the Roman army there was insufficient to oppose him. It is important to put this situation into context, however. The far more important war was on the eastern front with the Persians, and Justinian was clearly prioritizing it by not allowing Belisarius to draw soldiers from the Army of the East. The Roman army was probably still also suffering manpower shortages from the outbreak of the plague. There simply were not enough veteran soldiers to fight all the wars that needed to be fought.[2]

To make up for the shortfall, Justinian authorized Belisarius to go on a recruiting drive through Thrace, where he could gather enough volunteers to form some kind of an army. On this recruiting drive, Belisarius was to be accompanied by Vitalios, the General of Illyricum. It is not clear why. Perhaps the emperor hoped Vitalios could help attract recruits, or perhaps Vitalios was supposed to watch Belisarius and make sure he did nothing inappropriate, such as try to raise a rebel army. Procopius suggests, sotto voce, in the *Secret History*, that some expected Belisarius to do this. He alleges that Belisarius promised to finance the whole campaign against the Ostrogoths himself and to never ask the emperor for money, and he states that "everyone" imagined that this promise was made only so that Belisarius could get out of Constantinople, "take up arms and do something noble and befitting a man." It is unlikely that Belisarius promised to finance the whole campaign himself, or swore to never ask the emperor to fund the war against the Ostrogoths. Doing so would have hamstrung his campaign before it started. At most, Belisarius might have promised to pay initial recruitment bonuses to the new recruits he found in Thrace with his own funds. As to the other rumor, if any contemporary observers expected Belisarius to raise the standard of rebellion, they cannot have known the loyal general very well.[3]

So, sometime in spring 544, Belisarius set out from Constantinople and made his way through Thrace, accompanied by a very few soldiers, the General Vitalios, and Antonina. Although Procopius does not state explicitly that Antonina accompanied Belisarius at this point, it seems very likely that she did, since Procopius mentions her presence in Italy in 546, and there is no mention of her setting out later to join the army. So in all probability, she was with Belisarius on this campaign from the very moment he left Constantinople in 544. The presence of Antonina on this journey is significant and important for our understanding of the degree to which the couple had repaired their relationship. After their blowup family argument in 541, it is not clear that Antonina traveled with Belisarius to the East in 542. Yet, a key part of their relationship prior to 541 is that Antonina almost always went on campaign with Belisarius. In 544, Antonina might have easily stayed behind in Constantinople. She was probably almost 50 years old and had earned the rest. However, she chose to accompany Belisarius on what she and he must have both known would be a difficult campaign, against a determined foe, with relatively little imperial support. This decision points to two features of their marriage. First, despite all the ups and downs of Belisarius' career, he still considered Antonina an indispensable part of his military life. He must have valued her counsel and seen her as integral to his success. Antonina must have equally considered herself to have a part to play in her husband's campaign. Second, that the two refused to let distance separate them even in this later stage of their lives perhaps speaks to the degree of affection the two held for each other. In the *Secret History*, Procopius attests to this love by claiming that Belisarius "was so extraordinarily infatuated with her." He offers the observation mean-spiritedly, and he twists it to suggest that the love was only one way, from Belisarius to Antonina, but it is an affirmation of the strength of their bond in spite of that. Antonina's decision to accompany Belisarius to Italy in 544, after all the two had been through, when she might have easily just stayed in Constantinople and enjoyed retirement and a life of leisure, is a strong indication that she was as infatuated with Belisarius as Procopius says he was with her.[4]

Residing in Ravenna

Belisarius, Antonina, and Vitalios spent some weeks in Thrace, where they managed to attract 4,000 fresh recruits. These young men were completely inexperienced, but had at least the potential to be molded into a force that could fight in Italy. From Thrace, Belisarius marched his green army overland across the Balkans, arriving at the port city of Salona in late spring or early summer of 544. At Salona, Belisarius and Vitalios conferred about what to do. They received a report that the Roman garrison of Otranto (in Apulia), currently besieged by Gothic forces, was on the verge of surrender. Belisarius dispatched the commander Valentinos with ships full of provisions, and he was able to effect the resupply and salvation of Otranto. In the meantime,

Belisarius embarked his army upon other ships and sailed north to Pula, where he began to put his army into order, presumably by equipping and drilling his new recruits. Although Procopius does not offer additional explanation, it is interesting that Belisarius was immediately furnished with ships to carry more than 4,000 men when he reached Salona. This suggests that there was more care and planning put into the start of this campaign than Procopius had implied. As Belisarius trained his new army, Totila besieged Tivoli, less than 20 miles east of Rome. Hearing of Belisarius' arrival in the area and perhaps alarmed, Totila dispatched spies to discover the strength of the Roman army, who succeeded in their mission undetected by Belisarius. Meanwhile, Belisarius conferred with Vitalios and the two agreed to move to Ravenna. The Roman armada sailed into Ravenna, perhaps in late summer 544. Thus Belisarius and Antonina returned to the city they had left in 540, although the situation now was quite changed. While they had been sailing, Totila captured Tivoli, which began to tighten the noose around Rome.[5]

Safely ensconced in Ravenna, Belisarius began to dispatch his meager forces around Italy, in an attempt not to defeat Totila but to at least slow the rate at which he was seizing Roman-held cities. He first dispatched his guardsman Thurimuth with the General Vitalios and some soldiers to Bologna. Thurimuth then returned to Ravenna, and Belisarius sent him, other guardsmen, and a thousand of his soldiers to Osimo to try to break the Gothic siege of the city. They failed to do so. Belisarius next sent Thurimuth and Sabinianos to take control of Pisaurum (Pesaro). Finally, Belisarius dispatched two of his guardsmen and some soldiers to Rome itself, to assist the General Bessas, who was in command there, in defending the city. These actions reveal a very different plan than in Belisarius' first campaign in Italy, when he had marched at the head of his army and methodically conquered cities one by one, going from Syracuse, to Naples, to Rome. This time the general must have felt that he did not have a large enough army to mount a significant campaign or to risk open battle with Totila, so he resorted instead to sending out small units, much as he had while bottled up in Rome during the siege of 537. Belisarius and Antonina remained in Ravenna through the winter of 544/545. It was probably during this period that the pair featured in a remarkable set of mosaics that were executed upon the walls of the church of San Vitale. These mosaics are the most famous and instantly recognizable depictions of the Emperor Justinian and Empress Theodora, shown standing with their retainers and preparing to present their gifts to the church. It is believed that the mosaics were set under the leadership of Victor, bishop of Ravenna (537–544). Possibly they were created in fall 544, while Belisarius and Antonina were present in the city, although they could have been planned as early as 540, when the couple entered the city for the first time. The general and his wife are not identified on the mosaics, but it seems likely that Belisarius is the figure on Justinian's right, and Antonina is the figure on Theodora's left. Because there are no labels, this identification cannot be certain, but the timing of the mosaics' creation is highly indicative. Belisarius and Antonina were the key figures linking Ravenna to the imperial couple in this decade. Moreover, they would have desired their own close relationship with Justinian and Theodora to be known to the people of Italy as they geared up for this second campaign.[6]

FIGURE 14 The imperial mosaic panel of Justinian in San Vitale, Ravenna. Photo by Steven Zucker.

FIGURE 15 The imperial mosaic panel of Theodora in San Vitale, Ravenna. Photo by Steven Zucker.

By early 545, Belisarius was becoming desperate about the military situation in Italy. Totila still had the initiative and was moving into Tuscany, seeking to capture the cities of the region and further isolate Rome. Unable to do more with the forces at his disposal, Belisarius crafted a plaintive letter to Justinian. In this missive he denigrated the soldiers he had recruited in Thrace as "a small and pitiful band ... altogether unpracticed in fighting" and reproached the emperor with top-rate sarcasm, "if it sufficed to merely send Belisarius to Italy, then you have made the best plan possible for the war, for I am here in Italy. But if you want to overcome your foes in the war, it is necessary to make other provisions too." Belisarius went on to demand that his guardsmen and other soldiers be sent to him, along with money to pay them. He entrusted this letter to John, the nephew of Vitalian, the general who had once opposed him in the first campaign in Italy in 538, and sent him to Constantinople. John was an interesting choice as a courier. Belisarius did not get along well with John. Perhaps Belisarius sent him as the messenger to get him out of the way, while also seeking reinforcements. We have other evidence of Belisarius' activities at this time. In May 545, Pope Vigilius sent a letter to Auxanius, the bishop of Arles, in which the pope credits "our most glorious and most excellent son, the patrician Belisarius" for interceding with Justinian and Theodora to confirm privileges for his bishopric. It seems that Belisarius was maintaining communication with Vigilius, who probably also kept the general appraised of the increasingly concerning situation in and around Rome. In the summer of 545, while John was in Constantinople attempting to pry additional soldiers and money out of Justinian, Totila captured Fermo and Ascoli in Marche, and then moved west and took Spoleto and Assisi in Perugia. The Gothic stranglehold over the Italian countryside around the region of Rome was nearly complete.[7]

John's sojourn in Constantinople was of long duration and was not immediately successful. He spent nearly a year in the city and evidently passed the time by courting and marrying Iustina, the daughter of Germanos. That John was unable to immediately secure significant reinforcements is not surprising when considering the manpower shortages the Roman army must have been facing at the time. The war with the Persians was still raging, there was also war in North Africa with the Berbers, a group of Huns had just stormed through Illyricum, and on top of that the first outbreak of the plague had only just ended. Although Procopius thinks that Justinian was negligent in not immediately sending reinforcements to Italy, the simple fact is that Italy was not a top priority and the emperor was probably having a hard time finding soldiers he could spare. Meanwhile, the Roman position in

Italy continued to deteriorate. Perhaps in November 545, Totila left Perugia and brought his army south to Rome, which he surrounded and placed under siege. Just before the siege began, Roman soldiers abducted Pope Vigilius and smuggled him out of the city, taking him to safety in Sicily. When Bessas, in command in Rome, failed to oppose Totila's encirclement of the city, the king grew bold and divided his army, dispatching a unit into Emilia to besiege Piacenza, while maintaining the siege of Rome with his main force. It is clear that Totila and the Goths had complete control of the field by this point. In Ravenna, Belisarius and Antonina must have been growing increasingly alarmed. They did not have enough soldiers to oppose Totila's army, John had still not returned from Constantinople, and now Totila was at the gates of Rome itself. According to Procopius, Belisarius regretted coming to Ravenna in the first place, where he felt he was doing no good. The general allegedly blamed Vitalios for advising this move. Although Procopius reports that Belisarius wished to move immediately to Rome to help relieve the siege, he did not do so, so this is perhaps simply foreshadowing on the author's part. In fact, Belisarius and Antonina moved farther away, sailing across the Adriatic to Dyrrachium (modern Durrës, Albania), there to greet John and the hoped-for reinforcements as soon as they should appear. At the same time, Belisarius dispatched a small force, perhaps 500 men, under the command of his guardsman Phokas and the commander Valentinos. Their orders were to link up with the Roman garrison at Portus, and then make sallies and harass Totila's forces as they lay in siege around Rome. So matters stood as 545 came to an end.[8]

Totila in the Ascendant

In early 546, Belisarius received good news and bad news. The bad news was that Phokas and Valentinos had been killed and most of their force wiped out in a battle outside of Rome, when they sallied forth to attack the Goths and Bessas did not support them by sending his own garrison troops out to join the attack. Equally bad, the inhabitants of Rome were hard pressed by the siege. Procopius paints a doleful picture. Pope Vigilius arranged for a fleet of grain ships to come from Sicily to resupply the city, but the Goths captured the vessels. The deacon and future pope Pelagius went to Totila to beg for mercy and a truce, but received neither. The people in Rome were suffering from a famine, and the General Bessas profiteered off this crisis by selling the increasingly scarce food in the city for enormous sums to those who could pay. There was, however, good news to offset the increasingly panicked reports from Rome. About this time, John, the nephew of Vitalian, finally returned from his long sojourn in Constantinople at the head of an army. Frustratingly, Procopius does not know the size of this force, describing it generically only as "an army of barbarian and Roman soldiers." Given that Belisarius was unable to do much with these reinforcements, it is unlikely that they exceeded one or two thousand men. In Dyrrachium, Belisarius and John conferred on how to proceed. Perhaps not surprisingly, given past disputes between the two, they did not see eye to eye. John wished to ferry the army across the Adriatic to Otranto, and from there march to Rome, establishing control over Apulia along the way. Belisarius argued that Rome would be taken before the army could reach it by this route, and instead advocated sailing directly to Portus to try to lift the siege and save the city as soon as possible. There was a real time difference involved in the two options. Including ferrying from Dyrrachium to Otranto, and assuming constant marching after that, the army would take perhaps 40 days to get to Rome, even if it was not bogged down in battles along the way. Meanwhile, sailing directly from Dyrrachium to Rome, the army could reach Portus in as quick as five days. Assuming time was of the essence, and saving Rome was the goal, Belisarius' plan was better. Perhaps John was already writing off Rome and was thinking of a wholesale reconquest of the peninsula from south to north. Surprisingly, Belisarius did not compel John to accept his plan. Perhaps he was simply unable to do so. Their army, already meager enough, was divided into two. Belisarius was to sail with a portion of the army straight to Portus, while John was to take his army into Apulia and proceed overland as he preferred, ostensibly to eventually meet up with Belisarius outside of Rome.[9]

Belisarius, Antonina, and the fleet sailed out from Dyrrachium and, after putting in briefly at Otranto on account of adverse winds, proceeded directly to Portus. In the meantime, John ferried his forces over to Apulia. There, he defeated a small Gothic army outside Brindisi and captured Canosa. When he became aware that Totila had sent 300 Gothic soldiers to Capua to keep an eye on his forces, John lost his nerve and discontinued his march toward Rome, instead turning back into Calabria. From Portus, Belisarius sent to John, reproaching him for his failure to come to Rome, but the junior general was not to be persuaded to change his mind. In the *Secret History*, Procopius provides a potential explanation for this truculence. He weaves a narrative based on an assertion that the Empress Theodora hated Germanos, the cousin of Justinian. Because she hated Germanos, nobody would dare to form an alliance with him by marrying his children. Only John, the nephew of Vitalian, was bold enough to marry Germanos' daughter Iustina, who was

18 years old at the time they wed in 545. Allegedly, Theodora was so outraged by this that she made threats on John's life. Therefore, once he arrived in Italy, John avoided Belisarius, because it was well known that Antonina was close to Theodora and willing to do her bidding, which Procopius implies might have included arranging the murder of John. This story of intrigue falls apart when subjected to close scrutiny. In particular, the allegation that John wanted to avoid Antonina seems preposterous because John joined Belisarius and Antonina at Dyrrachium when he first arrived with the reinforcement army and spent some time in their presence debating where the army should go first. If John was so afraid of Antonina, why would that fear only manifest once Belisarius and Antonina were in Portus waiting for John, instead of just a few weeks earlier when they were all together in Dyrrachium? John's refusal to march to Rome at this time also mirrors his earlier insubordination in 538, when he refused to evacuate Rimini on Belisarius' orders. The general, for whatever reason, had a history of refusing to cooperate with Belisarius, so that he should again prove difficult is not surprising and requires no convoluted story about Theodora wanting Antonina to arrange his death. The story Procopius presents in the *Secret History* is therefore just another groundless way for the author to complain about the power and influence of Theodora and Antonina.[10]

Without John's force, Belisarius felt unable to face Totila's army directly, another indication that the number of soldiers available to the general at this time could not have been very large. However, Belisarius did feel that he had sufficient troops to attempt to cut through some of the besieging Gothic forces in order to deliver food and supplies to the beleaguered inhabitants of Rome. Totila had prepared for this by constructing a sort of wooden boom across the Tiber River, about 10 miles outside of the city, and anchoring it with two wooden towers on either river bank. This interesting fortification was designed to prevent the Romans from bringing in supplies via ship to the besieged city, as they had done in late 537. However, Procopius reports that Belisarius came up with a clever plan to break through this obstacle. He lashed together two skiffs and built upon them a wooden tower. This vessel would take the lead in sailing up the Tiber, and behind it were 200 other ships, walled in to protect the passengers, and stuffed with food, supplies, and soldiers. The remainder of Belisarius' available forces would march beside this armada on the riverbanks. Finally, a small garrison force was left in Portus under the command of an officer named Isaac. Here also Antonina was to remain to await the outcome of this remarkable operation. It is significant that this is the first moment in this campaign that Procopius has explicitly mentioned the presence of Antonina. As explained earlier, it seems likely that she was at Belisarius' side from the moment he left Constantinople, but she is first attested here. Although Procopius gives her no credit, it is very possible that Antonina was deeply involved in the planning of this operation. After all, Antonina had personal experience with supplying Rome via the Tiber. In late 537, when Belisarius and the Roman army was besieged in Rome, Antonina had helped to direct a resupply operation up the Tiber from Ostia. It is hard to believe that Belisarius would ignore her expertise in planning out the current operation. Procopius was not present, and perhaps did not know, but that Belisarius and Antonina worked together to arrange for this resupply fleet is not at all hard to imagine. However, she did remain in Portus as the plan unfolded. There were limitations to her contributions to the running of the army, which apparently stopped short of participating in combat operations.[11]

Although well conceived, the attempt to break into Rome and resupply it was ultimately a failure. Bessas, in command of the garrison of Rome, refused to participate by having his forces sally forth in support. Even without them, Belisarius' troops successfully broke the Gothic barrier and destroyed one of the wooden towers, which allowed the resupply fleet to keep inching up the Tiber toward Rome. Unfortunately, Isaac back in Portus grew restless and unwisely decided to leave the walled port and conduct his own sally with the garrison soldiers he had available. He was captured by the Goths. When word reached Belisarius that Isaac was captured, Procopius says that the general believed that Portus itself had been taken and was so decimated by the news that he experienced temporary aphasia. When he recovered, he gave orders for the Roman forces to abandon the attempt to sail up the Tiber and to return at all speed to Portus in order to recover the city. Of course, when they arrived, they found Portus still in Roman hands after all and learned of Isaac's foolish decision. Procopius reports that Belisarius was so overcome with sorrow at this that he fell ill and developed a fever that lasted a long time and nearly killed him. The plan had fallen apart, and Rome remained starving under a tight Gothic siege. It is not hard to see how Belisarius' subordinate commanders had failed him here, but it also seems likely that part of the explanation for the failure of this raid lies in some sort of medical emergency. Belisarius' aphasia, followed by a severe fever, suggests that the general might have suffered a stroke in the midst of this operation. Aphasia is a well-known symptom of a stroke, and about half of stroke victims subsequently develop a fever, which exactly mirrors the way that Procopius describes the progression of Belisarius' symptoms during this operation. A stroke would have incapacitated the general and brought the advance of the relief force to a halt while Belisarius' subordinates tried to figure out what was going on: a measure of their reliance on his leadership during this critical moment. If this is the case, the failure of the operation would have been partially unrelated to Isaac's foolhardy venture, which Procopius (who was not present himself) highlights as the main reason for Belisarius' withdrawal.[12]

Belisarius ultimately recovered, but during his illness and convalescence the opportunity had been lost. It is interesting that none of his subordinates seem to have done very much while Belisarius was recovering. Perhaps he simply had fewer trustworthy commanders than he had earlier in his career. The rashness of Isaac, the disobedience of Bessas, and the apparent failure of any other subordinate to step up during Belisarius' illness make for a stark contrast to the general's cheerful reliance on commanders like John the Armenian in the Vandal campaign. The failure to resupply Rome meant that the city was doomed. In December 546, Totila and the Ostrogoths took the city after a lengthy siege. Four of Bessas' soldiers, in exchange for a payment, allowed the Gothic army to enter the city via the Asinarian Gate. Bessas and some of the senators escaped the city on horses through another gate, but the commoners of the city, who had dwindled to only 500, were unable to flee. The deacon Pelagius successfully petitioned Totila to have mercy on these people. After reproaching the remaining senators for turning traitor to the Goths and accepting the Roman forces, Totila sent Pelagius to Justinian as an envoy, requesting peace. The emperor dismissed the deacon, saying that Belisarius had the power to make settlements, probably an indication that the only settlement Justinian sought was a military one. In the meantime, John, the nephew of Vitalian, was continuing to hold Calabria to the south, and in early 547 Totila thought the time right to move against him. In preparation for this move, Totila allegedly decided to destroy Rome rather than hold it. His troops began to tear down the walls of Rome and were on the verge of burning the great, ancient buildings of the city as well. Here, Belisarius intervened, somehow getting word of this plan and deciding to plead with Totila to spare the Eternal City. He sent the Gothic king a letter in which he urged him to save Rome, because it would redound to his credit whether he won or lost in this war. Totila agreed and, instead of destroying the ancient capital, decided to desert it. When he marched out with his army, he brought the senators with him as captives and expelled all the other inhabitants, refusing to allow a single person to remain in Rome. This is an extraordinary sequence of events. It is not surprising that Totila should be uninterested in garrisoning Rome. He was probably wary of diluting his army by leaving behind a substantial force, and Rome was not strategic enough of a location to really be worth the investment of troops. However, that he should decide to destroy the whole city seems unlikely. This might be an instance of Procopius attempting to fictionalize a contrast between the barbarian king and the civilized Roman general who urges restraint. On the other hand, that Totila depopulated the city certainly seems plausible as a way of denying manpower to Belisarius at a time when the general needed it badly. So as Totila marched south with his army to deal with John's forces in Calabria, Rome lay empty.[13]

Rome Restored

Belisarius, by now apparently fully recovered from his severe illness, decided to occupy the vacant city. He would have had to make the same calculations that Totila did: Rome was not strategically important, and garrisoning it would essentially root him there and prevent him from taking the field elsewhere in Italy. However, Belisarius did not have a sufficiently large army to take the field anyway, and he saw what Totila did not—that Rome's importance transcended strategic considerations. Holding Rome was a symbol. The polity that held Rome was the legitimate ruler of Italy. In some way, Rome was the Roman world, and the Roman world was Rome. That Totila had left the city abandoned must have made retaking it even more tempting, because it would not be necessary to conduct a long siege. Perhaps in the early spring of 547, Belisarius led out a thousand men from the garrison at Portus in a reconnaissance in force to determine if Rome could be easily occupied. They ran into a Gothic ambush outside of the city, and although they successfully defeated the Gothic troops, Belisarius decided to return to Portus to regroup. Some days later, Belisarius tried again, this time bringing every soldier he could spare and leaving only a small garrison in Portus. Procopius does not number this enlarged force, but it seems unlikely to have exceeded 2,000 men. This time Belisarius' army faced no ambushes, and entered Rome unopposed, finding the city deserted. The *Chronicle* of Marcellinus Comes records that the city "was so desolated that for forty days or more neither man nor beast stayed there." Belisarius immediately set his soldiers to rebuilding the walls of Rome, a slow process that was mostly complete within 25 days of the occupation. The natives who lived in the area then moved into the city, because, as Procopius says, they both wanted to live in Rome and also because Belisarius had brought abundant food and supplies. It was perhaps now April 547. From a distance of nearly 1,500 years, this does not sound like the most heroic achievement of Belisarius. He successfully occupied, garrisoned, and repopulated an abandoned city. However, it made an impression on contemporaries. Procopius exclaims that this was "a daring and farseeing plan, which seemed insane to those who first saw and heard of his actions, but its outcome proved to be a splendid achievement of virtue and almost supernaturally magnificent." Procopius is not prone to hyperbolic praise in describing this campaign, which he generally thought poorly run, so this paean particularly stands out in the *Wars* as evidence of what the city of Rome meant to the Romans. Perhaps the retaking of the city was made the more impressive by the fact that Belisarius soon had to defend it. Hearing word of the Roman occupation, Totila immediately marched back to Rome with his army. The Goths attempted to storm the city, focusing on the gates, which Belisarius had been unable to repair or replace due to a lack of skilled workers. Belisarius stationed his bravest soldiers in the gaps of the walls that previously held the gates. The battle was fierce, but Belisarius' forces prevailed, forcing back the Goths. The next day, the Goths tried again, and were again repulsed. After several days of resting, the Goths prepared for a third attempt to storm the city, but this time Belisarius' men rushed out to meet them and defeated them in a pitched battle beside the city walls. Repulsed three times, and no doubt furious, Totila and the Goths then withdrew to Tivoli, where they built up a fortress camp. Belisarius meanwhile had time to finish the gates of the walls of Rome, and then sent the keys of the city to Justinian as proof of his success. The holding of Rome, when its fortifications were incomplete and his forces were small, was indeed a triumph for Belisarius, even if not on as grand a scale as some of his earlier victories.[14]

Triumph it might have been, but reoccupying Rome did not change the trajectory of the war. As he must have known beforehand, taking Rome had merely locked Belisarius and his forces in the city. He did not have sufficient men to both garrison Rome and to pursue the war with Totila elsewhere in Italy. Therefore, Belisarius was reduced to sitting in recaptured Rome for the majority of the remainder of 547. Antonina must have come from Portus and joined him at this time, if she had not come earlier in the year when he first reoccupied the city. Belisarius perhaps kept himself busy governing the city, and he frequently sent Justinian letters urging the emperor to send reinforcements to enable him to prosecute the war more completely. Belisarius' relative inactivity in Rome left Totila to continue to take the initiative in the war. Taking advantage, the Gothic king led his army north to Perugia to establish a tight siege around the city. In the meantime, John continued to be active in southern Italy, where he led a contingent of cavalry in a daring raid on Capua to free the senators and their families whom had been

stashed there by Totila after his earlier capture of Rome. News of this success enraged Totila, who headed south from Perugia in the summer of 547
with the majority of his force and ambushed John's army at night in Calabria.
John's forces scattered and fled southeast all the way to Otranto, leaving their
camp behind for the Goths to plunder. Belisarius and Antonina were in the
meantime remaining quiet in Rome. However, their pleas to Justinian were finally having an effect. By the fall of 547, they received word that Justinian was
sending reinforcements. They seem to have totaled a little more than 2,000
soldiers, and so, while helpful, were not going to significantly change the
course of the war. First to arrive, perhaps at Rome itself, were the commanders
Pakourios and Sergios, whom Procopius says had only a few men. After
them came Vera and Varazes, with 1,100 men between them. Sent last was
Valerianos, the General of Armenia, and an old compatriot of Belisarius,
with his own guardsmen, who numbered more than 1,000. Vera and his 300
soldiers were almost instantly defeated in battle with Totila's forces in Apulia,
while Varazes with his 800 men joined up with the troops of John at Taranto.
These numbers serve to illustrate how small the armies fighting for control of
Italy in the 540s were.[15]

It seems that Justinian hoped that if all of these small armies were united
together, they might be able to oppose Totila, so he wrote to Belisarius to
leave Rome and meet up in Apulia with Varazes, John, and Valerianos, who
was wintering on the coast of the Adriatic Sea, perhaps in Dyrrachium.
Belisarius received this letter, maybe in December 547, and immediately
made preparations to depart. He named Konon the commander of the garrison at Rome. Belisarius and Antonina took with them the best 700 cavalry
and 200 infantry he had available and left the rest of the army with Konon.
Belisarius, Antonina, and their small fleet sailed first to Sicily, putting in
perhaps at Messina, and then set forth from there intending to sail directly
to Taranto to join up with the rest of the army. However, along the way the
fleet was blown aside by a storm and forced to put in at Crotone, across the
Gulf of Taranto from their intended destination. It was now winter, and sea
travel was more hazardous. Crotone was unfortified, so while Belisarius and
Antonina remained in the town with the infantry, he dispatched the 700
cavalry out under the command of Phazas to scout the countryside, collect
supplies, and to provide a screen for the town in case of an attack by Totila's
cavalry. Phazas and his troops did happen upon a unit of Gothic soldiers and
defeated them in a pitched battle, but this encouraged them to get careless.
They were thus unprepared when a second Gothic force of 3,000 horsemen
arrived and ambushed them. Phazas died trying to hold off the Goths, and

with him died most of the Roman cavalry, with only a few surviving to report the bad news to Belisarius. The general was so shaken by the news that he ordered an immediate withdrawal all the way back to Messina. The surviving cavalry, the infantry, and Belisarius and Antonina thus boarded their ships and ignominiously retreated to the safety of Sicily. This was surely a low point in the general's career. He who had stood strong against tens of thousands of Persians was reduced to fleeing with a few hundred soldiers to a different landmass to avoid a small force of Gothic raiders. While this must have been frustrating, the retreat was understandable. Crotone was not defensible, and Belisarius must have known that any force which could defeat his 700 cavalry would also chew up his 200 infantry.[16]

Desperate Measures

It is possible that Belisarius and Antonina now wintered in Sicily, because they are not reported in Italy until spring 548. It is worthwhile mentioning that Sicily remained secure in Roman hands, a bright spot amongst the gloomy picture of the Italian theater. In the spring, Justinian sent another 2,000 infantry by ship to reinforce Belisarius, and also ordered Valerianos and his guardsmen to proceed across the Adriatic to Italy. He arrived at Otranto in early summer 548, and found there Belisarius and Antonina. Belisarius summoned John and his forces also to Otranto, and the other commanders as well, presumably including the recently arrived Varazes. The meeting at Otranto must have been bittersweet. Belisarius and Valerianos had served together in the campaign against the Vandals in 533, when a comparatively enormous army was under their command. The forces available to them now in 548 were relatively meager. Procopius does not number this united army, but a reasonable guess is that it totaled about 5,000 if the infantry reinforcements recently sent by Justinian are included. Belisarius was painfully aware that this force would not be sufficient to both garrison Italy's cities and defeat Totila in the field. Belisarius and Antonina therefore resolved upon a desperate plan to try to increase the size of the army. They decided that Antonina should return to Constantinople in person, meet with Theodora, and attempt to persuade the empress to lean on Justinian to better fund the war in Italy. This was a plan of last resort. Belisarius knew that the appropriate channel was that he write a letter to the emperor in his capacity as general explaining the situation and requesting reinforcements. But Belisarius had been doing this for years at this point without significant results. Clearly the couple hoped that Antonina could use her personal friendship with the empress in order to secure the reinforcements that Belisarius' letters had been unable to pry loose. She perhaps set off for Constantinople in June 548. The journey by sea would have taken about three weeks.[17]

In the meantime, Belisarius, John, Valerianos, and the other commanders had to make do with the forces available to them. Small as this army was, it was still the largest Roman force Italy had seen since Belisarius' arrival in 544, and so surely, the generals reasoned, it should be able to accomplish something. Totila and the Ostrogoths were still setting the terms of the war, however. After his cavalry had successfully ambushed Belisarius' troops outside of Crotone, Totila moved his army to Rusciane (perhaps modern Rossano, Calabria) and established a strict siege of the fortress there. By June, the Roman garrison was hard pressed and agreed to surrender to Totila by midsummer if they had not been relieved. Belisarius therefore decided to first turn his united army to the relief of Rusciane. He gathered together a fleet, embarked the combined army, and they set sail in midsummer 548. However, a huge storm pushed the fleet back and scattered its ships far and wide before they could reach Rusciane. After regrouping at Crotone, the fleet set out again, but Totila was prepared this time and lined the beach outside of Rusciane with spearmen and archers. Unwilling to conduct a contested landing and amphibious assault, the fleet again withdrew to Crotone. This was a failure, to be sure, but it is not altogether surprising. The Romans of the sixth century were relatively inexperienced in launching successful amphibious assaults. Landing troops was a difficult enough maneuver without also having to account for fighting a prepared, potentially more numerous enemy ensconced on the beach. Belisarius, John, and Valerianos now again took council at Crotone. They decided that John and Valerianos should take their forces and march overland all the way north to Picenum, with the hope that doing so would cause Totila to break the siege of Rusciane and follow them. The plan failed. Totila, with a larger army at his disposal, simply detached 2,000 cavalry to chase John and Valerianos' troops northward, while he maintained the siege. Rusciane soon surrendered to the Gothic king.[18]

And what of Belisarius himself? Apparently, in conference with John and Valerianos, he decided that it was best for him to return to Rome, there to lay in provisions, set matters in order, and await the return of Antonina and hopefully additional reinforcements. On first glance, this seems like a strange decision. The war was currently hot in Calabria, with Totila and his army there about to take a key fortification. Belisarius might have stayed there to shadow Totila. He might have moved with John and Valerianos into Picenum to keep the Roman army together. Instead, he moved to Rome. One part of the explanation must be that the garrison in Rome had recently mutinied against its commander, Konon, and murdered him. The soldiers had accused Konon of trafficking in grain and enriching himself to their detriment. So clearly the city needed a new garrison commander, and one that could command the respect of the soldiers there. Belisarius certainly fit the bill. There was probably also some defeatism in this decision. Clearly, Belisarius had decided that there was no way for his army to oppose Totila in its current size, so he had reverted to a strategy of garrisoning key cities and sending out small raiding parties to distract the Gothic king. Finally, one wonders if Belisarius returned to Rome at least in part because he liked the city. He had spent more time in Rome than any city in Italy. He clearly saw its symbolic importance. Perhaps all of these reasons played into the decision. It is probably during these months in Rome that Belisarius made additional religious benefactions in the city, beyond the gifts he had already given to Pope Vigilius in the 530s. The *Liber Pontificalis* records that Belisarius built a hostel for visitors on the Via Lata, and endowed the Monastery of St. Juvenal on the Via Flaminia, north of Rome and near the modern town of Orte. These gifts are a reminder of Belisarius' devotion to his Christian faith and an indication of his belief in charitable works. He is unlikely to have engaged in such philanthropy when he was last in Rome between 537 and 538 during a major Gothic siege, so these constructions probably belong to this later period.[19]

While these events were unfolding in Italy, Antonina had arrived in Constantinople, perhaps in early July 548. She found a court in mourning. She was no doubt shocked to learn that the Empress Theodora had died on June 28, while Antonina was en route to visit her. The empress was about 48 years old, and the cause of death might have been cancer. This was devastating news. Justinian lost his partner and the love of his life. Antonina lost a friend and patron. Belisarius lost his unofficial backchannel to Justinian. After two decades of success and occasionally contention, the quadripartite alliance of the two couples was broken. When Antonina was able to secure an audience with the grieving Justinian, she allegedly skipped the petition for reinforcements for her husband's army, and instead begged the emperor to recall him to Constantinople. Procopius suggests two alternative versions of this request: in the *Wars*, he gives the initiative for the recall to Antonina, while in the *Secret History*, he claims the petition originated with Belisarius. Perhaps Belisarius and Antonina had worked out a plan before she set sail, according to which Antonina was to press hard for reinforcements and, if unable to secure them, was to instead request recall. This is not hard to imagine. Belisarius was likely tired of toiling hopelessly in Italy and well aware of his inability to make a difference without a significant investment of imperial resources. On the ground in Constantinople, it would have been up to Antonina to decide when to switch from plan A (requesting reinforcements) to plan B (requesting recall). Perhaps Antonina did tentatively broach the subject of reinforcements with Justinian himself, or perhaps she determined that with Theodora dead and Justinian grieving such a request was unlikely to go anywhere. In either case, Antonina ultimately pursued plan B, begging Justinian to bring Belisarius home. The emperor granted the request and by doing so confirmed he had no plan to significantly invest in the war in Italy at the time.[20]

The recall message was sent out too late to catch Belisarius at Crotone, and the general therefore received it at Rome, perhaps in fall 548. It appears that Belisarius tarried in Rome for a few months, setting the city's defenses in order, before he heeded the recall and began the return trip to Constantinople. He left behind a garrison of 3,000 men under the command of Diogenes, one of his own guardsmen, whom Procopius praised as "a man of unusual prudence and an able warrior." The amount of time he spent establishing this garrison is perhaps indicative of Belisarius' guilt over abandoning the war unwon, or of his love for the Eternal City, or both. It seems likely that Belisarius left Rome at the beginning of 549. He perhaps sailed around Italy and landed at Dyrrachium and from here he proceeded overland through Illyricum and Thrace to Constantinople. The journey would have taken at least six weeks, although possibly more if Belisarius was not motivated to travel quickly. During his trip, Belisarius was unwittingly one of the targets of a conspiracy. A group of malcontents led by the General Artabanes plotted to murder Justinian and Belisarius at one stroke, and so they were intending to time the plot for Belisarius' return to Constantinople. This suggests that Belisarius' loyalty to Justinian was well known, as was the threat of his reputation, even after the recent struggles in Italy. The conspirators feared that if they killed Justinian while Belisarius was en route, the general "would muster a large army in the towns of Thrace" and then move against them. Therefore, they determined to wait until Belisarius arrived at Constantinople and kill him and the emperor at the same time. However, the conspiracy was detected and the plotters arrested before Belisarius got too close to the city, so the plot ended up having no direct impact upon him. Belisarius arrived in Constantinople by April 549 at the latest and was reunited with Antonina.[21]

By all accounts, Belisarius' second campaign in Italy had been a failure. Even the historian of the Franks, Gregory of Tours, includes in his history a confused description of the defeat of Belisarius and his recall to

Constantinople. Belisarius' constant historian, Procopius, is quite hard on the general for this campaign. He complains that "for five years he had not disembarked anywhere on the soil of Italy nor had he succeeded in making a single march there by land, but he had taken refuge in concealed flight during this whole time, always sailing without interruption from one coastal fort to another stronghold along the shore" and adds in the *Secret History* that this was a "total disgrace" and that Belisarius was simply "too terrified" to fight. The historian also charges that "the will of God was manifestly opposed to him" in this campaign. To round out the accusations, Procopius claims that during this period Belisarius "became the most greedy person in the world" and squeezed money out of his subordinates and the Italians on the pretext that the emperor was not funding the war properly.[22]

In all of these charges, Procopius is trying to make sense of Belisarius' abject failure, especially compared to his brilliant successes in the 530s. His overall characterization of Belisarius' campaign as one focused on sailing around the coast and attempting to hold fortified cities is a fair summary of what Belisarius did. However, it seems unlikely that Belisarius adopted this strategy because he was scared. In fact, Procopius knows the reason why Belisarius could not face Totila in the field, and the reason why Belisarius tried to raise funds in Italy; he even mentions it, although he only calls it a pretext. Belisarius never had the imperial support he needed to make a difference in Italy. Justinian never sent a large enough army of seasoned soldiers, nor the money required for Belisarius to raise an army of mercenaries. From the beginning of the campaign in 544 to its end in 549, it seems unlikely that Belisarius ever commanded more than a few thousand soldiers at a time. When he left Rome in 549 to return to Constantinople, he left behind 3,000 men, and that was probably the entire fighting force available to him. This was not enough men to both hold the critical cities of Italy and face Totila in the kind of pitched battle that would be needed to bring about the beginning of the end of Gothic resistance. Curiously, Procopius fails to cut Belisarius any slack for this, or to even acknowledge that it might have been a problem. While it is true that Justinian failed to reinforce Belisarius in Italy, blaming the emperor requires considering his choice in context. Italy simply did not rank high enough on Justinian's list of priorities. The war with Persia was ongoing, there were probably lingering demographic impacts on the Roman army from the ravages of the plague, and various enemy armies were operating in the northern Balkans at the time, threatening Roman possessions near Sirmium (in today's northern Serbia). Justinian prioritized all of these threats over the war in Italy. As a result, Totila ran free in Italy after Belisarius' recall, recapturing Rome and other cities as well. The Roman cause would not be restored until Justinian appointed Narses the eunuch as general in 551. The emperor gave Narses a large army and a substantial amount of money, with the result that Narses would defeat Totila in battle in 552 and eventually secure Italy for the emperor. Thus, too late for it to help Belisarius, Justinian did at length prioritize Italy and Narses demonstrated that Totila and the Goths were beatable given the appropriate resources.[23]

FIGURE 16 A sixth-century lead seal, obverse: Virgin and Child,
reverse: monogram of Belisarius. © Dumbarton Oaks, Byzantine
Coins and Seals Collection, Washington, DC.

8

Twilight of a Power Couple

WHEN BELISARIUS REACHED Constantinople in 549, he must have been both exhausted and dispirited after his failed five-year campaign in Italy. Unfortunately, rest was not an option, for he arrived in the city in the midst of yet another family argument. Belisarius and Antonina's daughter, Ioannina, had been betrothed to Anastasios, the grandson of the Empress Theodora, since perhaps 543. As soon as Antonina had found out that Theodora had died (so perhaps in July 548), she had begun to work to formally break her daughter's engagement. The only source for this story is the *Secret History*. According to Procopius, Theodora wanted Ioannina and Anastasios to marry so that her grandson would become the heir of Belisarius' wealth. As 548 approached and Theodora perhaps knew she was ill, she pressed Belisarius and Antonina to return from Italy so there could be a wedding. The author claims that Belisarius and Antonina pretended they could not come to Constantinople because they did not wish Ioannina to marry Anastasios, which is an unfair blow, because of course the couple really were detained by the campaign in Italy, which was not going well. Procopius charges that Theodora then took matters into her own hands, forcing Ioannina to sleep with Anastasios and then, having ordered this rape, requiring them to live together. This situation persisted for eight months, until Theodora's death. When Antonina arrived in Constantinople, she was horrified and immediately separated Ioannina and Anastasios and sought to call off the engagement. Procopius argues that this showed "immense ingratitude." When Belisarius reached Constantinople in 549, Antonina persuaded him to support her in breaking off the engagement of their daughter. Procopius uses this incident as further evidence to support his claim that Belisarius' wife was his mistress and ruled over him.[1]

Belisarius & Antonina. David Alan Parnell, Oxford University Press. © Oxford University Press 2023.
DOI: 10.1093/oso/9780197574706.003.0009

It is difficult to know what to make of this latest round of family drama. On the one hand, it is unlikely that the entire story is fiction. Certainly, an engagement between the daughter of Belisarius and the grandson of Theodora would have been rather well known at the time, so it seems unlikely that Procopius is making that part up. However, it is quite likely that some of the more salacious details in the story are simply fictitious. That Theodora forced the young Ioannina to be raped by her grandson too neatly fits into gendered tropes about out-of-control women violating sexual taboos. It reeks of a detail that Procopius invented to make the empress look bad. Similarly, the suggestion that ending the engagement was primarily Antonina's idea and that Belisarius was being servile to his wife in agreeing with her also fits all too perfectly into the theme of Antonina's unnatural power over her husband that Procopius weaves throughout the entire *Secret History*. In short, the breaking of Ioannina's engagement has all the hallmarks of a classic Procopian smear job. The author takes what was probably a real event, that many Constantinopolitan grandees knew of, and adds a gendered, invective spin to it.[2]

The real history of Ioannina's betrothal was probably less salacious, if not any less scandalous. Belisarius and Antonina agreed to an engagement between Ioannina and Anastasios, perhaps in 543, but by 548/549 they decided to call it off. As described in Chapter 6, the engagement was probably initially politically motivated, a sign of the renewed amity between the two powerful couples. That Theodora wished to see this marriage alliance consummated, especially as she perhaps began to feel she was growing ill, is not at all surprising. That Belisarius and Antonina put off the empress because they desired to be present in person for the wedding is also not surprising and does not require any hostile explanation that they secretly did not want the marriage to happen. Belisarius and Antonina had already seen their family implode earlier in the decade, and Ioannina was their only daughter. Of course they would wish to be present at her wedding. Nor could the general and his wife easily get away from Italy so that the wedding could happen sooner, given how perilous the situation was there. However, it seems likely that the failure of Belisarius' campaign in Italy and the concurrent death of Theodora did dramatically change the situation. Belisarius and Antonina, shrewd political operators, would have understood well that the marriage of Ioannina and Anastasios would be of no benefit to them once Theodora was dead. With Theodora dead, Anastasios, related only to Theodora and not to Justinian, was a relative nobody. And now that Belisarius' campaign in Italy had ended in failure, would it not be more beneficial for the general to seek to ally himself with another influential family? Thus, cold political calculus on the part of Belisarius and Antonina told them that there was no reason for Ioannina to marry Anastasios, and that instead they should seek out a more politically profitable alliance for their daughter. In one editorial comment, then, Procopius was not far wrong: this was indeed an act of immense ingratitude on the part of Belisarius and Antonina, even if it might have made political sense. Thus, the true core of this story is Belisarius and Antonina using their daughter's hand in marriage as a political tool to cement their place in the Constantinopolitan hierarchy, and Procopius' claims of out-of-control empresses, rape of fiancées, and servile men are simply sensational window dressing. Ironically, since the *Secret History* is the only source that records this story and it does not provide a follow up, it is not clear if Belisarius and Antonina succeeded in making a more advantageous match for Ioannina. This is her last mention in any source. She, and with her the future of Belisarius and Antonina's family, fades from view.[3]

General of the East Again

While sorting through this family drama with Antonina, Belisarius must also have found the time to present himself before Justinian and formally resign his commission as commander of the war in Italy and his title of Count of the Sacred Stables. He soon replaced this title with another, older and more familiar. Procopius suggests in the *Wars* that Justinian agreed to recall Belisarius from Italy in part because the Persian war was heating up, and additional evidence exists that suggests that this is true and not merely a cover for the general's disappointing recall after an unsuccessful Italian campaign. When Belisarius arrived in Constantinople, Justinian "appointed him commander of the imperial guards in his capacity as General of the East." This sentence is evidence that Belisarius regained his position as General of the East at this time and received the additional, honorary title of some sort of commander of the guards, perhaps Count of the Protectors (*comes protectorum*). Despite these appointments, neither Procopius nor any other surviving source suggests that Belisarius actually left Constantinople and traveled to the eastern front. This has led some modern historians to conclude that Belisarius' reinstatement as General of the East in 549 was nothing more than a reward for his many years of service and that the title was honorary, like the commander of the guards title. However, comparing the timeline of the Roman war with Persia with the timing of Belisarius' reappointment reveals that this was likely to have been more than an honorary recognition.[4]

While Belisarius and Antonina were in Italy in 545, Justinian had signed a five-year truce with the Persian Empire. In 548, Justinian had dispatched a Roman army into Lazica (modern Georgia in the Caucasus) to try to protect the Lazican King Goubazes from Persian attack. War between Roman and Persian forces in Lazica was heating up considerably by late 548, and it is possible that the emperor feared it might spill over into the traditional arena of Roman-Persian competition, Mesopotamia. Procopius mentions an incident that might have raised Justinian's suspicions. In 548, Khusro made an attempt to seize the Roman stronghold of Dara by deception. A Persian ambassador, Yazdgushnasp, attempted to gain entry to Dara on his way to Constantinople to speak with Justinian. Unusually, the ambassador tried to enter with 500 attendants. These men were to set fires in the city and, while the Romans were distracted by the fires, to open the gates and let in hidden Persian soldiers. But the attempt was betrayed to the Romans, who only allowed Yazdgushnasp to enter with 20 attendants, thus foiling the plan. Although the Persian attempt on Dara did not succeed, it would have alarmed Justinian and alerted him to the possibility that the hostilities with the Persians in Lazica might spread to Mesopotamia. Perhaps not coincidentally, this is roughly the time period in which Belisarius returned from Italy and was reinstated as General of the East. It is entirely possible that Justinian appointed Belisarius to this position in preparation for all-out war with the Persians in Mesopotamia, the domain of the General of the East. However, the attempt on Dara turned out to be an isolated incident, and war with Persia did not end up expanding beyond Lazica. In late 551, Justinian signed a five-year extension of the truce with Persia, exempting the hostilities in Lazica. With this extension, there was no longer any concern that the war would extend to Mesopotamia. It also seems, again perhaps not coincidentally, that Belisarius around this time resigned his commission as General of the East. In a document dated February 5, 552, Belisarius is described only as ex-consul and patrician, not as General of the East, which would imply that by this time he had laid aside his active military career.[5]

This evidence suggests that when Belisarius arrived in Constantinople in April 549, Justinian asked him to resume his position as General of the East to defend Dara and prepare for the possibility of an expanded war with Persia. Belisarius agreed and served in this position for between one and two years, until the crisis passed and the extension of the truce was either expected or actually signed. Belisarius' whereabouts during this period are unknown. While Procopius suggests that Justinian detained Belisarius at Constantinople and no source records him leaving the city and moving to the East, it is entirely possible that he might have done so at some point, especially at the beginning of this appointment. Perhaps his job during this term of office was to organize and drill the Army of the East in preparation for war, much as he had done in spring 541. It is not hard to imagine Belisarius traveling to Dara in summer 549 and spending a campaign season with his old troops, preparing them for potential war. Since no war actually ended up breaking out in Mesopotamia and there was no fighting, this could have easily gone unremarked in Procopius' *Wars* and other contemporary histories. On the other hand, it is perhaps possible that Belisarius spent this term as General of the East in Constantinople, sending commands via post to the East and waiting on developments, only intending to travel to the frontier if fighting actually broke out. This scenario is a little less likely, given the travel time for messages to arrive via post and for Belisarius to react, but perhaps the general demanded it as a condition of accepting the position.[6]

However Belisarius spent this last year or two in the military, it is clear that, probably sometime in 551, and at the very latest by the beginning of 552, he had retired from active service. This withdrawal has traditionally been met with consternation and handwringing by modern historians, who seem confused that the general retired. They frame the decision as being forced upon Belisarius by a jealous Justinian. Belisarius must have longed to continue his career and pursue additional military glory, but he was denied this by the emperor, or so the argument goes. This argument approaches the retirement of Belisarius from the wrong angle. It would actually have been a surprise if Belisarius had not retired at this point. By 551, Belisarius was about 50 years old and had served in the army for more than 25 years. The standard term of service required for a Roman soldier in the field army during this period to receive an honorable discharge was 20 years. So Belisarius had more than served his term. It is true that other generals in Justinian's service chose to continue their careers into old age. Bessas, Narses the eunuch, and Liberius were all still holding commands while in their 70s or older. However, the very fact that contemporaries make a point of mentioning their extreme age suggests that they were outliers in this respect. As for Belisarius, just because other generals continued to serve into old age did not mean that he felt compelled to do so. After all, Belisarius had won his fame and fortune. What was left for him to prove? Why should he not settle into a comfortable retirement and enjoy the life of a rich Constantinopolitan grandee? There was also Antonina to consider. She was older than Belisarius and traditionally accompanied him on campaign. Belisarius clearly cared for her, and she had surely also earned retirement, not more years spent in the saddle. In fact, far from Justinian forcing

Belisarius to retire, it is possible that the emperor hampered Belisarius' retirement plans. When the general arrived at Constantinople in April 549, he perhaps intended to retire on the spot and only agreed to serve another brief stint as General of the East because Justinian begged him to do so. Seen in this light, Belisarius' final commission as General of the East becomes a favor the tired general did for his emperor, to whom he had been loyal for so long, rather than a reward that Justinian bestowed upon his long-serving subject.[7]

First Place

Belisarius' retirement from the military did not mean the end of his fame nor of his service to Justinian. In the *Wars*, Procopius makes clear that Belisarius was greatly admired by the people of Constantinople in this phase of his life, suggesting that "all yielded first place to him." Indeed, perhaps the completion and distribution of the first seven books of the *Wars* at around this time (551) contributed to the high reputation of Belisarius and his place amongst the elite. Contrarily, in the *Secret History*, the author claims that Belisarius was "mocked in the streets and reviled as a confirmed fool," but this can be dismissed as invective related to Procopius' claims that everyone thought of Belisarius as subservient to Antonina. It was not just the average people or even merely the elite that admired Belisarius in his retirement. Procopius claims that Justinian "held him in honor." While this is a vague claim, it is perhaps evidence that Belisarius became an integral part of the inner circle of Justinian in his later years. The retired general might have been an important adviser to the emperor. It has been suggested that Justinian may have particularly valued Belisarius as an adviser at this time to fill the gap left by the death of Theodora. While this assertion cannot be conclusively proved, there does exist some evidence that Belisarius was a critical part of Justinian's inner circle in the 550s.[8]

Ecclesiastical sources from this decade point to Belisarius playing a role as mediator between Justinian and Pope Vigilius in their ongoing theological dispute. Of course, the retired general and the pope had a long history with each other. Belisarius and Antonina had confronted and deposed Silverius as pope in March 537 and then immediately thereafter supported the election of Vigilius. In 543 or 544, before Belisarius returned to Italy for his second campaign there, Justinian published a religious edict against the so-called Three Chapters, which was to be the start of a long theological quarrel. The Three Chapters were the writings of Theodore of Mopsuestia, some writings of Theodoret of Cyrus, and a letter from Ibas of Edessa. The emperor intended, through condemnation of these ecclesiastical authors, to appeal to moderate anti-Chalcedonian, or Monophysite, religious leaders. This was a part of Justinian's longstanding search for unity in the church between the Chalcedonian religious establishment and the moderate Monophysite resisters. The edict rankled many senior Chalcedonian bishops in the West, who saw the condemnation of these authors as critical of the Council of Chalcedon. In Rome, Pope Vigilius ignored the edict, neither condemning nor confirming it. However, in November 545, Roman soldiers abducted the pope in Rome and carried him to Sicily, just before Totila and the Goths besieged the city. Vigilius spent almost a year in Sicily and was then moved to Constantinople in late 546. Here, the pope and emperor engaged in a struggle of wills over the next several years, with Justinian trying to convince Vigilius to accept his condemnation of the Three Chapters, and Vigilius trying to get the emperor to withdraw the condemnation.[9]

Seeking to force the issue, in July 551, Justinian issued another edict condemning the Three Chapters. Rather than respond to it, in August Vigilius left his residence and fled to the Church of Saints Peter and Paul near the imperial palace of Hormisdas. After Justinian failed to extract Vigilius from the church with a unit of soldiers, he sent a group of high-ranking officials and advisors to mediate with the pope. A letter written by Vigilius on February 5, 552, identifies the members of this group: Belisarius and Cethegus, ex-consuls and patricians; Peter the ex-consul, patrician, and *magister*; Justin the ex-consul and *cura palatii*; Marcellus the ex-consul and *comes excubitorum*; and Constantine the *quaestor*. This list places Belisarius at the head of a roster of important officials and confidants of the emperor and is also the first mention of Belisarius in the sources without a military title, indicating that his retirement was complete by this point. The delegation successfully convinced Vigilius to leave the sanctuary and return to his living quarters. However, by the end of the year, Vigilius fled again, this time crossing the Bosporus and taking refuge in the Church of St. Euphemia in Chalcedon. On January 28, 552, Belisarius and the same group of officials were dispatched again to negotiate with the pope and convince him to return. This time they were unsuccessful, and Vigilius remained in Chalcedon for many months. Perhaps Belisarius had burned whatever influence he had with Vigilius on the first negotiation in August 551. Sometime in late 552, Vigilius and Justinian agreed to call together an ecumenical council of the church to debate the emperor's condemnation of the Three Chapters. But when the council began in May 553, Vigilius refused to attend. Justinian again called on Belisarius to negotiate with the pope, with some of the same officials from the first two visits and some new ones. Belisarius, Liberius the patrician, Peter, Patricius the patrician, Constantine, Cethegus, and Rusticus the patrician were all dispatched to attempt to convince the pope to come to the council. They failed. By the end of May 553, Vigilius had composed his own document on the Three Chapters, which he called the *Constitutum*, and he summoned a group of Roman notables to accept the document and deliver it to Justinian. This group consisted of Belisarius and Cethegus, the ex-consuls Justin and Constantianus, and the bishops Theodore, Benignus, and Phocas. The men politely declined to deliver the pope's message, which all of them must have understood would upset the emperor. This is the last time that we know Belisarius was involved in this story. In 554, Vigilius finally caved and condemned the Three Chapters as the emperor wished, but died in 555 on his journey back to Rome.[10]

While he was only a peripheral actor in this ecclesiastical drama, the story is important to the life of Belisarius because it is one of the few glimpses of his activities in the 550s that the surviving sources provide us. The lists of officials who attempted to negotiate with Vigilius demonstrate that although Belisarius was now decisively retired from military service, he remained an important fixture in the elite ruling circles of Justinian's government. The pride of place given to Belisarius in these lists supports Procopius' claim that "all yielded first place" to the retired general. Belisarius was perhaps uniquely positioned to lean on Vigilius to do the emperor's bidding since he and his wife had ensured the election of the pope in 537, but this does not mean that Belisarius was important only in ecclesiastical negotiations with Vigilius. It is possible that this was just one of many areas in which Belisarius advised Justinian. The other activities of the civilian Belisarius in the 550s may simply not have been recorded, or recorded in sources that have since been lost. The continuing involvement of Belisarius in imperial affairs at a high level in the early 550s points to both the importance of the retired general and to his ongoing, amicable relationship with Justinian.

The Last Bow

In 559, six years after his last appearance in the sources with Pope Vigilius, Belisarius resurfaced in the historical record for one final flourish of military glory. This time the setting was not Mesopotamia, or North Africa, or even Italy, but much closer to home. A group of Kutrigurs, nomadic people perhaps descended from Attila's Huns, led by a ruler named Zabergan, had crossed the Danube in late 558 to raid south into the Balkans. Once in imperial territory,

Zabergan and his forces evidently defeated a Roman army under the command of the General Sergios. By March 559, Zabergan's army had entered Thrace, penetrated the Long Wall, and reached as close as 20 miles away from Constantinople. At this point, Justinian was forced to turn to ad hoc measures for defense against the Kutrigurs. The emperor called upon his old, loyal subordinate and confidant, Belisarius. The historian Agathias describes the former general as "aged." He was perhaps about 60 years old. The chronicler John Malalas gives Belisarius' title as "the patrician," which serves again as a reminder that he was a civilian retired from military service. Conspicuously missing from this list of historians of Belisarius' last campaign is his former secretary, Procopius. Although no source records the date of his death, the consensus among modern scholars of Procopius is that the author likely died shortly after working on his last known book, *On Buildings*, in 554. This early death for Procopius seems all the more likely because he does not seem to have ever written a church history of the reign of Justinian, which he had promised when discussing the deposition of Pope Silverius in 537. Procopius therefore did not live to see the final flourish of Belisarius' career, about which he might have provided an interesting account.[11]

Back in 559, Justinian evidently charged the "aged" patrician Belisarius with gathering a scratch force to meet and turn away Zabergan before his army could get too close to Constantinople. It is unlikely that the walled city itself was in much danger, but the rich suburbs of the city would have made a tempting target for plundering. Belisarius, roused to one last act of military service for an emperor to whom he had already given so much, did his best to scrape together a small army. Agathias reports that he had 300 heavily armed soldiers and also collected some untrained civilians, perhaps city dwellers or peasants from the surrounding farmland. While the number 300 neatly conjures up images of the Spartan contingent at Thermopylae, it is also a common number for a detachment of soldiers in the sixth century, so it should not be dismissed out of hand. That Belisarius had some core of well-armed soldiers in his scratch force is also not at all hard to believe. Even in retirement, the general probably retained some guardsmen, and other retired veterans who still possessed their arms and armor and lived in the area might have heeded his call. Malalas paints a rich portrait of Belisarius commandeering every available horse in Constantinople to mount as many soldiers and volunteers as he could. When he had gathered as many men as was possible and waited as long as he dared, Belisarius led them out of Constantinople to a village named Chiton, some 15 miles west of the city. Here he set his forces to work digging an entrenched camp. Soon after, Zabergan dispatched 2,000 of his cavalry to probe Belisarius' position. The general used the terrain to his advantage, stationing some of his cavalry on the wings of his main force and out of sight, a call back to his tactics at the Battle of Dara, almost 30 years before. The Kutrigur force charged Belisarius at the center of his line, and then the Roman cavalry sprang from ambush and helped to rout the Kutrigurs. According to Agathias, there were some 400 casualties for the Kutrigurs and none for the Romans. Malalas adds in the key detail that Belisarius ordered trees to be cut and dragged behind his army, which blew up a large cloud of dust and suggested that his scratch force was bigger than it actually was, or at least prevented the enemy from being able to accurately number his troops. In doing this, Belisarius was following a maxim of contemporary strategy that a good general should seek to prevent the enemy from accurate reconnaissance of his army. This shows that the retired general had lost very little of his military acumen in the past decade. The combination of their defeat in battle and their uncertainty about the total size of Belisarius' army was enough to chase off the remains of the Kutrigur raiding party and then to convince Zabergan to pull back his main force as well. This was no grand battle on the scale of Dara (530) or Ad Decimum (533), but Belisarius and his scratch force did fight a small engagement with some of Zabergan's cavalry and did force them to fall back. Under the circumstances, for a retired general with a cobbled-together army, this was an achievement that impressed contemporaries. Agathias, perhaps with a touch of hyperbole, exclaimed, "by this feat of arms, which was to be the last in his life, he won as great a measure of glory as he had done by his earlier victories over the Vandals and the Goths."[12]

Once it became clear that the Kutrigurs were pulling back and would no longer be an imminent threat to Constantinople and its suburbs, Justinian recalled Belisarius. Agathias alleges that this recall was not Belisarius' choice. The historian blames the jealousy of Belisarius' political enemies, whom, he says, whispered that Belisarius aspired to a higher position. It seems likely that here Agathias is drawing on the earlier works of Procopius, which had suggested that Belisarius' enemies whispered against him after his great victories, in order to dramatize and spice up his history of this campaign. But Belisarius had only been called into service in this moment as an emergency measure. Both he and Justinian must have assumed this command would be of extremely brief duration. Belisarius' job had been to hold off Zabergan's forces until more permanent plans had been put in place. He had done so, and therefore the job was done. So it is unlikely that Belisarius' recall irked him. It is equally unlikely that there were lots of whispers from the general's political enemies, or that Justinian recalled Belisarius because of such whispers. The truth was much simpler: the situation was now under control, and Justinian was happy to let his old friend return to his retirement. Justinian himself supervised the reoccupation and repair of the Long Wall and then paid Zabergan to retreat out of the empire. Later, the emperor paid the Utigurs to attack the Kutrigurs, with the result that the two peoples virtually wiped each other out.[13]

Meanwhile, Belisarius slipped back into his retirement. For the next few years, he again disappears from the sources. As with the 550s, this is not proof that he was doing nothing or was completely disengaged from politics. He perhaps continued to serve Justinian as an advisor during this time. That he continued to be an important person in the Constantinopolitan elite is confirmed by the fact that the next mention of Belisarius in the surviving sources is in connection with a plot against the emperor. In November 562, three men devised a conspiracy to murder Justinian. Ablabios, a musician; Marcellos, a banker; and Sergios, the nephew of a leading senator named Aitherios, were the leaders. Their plot was amateurish and quickly detected. Under questioning, Sergios accused three other men of participating in the conspiracy. They were Isaakios, Vitus, and Paul, who all belonged to the household of Belisarius as accountants and assistants. Soon Belisarius himself was implicated. On the fifth of December, the depositions of all these men were read out in a special sitting of the imperial court, and Justinian became angry with Belisarius. The emperor stripped the retired general of all his household men, and presumably also of his titles as well. Belisarius found himself again in dishonor, roughly 20 years after his last disgrace.[14]

It is difficult to know what to make of this story. Malalas, our source for the event, is characteristically terse. On balance, it seems unlikely that Belisarius led, or even took part, in this failed conspiracy. The old general had so many opportunities to rebel against Justinian over the long course of his life and took none of them. It is not clear why he would have bypassed opportunities to plot against Justinian when he had military power at his fingertips, only to embrace a conspiracy against the emperor in his sixties as a civilian. Beyond this, to be quite frank, Ablabios, Marcellos, and Sergios were all beneath Belisarius. He was their social better in every way. There is no particular reason why Belisarius would reduce himself to playing a bit role in an amateur plot concocted by people who were his social inferiors and whom he must have known would have little chance of succeeding, or of gaining the throne even if they did manage to murder the emperor. And yet, as unlikely as it was that Belisarius was involved, it seems Justinian believed it enough to get angry and punish his old general. Some modern historians have presented this as evidence that Justinian was jealous of Belisarius, and always had been. He was ungrateful and willing to believe anything bad said about Belisarius. Perhaps this is true. The emperor had been willing to believe Belisarius would badmouth Theodora in 542 and had countenanced his punishment then. But that had been when Justinian was near death, Theodora was vulnerable, and Belisarius at the apex of his military strength. The situation in 562 was quite different in that Belisarius was no longer such a threat. The emperor himself was also quite different, however. It must be remembered that Justinian was 80 years old in 562. Perhaps his credulousness about the conspiracy, his anger at Belisarius, and his decision to punish him can be attributed to paranoia tinged with the onset of dementia. In other ways, Justinian was increasingly erratic in his last few years. For instance, the emperor bizarrely convinced himself that an extreme Monophysite doctrine known as Aphthartodocetism was the key to resolving religious conflicts between Chalcedonians and more moderate Monophysites, and he issued an edict in 564 declaring it orthodox.[15]

Whatever the reason that Justinian believed the accusations and punished Belisarius, his anger did not last. In a brief note, Malalas confirms that on July 19, 563, "the patrician Belisarius was received and given back all his honors." Belisarius' disgrace had lasted seven months. By restoring Belisarius to his position in society, Justinian once again exhibited the exercise of clemency that so often characterized his dealings with his generals. As with the disgrace in 542, this mercy was some time in coming. No doubt the months in between the hearing in December 562 and the restoration in July 563 had been difficult ones for Belisarius and Antonina. To be vindicated and restored to favor must have been a relief. Still, it is fair to wonder whether this final sequence of accusation, disgrace, and restoration perhaps drove, at last, a wedge between Justinian and Belisarius. Did the old general finally become disenchanted with his emperor? Although officially restored to honor, did Belisarius now stop coming to the Great Palace and retreat to private life? It is impossible to know, for the next thing that any source records about Belisarius is the date of his death.[16]

Belisarius the patrician, ex-consul, and former General of the East died in Constantinople in March 565. The circumstances of his death are not recorded. According to the chronicler Theophanes, his property was incorporated into an imperial estate known as Marina. It is not clear if this means some or all of his property. Even less is known of the fates of his closest family members, Antonina and Ioannina. No surviving, reliable source records their deaths. A late, fanciful, and legendary source suggests that Antonina outlived Belisarius, but as we will see in the next chapter, there are reasons to doubt this story. For Ioannina, there is not even this wisp of a tale. She simply disappears from the historical record following her separation from her betrothed, Anastasios, in 549. Perhaps both Antonina and Ioannina pre-deceased Belisarius, which would go some way to explaining why his property went to the emperor upon his death, instead of to them. It is impossible to know for sure. What is clear is that the historical record of Belisarius, Antonina, and Ioannina comes to an end with the death of Belisarius in March 565. The general's famous emperor, Justinian, reigned for 38 years, but outlived Belisarius by only a few months, dying on November 14, 565, at the age of 83. Thus passed the last member of the quadripartite alliance between the two powerful couples that had defined politics and military affairs in the middle of the sixth century. It was the end of an age.[17]

And yet, in a strange coda, one person from Belisarius' tight nuclear family survived to make a name for himself in the next generation. Antonina's son, Photios, who had been exiled from the family since 541, lived on in Jerusalem as a monk, apparently rising at some point to be the abbot of his monastery. There is no evidence that he ever had a rapprochement with Antonina or Belisarius. Perhaps he was persona non grata to Justinian as well, because Photios does not appear in imperial service again until the accession of the new Emperor Justin II, nephew of Justinian, in November 565. The abbot presented himself to Justin II and was immediately sent on an obscure mission to Alexandria, either to quell religious tensions or perhaps to slay the new emperor's closest rival, his cousin, also named Justin. Photios would go on to have a quasi-military career revival under Justin II. He commanded a host of monks, soldiers, and guardsmen, using them to crush a Samaritan revolt and perhaps to persecute Monophysite Christians in Syria in the 570s. His vague authority in this regard apparently lasted for 12 years. The ecclesiastical historian John of Ephesus describes Photios as "the son of Antonina," which both helps to clarify that this was the same Photios and emphasizes her lasting reputation as a formidable woman worth mentioning. Photios was dead by no later than 585 and thus ended the life of the last member of Belisarius and Antonina's nuclear family that our sources track.[18]

FIGURE 17 The album cover art for Judicator's *Let There Be Nothing*, showing Belisarius, Antonina, and Theodosios. Created by artist Mitchell Nolte.

9

Afterlife and Legend

FOR ALMOST 1,500 years, Belisarius and Antonina have lived on in legend through history, art, literature, music, and more. This curious afterlife is a fitting place to conclude a book about their lives and partnership. The immediate memory of their lives was no doubt primarily shaped by artwork, including the monumental ceiling mosaics of the Chalke, and literature, especially the works of Procopius and the other contemporary historians and chroniclers who mentioned them, as have been explored in previous chapters. However, gradually the heroic yet historic portrayal of Belisarius began to be overshadowed by new, fantastic constructions, as history became legend. The new legend of Belisarius might have begun as an oral folk tale or song. It first appears in writing in a text known as the *Patria of Constantinople*, a collection of works on the history and monuments of the city, which has been dated to the early reign of Basil II in the 10th century. In this tale, the investigation into the plot of 562, which implicated Belisarius, had a very different outcome. The relevant passage of the *Patria* reads, "And then later, [Justinian], bearing a grudge against Belisarius for the things he had said, dug out the eyes of that man who was most fit to be a general, and ordered him to sit in the Lauseion and a clay vessel to be given to him, for him to throw himself upon those who were passing by for an obol (a small coin)." No contemporary historian had spoken of such a punishment for the retired general, so it seems that here legend superseded history. The *Patria* also provides a note about the end of Antonina's life, claiming that after the blinding of Belisarius she made herself a habitation, presumably something akin to a convent, with Vigilantia, the sister of Justinian. As mentioned in the previous chapter, no sixth-century source says anything about the life of Antonina after 549. These stories in the *Patria* therefore have an earliest attestation of more than four centuries after the death of Belisarius and Antonina. And yet despite the brevity of these

Belisarius & Antonina. David Alan Parnell, Oxford University Press. © Oxford University Press 2023.
DOI: 10.1093/oso/9780197574706.003.0010

claims, the distance between the text and the individuals it purports to de-scribe, and the lack of corroboration by contemporary sixth-century sources, these passages became the germ of a legendary myth that persisted, expanded, and remained popular for centuries.[1]

The most complete manifestation of the legend that grew from this brief mention in the *Patria* is a late medieval Greek tradition known as the *Novel of Belisarius*. In this story, Belisarius takes command of an army and fleet and makes war on England, where he storms the citadel of the enemy. He returns to Constantinople and is received by Justinian with great honors. However, other noble families become envious and manufacture a charge of treason against Belisarius. Justinian has Belisarius blinded. Later, the Persians invade the empire and Belisarius' son, Alexios, is named commander of the army and defeats them. Belisarius makes a final appearance in the tale as a blind beggar, sought out by some foreign ambassadors in Constantinople. A version of this story appears in three different Greek texts that all date to the 15th century. This legend perhaps developed originally as a popular folk song and took on elements from medieval Roman history along the way. In particular, the blinding of Belisarius must come from the tradition recorded in the *Patria*, and the name of Belisarius' fictional son, Alexios, clearly comes from the fa-mous Komnenian emperor of the 11th century. Conspicuously absent in the *Novel of Belisarius* tradition is mention of Antonina in general (despite the fact that she is named in the *Patria*), and the *Secret History* criticism of the relationship of Belisarius and Antonina in particular.[2]

Moving beyond the 15th century, early modern popular portrayals of Belisarius also focused on the anachronistic story that he was blinded by Justinian and reduced to begging. The fictional tradition of the *Novel of Belisarius* enchanted playwrights, artists, and authors in western Europe from the early modern period into the 20th century. During the Italian Renaissance, the Greek legend passed into the West, with the first known Italian version of the novel being translated by Raphael Maffei of Volterra (1451–1522) in the late 15th century. Raphael also translated and published the *Wars* of Procopius about the same time, but the *Secret History*, on the other hand, was unpub-lished and unknown to Raphael, although not totally unknown to others who searched the Vatican archives. The text was consulted by historians in the archives only occasionally until 1623, when Nicolò Alemanni found it and published it, making it more accessible. After this publication, it would in theory have been possible for either the *Patria* blinding legend and the *Novel of Belisarius* to remain popular, or for the *Secret History* tradition of Belisarius and Antonina to grow in fame and displace it.[3]

In popular art and works of fiction, the legendary tradition of Belisarius' blinding absolutely dominated in this period, showing up in some format in almost every instance of fictional presentation of the general. However, artists and authors did not unapologetically adopt every aspect of this myth. They evidently started with the same legendary tradition of a great general's downfall and blinding, but built out of it slightly different storylines that often reflected their own interests. For example, one of the earliest works to utilize this legend in a creative way was the 1607 play *Belisarius* by Jakob Bidermann, a Jesuit priest who served as censor of books under Pope Gregory XV. His lengthy play ends with Belisarius blind and begging, but he adds an interesting moral twist: Belisarius recognizes that his blinding is a punishment for his deposition of Pope Silverius while in Italy in 537. It is not hard to imagine why a Jesuit priest with a close connection to the papacy might have seen it appropriate to emphasize Belisarius' clash with a pope in his play. This is an episode of Belisarius' career that is virtually ignored by future playwrights and authors, who had no such close connection to the papacy to inspire their storyline. While almost all creators followed the *Patria* tradition of Justinian blinding Belisarius, only some showed the retired general actually begging for alms. If he is not shown begging, then he suffers other fates. In *Le Belisaire* by Jean Rotrou (1643), Belisarius dies from the ordeal of blinding, and so there is no time for begging. In *Belisarius: A Tragedy* by William Philips (1758), Belisarius survives the blinding but is killed shortly after in a popular uprising in Constantinople. These differences may be ascribed to individual artistic interpretation of the source legend.[4]

The 1767 novel *Belisaire*, written by Jean-François Marmontel, was particularly influential. In this book, the reader learns of Belisarius' fate at the beginning: he is presented as old and blind. As the blinded general meets various characters on his journey from Constantinople to his ancestral home, the reader slowly learns that Belisarius was blinded because of the suspicion that he was the organizer of a plot against Justinian. The emperor himself visits the blinded general under a pseudonym, and this launches a long relationship. At the end of the book, Justinian reveals his true identity to Belisarius, who virtuously forgives the emperor for blinding him. The emperor then forces Belisarius to come to court and be his adviser. As a whole, the story presents Belisarius as impossibly virtuous and magnanimous, and Justinian as credulous and arrogant, although not necessarily evil. The moral of the story seems to be that rulers should be careful to not be too credulous of gossip or ungrateful for their virtuous and successful servants. Perhaps in writing it, Marmontel was indirectly indicting the reigning French monarch, Louis XV, who was known for abruptly dismissing powerful ministers after long service to his government.

It was probably Marmontel's novel that was responsible for an artistic explosion in the popularity of the Belisarius legend, which had previously been confined to literature. In the fifteen-year period between 1776 and 1791, at least four works of neoclassical art on Belisarius were created in France. *Belisarius* by Francois-Andre Vincent (1776) showed the blinded general receiving alms from a former soldier. *Belisarius Receiving Hospitality from a Peasant* by Jean-Francois Pierre Peyron (1779) showed, as the title implies, Belisarius in the home of a peasant, surrounded by solicitous helpers. This scene is actually pulled directly from chapter four of Marmontel's novel. *Belisarius Begging for Alms* by Jacques-Louis David (1781) is perhaps the most famous of these works of art. It shows Belisarius blind and begging, standing next to a stone inscribed "*Date obolum Belisario*" ("Give an obol to Belisarius"). This suggests that David actually researched the Greek legend of the *Patria* after reading Marmontel, since Marmontel's novel does not have Belisarius utter this phrase or even really beg. The last of the four works of art is *Belisarius* by Jean-Baptiste Stouf (1791). By its very nature as a bust, although it shows Belisarius aged and blind, it cannot show him in the act of begging.[5]

FIGURE 18 *Belisarius Begging for Alms* by Jacques-Louis David. Wikimedia Commons.

FIGURE 19 *Belisarius* by Jean-Baptiste Stouf. Getty Museum Collection.

The artistic and literary tradition of Belisarius in the 17th and 18th centuries is unanimous in its embrace of the myth that Belisarius was blinded in his old age. It is also unanimous in ignoring the *Secret History* tradition of the scandalous marriage between Belisarius and Antonina. In fact, Antonina is most remarkable in all these pieces by her absence. She does not appear in any of the four works of art we just examined. She is also completely absent in the plays by Bidermann and Philips. She appears briefly, with few spoken lines, in the play by Rotrou and the novel by Marmontel. Only in the opera *Belisario* by Gaetano Donizetti (1836) does she have an extended appearance, and here she appears as an antagonist, who arranges for Belisarius' arrest and blinding because of her mistaken belief that Belisarius got their fictional son killed. So even when Antonina is given a role in a creative work about Belisarius, and that role is a negative one, it is negative in a fashion contrived by the author, not according to the *Secret History* tradition of Procopius.[6]

At roughly the same time as artists and playwrights were engaging with the *Patria* tradition, professional historians were almost unanimously rejecting the legend of the blind and begging Belisarius. As early as 1722, the historian

John Oldmixon, in his short book titled *The Life of Belisarius*, acknowledged that the saying "*Date obolum Belisario*" was common, but stated he did not believe the story. Later in the century, Edward Gibbon, in *The Decline and Fall of the Roman Empire*, dismissed the legend with characteristic pithiness: "That he was deprived of his eyes, and reduced by envy to beg his bread, 'Give a penny to Belisarius the general!' is a fiction of later times, which has obtained credit, or rather favour, as a strange example of the vicissitudes of fortune." Only Philip Stanhope, known usually as Lord Mahon, gave credence to the blinding legend, in his 1848 biography *The Life of Belisarius*. He wrote, "Why should the Greeks, with these examples before their eyes, devise a new and groundless legend respecting the end of Belisarius?" He tracked the legend to the *Patria*, much as Gibbon had done, but unlike Gibbon decided that it was a trustworthy source. After Lord Mahon, no modern historian of Belisarius has followed him in accepting the story of Belisarius' blinding, and it has been roundly rejected as a later fiction.[7]

However, while historians are nearly unanimous in rejecting the *Patria* legend, so are they nearly unanimous in accepting the portrait of Belisarius and Antonina's marriage painted by Procopius in the *Secret History*. Gibbon set the tone for taking Procopius' story at its word. He cheerfully accepted every accusation against Antonina, including her affair with Theodosios and her domination and control of Belisarius. He wrote of Antonina, "she reigned with long and absolute power over the mind of her illustrious husband." For Gibbon, this did not reflect well on Belisarius: "the fame, and even the virtue, of Belisarius, were polluted by the lust and cruelty of his wife; and that hero deserved an appellation which may not drop from the pen of the decent historian." Perhaps the missing designation here was intended to be "cuckold." After Gibbon, modern historians throughout the 20th and into the 21st centuries have also been willing to take the *Secret History* more or less as truth with regards to the marriage of Belisarius and Antonina. While some scholars focusing on gender history have argued that the accusations of the *Secret History* are not to be trusted, its characterizations of their marriage have been repeated as historical truth in most general histories of the period and in studies of the lives of Belisarius, Antonina, Justinian, and Theodora.[8]

Why was there such a stark difference between the literary and artistic reception of Belisarius and Antonina and the historiographical reception of the pair? For historians, there is the perhaps obvious answer of primary source credibility. Historians looked into the primary sources of each legend and rejected the blinding tradition because of the late date of the *Patria* and the *Novel of Belisarius*, while accepting the marriage tradition of the *Secret*

History because of the proximity of Procopius to the couple. On the other hand, the blinding legend of the *Patria* caught the imagination of artists, novelists, and playwrights in the 17th and 18th centuries and beyond. It seems likely that the blinding legend became popular because it was a tale that formed a simple moral: rulers should not be ungrateful for their successful subjects. It could also be generalized even further: never take success or fate for granted, for it might be gone tomorrow. These morals seem to have been quite popular in 18th-century France, judging by Marmontel's novel and the rash of Belisarius artwork that followed it. The desire to lionize Belisarius in order to dramatize his fall perhaps also explains the relative unpopularity of the *Secret History* tradition for these artists, authors, playwrights. Showing Belisarius as subservient to his wife would have wrecked their attempts to present Belisarius as a perfectly virtuous hero by the standards of their time. Thus, historians discredited the *Patria* legend while accepting the *Secret History* tradition, and creatives ignored the *Secret History* tradition while trumpeting the *Patria* legend. However, the popularity of the legend of the blind and begging Belisarius began to peter out in the 20th century even among creatives. Its last major flourish was in the novel *Count Belisarius* by Robert Graves (1938). Graves titled his final chapter "The Last Ingratitude," with contents that are to be expected based on the *Patria* legend and other works of fiction discussed so far. After Graves' novel, the flood of modern historians dismissing the *Patria* legend as apocryphal seems to have had an effect. In the most recent literary and artistic reception of Belisarius, the general does not appear blind, and the *Secret History* tradition is instead in the ascendant.[9]

Belisarius and Antonina have continued to exert a powerful influence in some sectors of popular culture in the 21st century. They appear in fiction, video games, and heavy metal music. In all of these appearances, it is the *Secret History* tradition rather than the *Patria* legend that conditions description of their lives. The Belisarius series, six books published between 1998 and 2006, is far removed from historical realism. In these novels, authors David Drake and Eric Flint present an alternate history tinged with science fiction which finds Belisarius uniting with the Persians to fight an empire in Northern India that is being manipulated by divine alien beings. *Antonina: A Byzantine Slut* by Paul Kastenellos (2012) is a more traditional historical novel that follows the stories recorded by Procopius in both the *Wars* and the *Secret History* from the perspective of Antonina. In recent years, Belisarius and Antonina have broken free of literature to star in other forms of popular culture. In 2015, Creative Assembly released a campaign pack for the strategy video game *Total War: Attila* entitled *The Last Roman*. In the game, players take control of Belisarius and his army as they fight in North Africa and Italy, and they occasionally receive missions from Antonina, who ahistorically remains in Constantinople during these campaigns. Modern reception of Belisarius and Antonina struck a loud note in 2020 when the American power metal band Judicator released an album entitled *Let There Be Nothing*. The songs follow Belisarius and Antonina through their campaigns in North Africa and Italy, with a special focus on Antonina's alleged affair with Theodosios. While relying heavily upon the *Secret History* tradition, the lyrics also creatively explore the religious conviction of Belisarius and how it conditions his interactions with Antonina. In 2021, Belisarius and Antonina became the focus of a series of documentary videos released on YouTube by Epic History TV. These videos allow the viewer to delve deeply into the career of Belisarius, from his appointment as general to his death, and to learn directly from the writings of Procopius and other sixth-century sources. This brief overview of modern, popular receptions of Belisarius and Antonina shows that their story continues to inspire the imagination of contemporary artists and content creators. These individuals are eager to take up and build upon the historical tradition found in sixth-century sources and seek authentic history rather than legend. Perhaps in the future, artists, authors, musicians, and others will join historians in a critical examination of that historical tradition, and particularly of the accusations of Procopius in the *Secret History* regarding Belisarius and Antonina's relationship.[10]

Concluding Remarks

It is not easy to evaluate Belisarius and Antonina, who were remarkable but flawed people. We know more about the two of them than we do about most Romans of the sixth century, and for all that knowledge there are still large portions of their lives for which we know very little. The nature of the works of Procopius further complicates our knowledge of Belisarius and Antonina, who appear at times as titans (in parts of the *Wars*) and as repugnant (in the *Secret History*). However, as this book has hopefully made clear, neither the praise of the *Wars* nor the criticism of the *Secret History* should be accepted at face value. The true Belisarius and Antonina perhaps are to be found somewhere between these two portrayals, tantalizingly out of reach.

Belisarius was the most famous and successful general of his age. This is not the same as saying that he was the best or most talented general of his age, however. The former statement rests on his conquests in North Africa and Italy and the fame that these brought him in Constantinople during his lifetime and beyond. These conquests returned substantial lands to the Roman Empire to the extent that it is fair to mention Belisarius in the same sentence as famous Roman conquerors like Julius Caesar, Augustus, and Trajan. And yet, all this success does not make Belisarius the most talented general of Roman history, let alone of the sixth century. Some of this success was due to luck (the Vandal fleet being in Sardinia at the time of his landing in Africa) and some of it was due to deception (his capture of Ravenna). Moreover, other Roman generals, such as Sittas and Narses, won major victories in Belisarius' lifetime as well. Belisarius was uniquely successful and became justly famous for it, but as a battlefield commander he was not always remarkable. In many ways, he proved somewhat average as a general. He occasionally was brilliant at motivating his soldiers and subordinate officers, but at other times seems to have let them boss him around (the Battle of Callinicum). He was sympathetic to civilians and sought to form good relations with them in all the theaters in which he fought, but did not always succeed in doing so (the siege of Naples). He captured major metropolises like Carthage and Rome peacefully, but struggled to restrain the violence of his soldiers in the Nika Riot and at Naples. What stands out the most about Belisarius and makes him exceptional is his longstanding loyalty to Justinian and his partnership with Antonina. His loyalty to Justinian was questioned and tested on several occasions, but seems to have never wavered, and he stood by Antonina with remarkable fidelity through success and failure. Belisarius was characterized by long-term partnerships and loyalty. He comes across as remarkably stable in his relationships over the course of his long career.

Antonina was the most powerful uncrowned woman in the sixth-century Roman world. She deposed Pope Silverius, arranged for the sacking of John the Cappadocian, traveled across the Mediterranean with her husband, and even occasionally inserted herself into the running of his army. She knew soldiers, officers, the emperor, popes, bishops, and historians, and at various times commanded them, pleaded with them, and intimidated them. This is a remarkable resume, virtually unparalleled among Roman military wives, and certainly without parallel in the sixth century. She was a formidable woman and, like her friend and patron Theodora, one who was occasionally feared. If the reputation of Belisarius is sometimes inflated in modern evaluations, the reputation of Antonina has been chronically underappreciated. Historians have focused far too much on the *Secret History* story of Antonina's affair and her supposed domination of Belisarius, and far too little on her exceptional career. She is evidence that elite women in the sixth century could take on public roles alongside their husbands. This is a subject crying for more research, to determine whether Antonina was *sui generis* or is just one example of a trend of powerful elite women in this period.

While they were each important individuals, Belisarius and Antonina were truly exceptional because they were yoked together. A successful general of rural origin and an intelligent, cosmopolitan urbanite, they complemented each other well. Together, they managed their relationships with the imperial couple, Justinian and Theodora, through ups and downs over decades. Together, they deposed Pope Silverius, kept armies supplied, and cemented their status as the some of the wealthiest, most famous people in the Roman world. But their relationship was not perfect. They focused so much on their careers, wealth, and success that they ended up blowing up their family, as they neglected the festering rivalry between Photios and Theodosios in the late 530s and early 540s. Belisarius and Antonina, while largely successful in their military undertakings, seem also to have been a bit inept in some of their political maneuverings. They failed to manage the rumor mill in 542, with the catastrophic result that Belisarius was stripped of his position and wealth. They accepted appointment to Italy in 544, not perceiving that Justinian would not prioritize the campaign there anytime soon. They also seem to have bungled the engagement of their daughter, Ioannina, although to what degree it is hard to tell.

Belisarius and Antonina are an interesting study in contrasts. They were wildly successful in their public affairs, but their private lives were at various points in shambles. They were rich and powerful almost beyond imagination, but found this wealth and status difficult to maintain over the long term. What is most apparent from their story, however, is that Belisarius and Antonina stood together throughout their marriage. Their relationship was remarkably stable, suffering only occasional arguments, and their partnership seems to have sustained them through military campaigns, political intrigue, and personal trials. Perhaps the successes of these two powerful people should be partly attributed to their union, which was the most important nonroyal marriage of the century.

APPENDIX I

Dramatis Personae

Amalasuntha: She was queen of the Ostrogoths, ruling as regent for her son
   Athalaric, 526–535. Proposed to cede Italy to Justinian before she was murdered
   by her cousin Theodahad.

Anastasios: The grandson of Theodora, perhaps the son of an illegitimate daughter
   of the empress. He was betrothed to Ioannina, the daughter of Belisarius and
   Antonina.

Antonina: Deposer of Pope Silverius, political operative, and supply-chain expert.
   Wife of Belisarius.

Belisarius: Duke of Mesopotamia, General of the East, Count of the Sacred Stables,
   and victor over the Persians, Vandals, and Goths. Husband of Antonina.

Bouzes: A fellow officer of Belisarius, he fought with the general at Mindouos (528)
   and Dara (530), and in 542 was disgraced with Belisarius for allegedly plotting
   during the plague. Restored to favor in 549 and still serving actively in 556.

Constantine: A fellow officer of Belisarius, he was a subordinate commander at
   the start of the first Italian campaign in 535. He fought in Tuscany in early 537.
   Belisarius had him arrested and executed for insubordination in 538.

Gelimer: He was king of the Vandals, 530–534. Belisarius defeated him at Ad
   Decimum and Tricamarum, and Gelimer surrendered himself in March 534.
   He marched as a captive in Belisarius' triumph in Constantinople in that
   same year.

Ildiger: The son-in-law of Antonina, married to a daughter whose name is unknown, but was from Antonina's previous marriage. He fought as an officer
   under Belisarius in the first Italian campaign.

Ioannina: The daughter, and only biological child of Belisarius and Antonina. She
   was betrothed to the grandson of Theodora, Anastasios.

John the Armenian: A member of the household staff of Belisarius who played a
   very prominent role in the campaign in Africa before being killed in an accident
   in late 533.

John the Cappadocian: Praetorian Prefect of the East, 531–532 and 532–541, and the most important civilian official in Justinian's government. He argued against the invasion of Vandal Africa and supplied poor quality bread for the expedition. Disgraced by the machinations of Antonina in May 541.

John the Glutton: A guardsman of Belisarius who commanded a raid in the East in 541, and in 542 betrayed Belisarius by accusing him of plotting for the event of Justinian's death. After this, served with Narses the eunuch until at least 552.

John the nephew of Vitalian: An important general in Italy who argued with Belisarius and supported Narses the eunuch. He married the daughter of Germanos, cousin of Justinian. Served with Narses in Italy until at least 553.

Justinian: He was Roman emperor, 527–565. A famous conqueror, builder, and lawgiver. He had known Belisarius at least as early as 526, and probably earlier.

Khusro I: He was king of the Persians, 531–579, succeeding his father, Kavad I. He first negotiated the Endless Peace with the Romans in 532, but broke it in 540 and led a devastating invasion of the Roman East, sacking Antioch. Belisarius turned him and his army back in 542.

Narses the Eunuch: The chamberlain of Justinian, 531–552, entrusted with important operations such as disinformation during the Nika Riot, reinforcements for Belisarius in Italy in the 530s, and eventually with command of the war in Italy in 552. Commanded in Italy up to 568. Served as a rival to Belisarius' influence.

Pharas: An army officer of Herul origin who fought with Belisarius in the East at the Battle of Dara in June 530 and in North Africa in 533/534. Captured Gelimer in March 534. Killed in the North African mutiny of Stotzas in 535.

Photios: The son of Antonina by a previous marriage. He fought as an officer under Belisarius in Italy and in the East and seems to have been expelled from the family in 541/542. Reappeared under the reign of Justin II as a monk/general and died around 585.

Procopius: The legal adviser and personal secretary of Belisarius. He accompanied Belisarius between 527 and 540, and later wrote both the *Wars* and the *Secret History*. Died around 554.

Silverius: He was pope, June 536–March 537. He was irregularly appointed by the Ostrogothic King Theodahad, and deposed by Belisarius and Antonina on suspicion of Ostrogothic sympathies.

Sittas: A fellow guardsman of Justinian with Belisarius in the 520s, he received rapid promotion to General of Armenia and then General of the Army in the Emperor's Presence. Married Komito, sister of Empress Theodora. Killed in combat in Armenia in 539.

Theodoric: He was king of the Ostrogoths, ruled in Italy 493–526. He was succeeded by his grandson Athalaric under the regency of his daughter Amalasuntha.

Theodahad: He was king of the Ostrogoths, 534–536. A cousin of Amalasuntha, whom he deposed and murdered. Offered to cede Italy to Justinian before changing his mind in 535. Killed by his own men in November 536.

Theodora: She was Roman empress, 527–548. She was famed for partnering with Justinian in ruling and showed particular care for the circumstances of women. A patron and friend of Antonina.

Theodosios: The adopted son of Belisarius and Antonina. He accompanied the two of them to Africa and Italy, but never seems to have been a soldier. Died of natural causes around 542.

Valerianos: A fellow officer of Belisarius, he fought with the general in North Africa (533), in the first Italian campaign (537), in the East (541) when he became General of Armenia, and in the second Italian campaign (548). He served until at least 559.

Vigilius: He was pope, March 537–June 555. He became pope with the support of Belisarius and Antonina. Maintained a close relationship with Belisarius through the 550s, when he spoke with Belisarius several times during his detention in Constantinople.

Vittigis: He was king of the Ostrogoths, 536–540, succeeding Theodahad. He failed to dislodge Belisarius during the siege of Rome (537–538), and surrendered Ravenna to Belisarius in 540.

Zabergan: He was a chieftain of the Kutrigurs in 558/559, when he led a raiding party into the Roman Empire. Belisarius defeated part of his forces at the Battle of Chiton in March 559.

APPENDIX 2

Timeline of Their Lives

Origins

ca. 495–500 Birth of Antonina

ca. 500–505 Birth of Belisarius

ca. 515 Birth of an unnamed daughter to Antonina

ca. 520 Birth of Photios to Antonina

ca. 520–525 Belisarius enters the guardsmen of the future emperor Justinian

Early Career

526 Belisarius and Sittas lead two raids into Persian Armenia

527 Belisarius appointed Duke of Mesopotamia. Belisarius hires Procopius

ca. 527–528 Belisarius and Antonina are married

528 Belisarius defeated at Battle of Mindouos

529 (April) Belisarius is appointed General of the East. Antonina remains in Constantinople

530 (June) Belisarius victor at Battle of Dara

531 (April 19) Belisarius is defeated at Battle of Callinicum

531 (Summer) Belisarius relieved of command and recalled to Constantinople

ca. 531–532 Birth of Ioannina to Antonina and Belisarius

532 (January) Belisarius assists in putting down the Nika Riot

The Great Years

ca. 532 Belisarius reinstated as General of the East

533 (June) Belisarius and Antonina adopt Theodosios. The three sail to North Africa

533 Belisarius defeats the Vandals at Ad Decimum and Tricamarum

534 Belisarius captures Gelimer and marches in a triumph in Constantinople

535 Belisarius and Antonina sail to Italy for the first time. Belisarius is consul

536 Belisarius and Antonina argue over Theodosios in Sicily. Belisarius captures Naples and Rome

537 Siege of Rome. Antonina and Belisarius depose Pope Silverius. Antonina leads a supply convoy to Rome

538 Belisarius executes Constantine. End of the siege of Rome. Belisarius rescues John at Rimini. Belisarius struggles with Narses

539 The Goths sack Milan and Narses is recalled by Justinian. Belisarius captures Osimo and Fiesole

540 Belisarius captures Ravenna. Belisarius and Antonina return to Constantinople

Trying Times

541 Antonina orchestrates the downfall of John the Cappadocian. Belisarius returns to the East and captures the fortress of Sisauranon. Belisarius and Antonina argue over Theodosios and Photios. Photios expelled from the family. The Justinianic Plague emerges in Egypt

ca. 542 Theodosios dies of dysentery

542 Belisarius repulses an invasion by Khusro, hears that Justinian is ill with the plague, and is relieved of his command and recalled to Constantinople

ca. 543 Belisarius is restored to imperial favor and Ioannina betrothed to Anastasios

544 Belisarius appointed Count of the Sacred Stables and dispatched to Italy with Antonina

545 Belisarius and Antonina remain in Ravenna awaiting reinforcements

546 Belisarius sails to Portus, but fails to relieve the siege of Rome when he suffers a stroke

547 Belisarius reoccupies an abandoned Rome and remains in the city until late fall

548 Belisarius sails to Crotone, retreats to Sicily, then meets up with John and Valerianos in the spring. Antonina travels to Constantinople and finds Theodora has died. Belisarius fails to relieve Rusciane and returns to Rome

549 Belisarius, relieved of his command, departs Rome and travels back to Constantinople, arriving perhaps in April. Belisarius and Antonina break the engagement of Ioannina with Anastasios

The Twilight

549 Belisarius reappointed General of the East. It is not clear if he travels to the eastern front

ca. 550–551 Belisarius retires from the army for good

551 (August) Belisarius and others sent to Pope Vigilius by Justinian

552 (January 28) Belisarius and others sent again to Pope Vigilius

553 (May) Pope Vigilius tries to send Belisarius and others to Justinian

ca. 554 Death of Procopius

559 (March) Belisarius takes up arms to lead a defensive action against Zabergan in Thrace

562 (December 5) Belisarius is disgraced when his staff are accused of being involved in a plot against Justinian

563 (July 19) Belisarius is restored to imperial favor

565 (March) Death of Belisarius. Antonina and Ioannina had perhaps predeceased him

565 (November 14) Death of Justinian

ca. 585 Death of Photios

APPENDIX 3

The Wealth of Belisarius

Belisarius was one of the wealthiest Romans of the sixth century, and while we do not have a list of the richest people of the period, he might have been the wealthiest person who was not a part of the imperial family. We do not have a reliable figure for the total of his wealth. Procopius relates that Belisarius' wealth "was excessive and more suited to a royal court." When Belisarius was in disgrace in 542, his wealth was confiscated by the crown, and although most of it was restored upon his rehabilitation, the emperor kept 3,000 pounds of gold. Because the *nomismata*, the standard gold coin of the age, was minted at the rate of 72 to the pound of gold, this sum amounted to 216,000 *nomismata*. This number clearly represents only a portion of Belisarius' wealth at the time, kept as some sort of fine. Since we do not know how large of a fine this was, it is not possible to estimate Belisarius' total wealth before the confiscation, but it was presumably larger than 3,000 pounds. How does this figure hold up compared to the wealth of other elite Romans? Earlier in the sixth century, a sum of just 1,000 pounds of gold was considered enough by the Emperor Anastasios to restore the finances of a leading senator named Paul. The top-ranked senators in Constantinople therefore probably enjoyed incomes around 1,000 pounds of gold per year. By way of comparison with government activities, Justinian paid 11,000 pounds of gold for the Endless Peace with Persia in 532, and his prefect Phocas, in the same year, laid out 4,000 pounds of gold to begin the construction of Hagia Sophia. So it is likely that Belisarius' total wealth was comparable to that of major imperial expenditures and dwarfed the income of other leading senators.[1]

Another way of approaching the wealth of Belisarius is to consider his official salary. Belisarius served as General of the East between 529 and 531, 532/533 and 542, and again between 549 and 550/551. The holder of this position was perhaps paid 11,520 *nomismata* (160 pounds of gold) per year. For comparison purposes, it seems that the poverty wage in Constantinople at the time was about 5 *nomismata* per year. Therefore, the salary of Belisarius as General of the East was 2,304 times the poverty wage. To put it in modern terms, consider that the federal poverty guideline in the United States in 2021 was $12,880. Using this as a baseline, Belisarius' salary as General of the East was the equivalent of approximately $30 million per year in 2021 money. Belisarius was quite rich just from his military salary. And yet, he clearly banked money from other sources, because the fine of a portion of his wealth kept in 542 by the emperor represented nearly 19 years' worth of his salary as a general, and Belisarius did not even hold the position of General of the East for 19 years.[2]

One more way of considering just how rich Belisarius was is to think about his expenses. He famously employed thousands of guardsmen (*bucellarii*) to supplement his armies throughout his career. These guards were typically mounted archers. A cavalryman in the sixth-century army probably earned 24 *nomismata* per year. To maintain 1,000 guardsmen, Belisarius would have to spend a minimum of 24,000 *nomismata* per year (or twice his annual income from his salary as general). This is, however, just a minimum figure. Guardsmen were the cream of the crop, the best soldiers available, so it is not inconceivable that their employers had to pay them more than what they would have received in regular army service. If this is not expensive enough, consider that at the height of the Gothic War in 540, Belisarius allegedly employed 7,000 guardsmen at once, which would have cost a staggering 168,000 *nomismata* a year at minimum. This sum equates to around 2,300 pounds of gold per year, more than double the annual income of a top-ranked senator. So even considering only his expenses on the salaries of his guardsmen, Belisarius was living well beyond his salary as General of the East, and at times, well beyond the annual income of other wealthy senators. He was not just rich, but legendarily and fantastically wealthy. That wealth had to come from somewhere beyond his official salary, which makes it likely that Belisarius siphoned off significant portions of both the Vandal and Ostrogothic royal treasuries upon his captures of Carthage and Ravenna.[3]

Notes

INTRODUCTION

1. Previous monographs of Belisarius include Hughes 2009, Chassin 1957, and Stanhope (Lord Mahon) 1848, and in addition the entry of Belisarius in Jones et al. 1971 (3.181–224) is very detailed, and the treatment of Belisarius in Stein 1949 is extensive. Far less has been written on Antonina, but see Evans 2011, Fisher 1978, and Evert-Kappesowa 1964. For analysis of marriage in the Roman world, see Neville 2019, Herrin 2013, and Cooper 2007.

2. On the argument over the term "Byzantine" and the naming of this empire, see the discussion and bibliography provided by Kaldellis 2019, 3–37, but compare Cameron 2014, 26–45 and 65–67. More recent discussion may be found in the *Byzantium and Friends* podcast, "Is it time to abandon the rubric 'Byzantium'?, with Leonora Neville" (February 11, 2021) and in Theodoropoulos 2021.

3. Pope Vigilius describes Antonina as his "most Christian" daughter in a letter described by both Victor of Tunnuna 542.1.28 and Liberatus, *Breviarium* 22.70. Procopius, *Wars* 1.18.23 describes Belisarius fasting on Holy Saturday. The pair also stood as godparents for Theodosios, with Belisarius himself participating in the baptism (Procopius, *Secret History* 1.16)

4. Justinian and Theodora have been the subject of many important studies. On Justinian, see Parnell 2020a, Heather 2018, Leppin 2011, Sarris 2006, Maas 2005, Meier 2004, Moorhead 1994, Barker 1966, and Rubin 1960. On Theodora, see Potter 2015, Evans 2011, Evans 2002, Harvey 2001, and Fisher 1978.

5. The career and life of Procopius are described by Greatrex 2014, Treadgold 2007, Börm 2007, Kaldellis 2004, and Cameron 1985. The position of an *assessor* like Procopius is described by Jones 1964, 1.511–512. Scholarly consensus about the dating of Procopius' works is well explained by the overviews in Cristini 2021 and Greatrex 2014.

6. The two passages are Procopius, *Wars* 2.19.26–46 and Procopius, *Secret History* 2.18–23. For more on this situation, see Chapter 6.

7. On reconciling Procopius with Procopius, see Greatrex 2014, 96, but compare Kaldellis 2004, 45, who argued that there was only one Procopius. In general, one of the arguments of Kaldellis 2004 is that Procopius disliked Justinian and Theodora

throughout his writing career, but only felt free to express that dislike openly in the *Secret History*. For Procopius' familiarity with Thucydides, see Pazdernik 1997, 2000, and 2015. On the audience for the *Wars*, see Treadgold 2007, 189. Procopius claims in *Wars* 8.1.1 that his work had appeared in "every corner of the Roman world," which is probably an exaggeration. The passage in which Procopius implies that he received Justinian's favor is Procopius, *Buildings* 1.1.4. Stewart 2016, 257–258, argues that the gender ideologies and relations presented in the *Wars* were probably accepted by its readers as normal.

8. Brubaker 2004b, 101, argues that the *Secret History* is invective to such an extent that it says nothing true about the main characters it denigrates, which goes a bit far. Treadgold 2007, 209, argues that the *Secret History* resembles a legal argument. The argument that Procopius wrote the *Secret History* in preparation for a revolution against Justinian is made by Signes Codoner 2005, esp. 55–57. That argument is modified by Börm 2015, 329–330, who suggests further that we do not necessarily need to believe that Procopius himself believed any of his own invective, only that he wanted others to think he believed it. That the *Secret History* is first mentioned by the 10th-century *Suda*: Croke 2019, 6 and n. 13; Jones et al. 1971, 3.1064.

9. For other arguments over the nature of Procopius' works and his reason for writing them, see the very recent Meier and Montinaro 2022, as well as Stewart 2020, Greatrex 2014, Kaldellis 2009, Cesaretti 2008, Brodka 2004, Kaldellis 2004, and Howard-Johnston 2000. My argument that Procopius' invective in the *Secret History* is based on historical truth is spun off from Henning Börm, who argued that "an invective which is completely detached from reality does not develop any force, and a talented writer such as Procopius was, of course, aware of this" (Börm 2015, 330). On the portrayal of Theodora, see Potter 2015, 25–30 and Evans 2002, 15.

CHAPTER 1

1. The occupations of Antonina's parents are described in Procopius, *Secret History* 1.11.
2. The nature of theatrical performances in the period: Mango 1981, 341–344; Roueché 2008, 680–682; and Puk 2014. Theodora and the geese: Procopius, *Secret History* 9.20–23. The connection to Leda and Zeus: Kaldellis 2010, 43 n. 43; Evans 2011, 33–34; and Betancourt 2020, 61. Examples of adultery in sixth-century theater: Potter 2015, 42–44. The popularity of *Hippolytus*: Bowersock 2006, 55–59. Theater bans: John Malalas, *Chronographia* 17.12 (522) and 18.41 (529).
3. On chariot racing in this period, see Kazhdan 1991, 1.412, and Parnell 2020b, 234–238. On the mobility of charioteers and Porphyrius in particular, see Cameron 1973, 133 and 221. On hippodromes, see Humphrey 1986, 442; Kazhdan 1991, 2.934; and Dagron 2011.
4. On the organization of the factions, see Cameron 1976, 5–73; Jones 1964, 2.1016–1019; Parnell 2014, 633–637; and Puk 2014, 146–147. For fandom in Byzantium at hippodrome and theater, see Tougher 2010 and Webb 2008. For ecclesiastical

condemnation, see John of Ephesus, *Ecclesiastical History* 5.17, and Severus of Antioch, *Hymn* 269 (as quoted by Potter 2015, 45). On the paradox of raunchy entertainment in a Christian society, see Smith 2019, 103–138.

5. For the professions of Antonina's mother on the stage (θυμέλη) and father as a charioteer, see Procopius, *Secret History* 1.11 (translations of the *Secret History* are from Kaldellis 2010 unless otherwise noted). On the equation of actresses and prostitutes in Roman law, see Potter 2015, 39–40. For the relatively low position of chorus singers of among actresses, see Evans 2011, 12, and the career progression Procopius charts for Theodora's acting career in *Secret History*, 9.11–13. On the necessity of women working, see Herrin 2013, 96–101. The tenth-century evidence for the cash bonuses received by charioteers comes from Constantine, *De Cerimoniis* 2.55: charioteers of the Reds and Whites (μικροπανῖται) receive 5 miliaresion (silver coins), while charioteers of the Blues and Greens (φακτιονάριοι) receive 8. In comparison, palace stewards (διαιτάριοι) receive between 5 and 8 miliaresion and subdeacons in Hagia Sophia receive 6. For further discussion of these figures and titles, see Potter 2015, 11; Dagron 2011, 111; and Cameron 1976, 12–13. For elite Roman disdain for entertainers, see Jones 1964, 2.1020, and Kazhdan 1991, 1.16.

6. On Thessaloniki, see Kazhdan 1991, 3.2071–2073, and Vacalopoulos 1963. On Constantinople, see Dagron 1974; Kazhdan 1991, 1.508–512; Bassett 2004; Croke 2005, 76; and Vespignani 2010.

7. For Antonina being sixty in 544, see Procopius, *Secret History* 4.41, but compare to Stein 1949, 2.285 n. 6, who says this accusation of Antonina's age is "probably a malicious exaggeration." Another example of Procopius' exaggeration is the claim that Justinian killed millions of people in his reign (*Secret History* 18.4). For more on Procopius' invective in general, see Börm 2015, and for invective about this issue in particular, see Evert-Kappesowa 1964, 61. For the betrothal of Ioannina, see *Secret History* 4.37. For the wooing of Antonina's granddaughter, see *Secret History* 5.33.

8. Scenario 1: see the life cycle of Roman childhood described in Kazhdan 1991, 1.420–421, and Herrin 2013, 83–85. Scenario 2: see Evans 2011, 12–13, and Herrin 2013, 99. For Theodora's early life, see Procopius, *Secret History* 9.8–14, and Potter 2015, 41. For Greek as the chief language in both Thessaloniki and Constantinople, see Jones 1964, 2.986. For the use of Latin in the empire and Latin-speaking populations in Constantinople, see Kazhdan 1991, 2.1183, and Croke 2005, 74–76.

9. Procopius, *Secret History* 1.12 describes Antonina learning from φαρμακευσί. Historians who have believed Antonina was herself an actress: Barker 1966, 75; Evans 2011, 11–12; Herrin 2013, 99; and Potter 2015, 95. Evert-Kappesowa 1964, 56, points out that Procopius does not develop the same outrageous stories for Antonina's youth as he did for Theodora's youth. Antonina using spells to control Belisarius: Procopius, *Secret History* 1.13 and 3.2. For the ancient trope of female sorcery, see Graf 1997, 46–47, 189–190. Antonina's ability to preserve water is described in Procopius, *Wars* 3.13.23–24 (see Chapter 3).

10. The claim that Antonina was the mother of many children: Procopius, *Secret History* 1.12. Antonina's first marriage and the age of Photios: Procopius, *Wars* 5.5.5 (translations of the *Wars* are from Kaldellis 2014 unless otherwise noted); Liberatus, *Breviarium* 22; John of Ephesus, *Ecclesiastical History* 3.1.32. Unnamed daughter married to Ildiger: *Wars* 4.8.24. Infant mortality: Kazhdan 1991, 1.420, and Herrin 2013, 84.

11. Procopius, *Secret History* 2.6–7. For more on the context of Belisarius claiming to have raised Photios, see Chapter 6. Stanhope (Lord Mahon) 1848, 49, speculates that Antonina's first marriage was to a respectable husband.

12. On the marriage of Justinian and Theodora and their use of the Blues, see Potter 2015, 86–91. Justinian's power and wealth in this period was solidified by his holding the office of General of the Army in the Emperor's Presence—see Jones et al. 1971, 2.646. This office would have paid handsomely—see Treadgold 1995, 152. For Theodora helping women as empress, see Procopius, *Wars* 7.31.11–14, *Secret History* 17.24–26, and Evans 2002.

13. Belisarius' hometown is mentioned in Procopius, *Wars* 3.11.21, and identified with Sapareva Banya by Jireček 1886, 71–72. For the size and history of ancient Germania, see Koritarov 1990. For the denigration of the families of Antonina, Theodora, and Justinian, see Procopius, *Secret History* 1.11, 9.1–8 and 6.1–3. The claim that Belisarius' parents were noble comes from Stanhope (Lord Mahon) 1848, 3–4, and the claim that Belisarius' father was a decurion comes from Hughes 2009, 20. See also Stewart 2021, 255–259. On the types of late Roman villas in the Balkans, see Mulvin 2004.

14. The case for the name Belisarius having Thracian roots is made by Detschew 1957, 48. On the survival of Thracian and prevalence of either Latin or Greek in the Balkan provinces, see Jones 1964, 2.986–987, 993–996, and the older analysis of Jireček 1911. For the use of both Latin and Greek in the army, see Rance 2010, 63–67, Jones 1964, 2.989; and comments about multilingualism of soldiers in Amory 1997, 102–108. Belisarius could have easily found people with whom to speak Latin in Constantinople as well, see Croke 2001, 79–93 and Croke 2005, 75.

15. The age of Belisarius is determined via comments in Procopius, *Wars* 1.12.21, and Agathias, *Histories* 5.15.7, 5.16.1. Modern estimates of Belisarius' age are found in Stanhope (Lord Mahon) 1848, 2–3; Jones et al. 1971, 3.182; and Hughes 2009, 19. Procopius insinuates Antonina was much older than Belisarius in *Secret History* 4.41.

16. On the *bucellarii*, the best work is Schmitt 1994; see also Jones 1964, 1.666, and Parnell 2017, 17–18, for the title δορυφόρῳ. For the raids of Belisarius and Sittas into Persarmenia, see Procopius, *Wars* 1.12.20–22, and for their dating to 526, see Greatrex 1998, 147–148. On Justinian's role in directing these operations, see Koehn 2018a, 221–223.

17. Belisarius appointed as commander of troops at Dara: Procopius, *Wars* 1.12.24. The *Dux Mesopotamiae* stationed at Dara: *Wars* 1.22.3. Procopius joins the staff

of Belisarius: *Wars*, 1.12.24. For Procopius' job, see Treadgold 2007, 179, and for the position of *assessor* more generally, see Jones 1964, 1.512. On the early career of Belisarius, see also Evans 2011, 64.

18. For Justinian's position as general, see Procopius, *Wars* 1.12.21, Koehn 2018a, and Jones et al. 1971, 2.646. We do not know if Belisarius regularly left his post at Dara in winter during the period 527–529, but he did leave the eastern front and return to Constantinople for winter later in his career, e.g., in 541: see Procopius, *Wars* 2.19.49 and Chapter 6.

19. Procopius describes Antonina as Belisarius' wife in 533 at *Wars* 3.12.2. Belisarius claims to have raised Photios at *Secret History* 2.6–7. For the birth of Ioannina, see Chapter 2. The marriage of Sittas and Komito and promotion of Sittas are described in John Malalas, *Chronographia* 18.10. For more on the marriage of Sittas and Komito, see Stewart Forthcoming. Evert-Kappesowa 1964, 57–58, suggests that the wedding of Belisarius and Antonina might have taken place in either 531 or 527.

20. A friendship between Theodora and Antonina is mentioned by John of Ephesus, *Ecclesiastical History* 3.1.32; cf. Whitby 2021, 10. Hughes 2009, 21 speculates that Justinian and Belisarius were close friends at this time, although he may overstate it. Evans 2011, 64, speculates that Antonina was "Theodora's crony" at this time, and he is certainly overstating it. For elite Roman men "marrying down," see Cooper 2007, 155–158. Procopius refers to Belisarius being infatuated with Antonina in *Secret History* 1.20, 3.1, and 4.41, and praises Belisarius' restraint in *Wars* 7.1.11. Evert-Kappesowa 1964, 62, also thinks Belisarius and Antonina were a love match.

21. Justinian and Theodora's love story is well described by Potter 2015, 1, 91–95. The law for the marriage of Justinian and Theodora is *Codex Iustinianus* 5.4.23.

CHAPTER 2

1. For Persian-Roman relations from Crassus to Julian, see Greatrex 1998, 8–10, and Bonner 2020, 16–23, 71–89. The great Roman-Persian peace: Greatrex 1998, 11–18. The war of 502: Procopius, *Wars* 1.7–9; Greatrex 1998, 76–115; and Bonner 2020, 151–158. Construction of Dara: Procopius, *Wars* 1.10.13–19; Greatrex 1998, 116–121; and Bonner 2020, 163. The refusal of Justin to adopt Khusro: Procopius, *Wars* 1.11; Greatrex 1998, 135–138; and Börm 2007, 313–325. The defection of Iberia and Lazica: Procopius, *Wars* 1.12.1–19, and Greatrex 1998, 139–147. On Christians in the Persian Empire and its client kingdoms, see Payne 2015.

2. On the connection of the raids of Belisarius and Sittas to the situation in the Caucasus, see Greatrex 1998, 147–148. On Libelarios' raid to Nisibis, see Procopius, *Wars* 1.12.23, and Greatrex 1998, 148–150, and on Arab raids around this time, see John Malalas, *Chronographia* 17.20. On the *limitanei*, see Parnell 2017, 14–16, and Isaac 1992. For an estimate of the number of soldiers commanded by the *Dux Mesopotomiae*, see Treadgold 1995, 51.

3. The sources for the campaign of 528: Procopius, *Wars* 1.13.2–8; John Malalas, *Chronographia* 18.26; and Pseudo-Zachariah, *Historia Ecclesiastica* 9.2. Rubin 1960, 264–265, proposes after Pseudo-Zachariah that there were two battles in 528, one at Thannuris and one at Mindouos (see also Jones et al. 1971, 3.183–184; Hughes 2009, 44–45; and Whitby 2021, 122–125, but compare Greatrex 1998, 156–159). It is unlikely that Belisarius had time in a single campaigning season (528) to attempt to fortify, and fight battles over, two different sites. Other battles or attempts to fortify, including at a site like Thannuris, could possibly have happened the previous year, although neither Procopius nor Malalas confirms that. The location of Mindouos, about 4 miles southeast of Dara, is cleverly proposed by Lillington-Martin 2012 (see also Lillington-Martin 2013, 603–606).

4. Only John Malalas, *Chronographia* 18.26, records the number of Persian troops involved in the battle (30,000). Treadgold 1995, 51, suggests that the two dukes of Phoenice might have had 14,000 soldiers between them, although it is unlikely they showed up at Mindouos with that full strength.

5. On Justinian perhaps not expecting the fortlet building at Mindouos to succeed, see Greatrex 1998, 156. Stanhope (Lord Mahon) 1848, 34, noted that Belisarius would not have been promoted if Justinian had blamed him for Mindouos.

6. The salary of a duke was about 1,582 *nomismata* (Treadgold 1995, 151, and *Codex Iustinianus* 1.27.2.20) while the salary of a general was about 11,520 *nomismata* (Treadgold, 1995, 152). For more on the wealth of Belisarius, see Appendix 3. Belisarius' promotion to general is described in Procopius, *Wars* 1.13.9; John Malalas, *Chronographia* 18.34; and Theophanes, *Chronicle* AM 6021. See Koehn 2018a, 223–225, on the promotion of Belisarius and its connection to Justinian's previous work as a general. For Hypatios, see Jones et al. 1971, 2.580.

7. The illustrious dignity of a general is described by Jones 1964, 1.378. Appointment via imperial codicil is explained by Jones 1964, 1.528–535. John Malalas, *Chronographia* 18.26, describes the harsh winter, suspension of hostilities, and dispatching of senators and their forces. Throughout this period, wars in Mesopotamia were rarely waged in winter, so even without the suspension of hostilities it might have been considered a safe time to be absent.

8. Procopius, *Secret History* 2.2, discusses Antonina accompanying Belisarius. The home of Belisarius and Antonina in Constantinople is mentioned in Procopius, *Wars* 1.25.12, 20–21.

9. That Ioannina cannot be older than 12 in circa 543 is established by Procopius, *Secret History* 4.37 (and see Chapter 1). Antonina departed with Belisarius in June 533: Procopius, *Wars* 3.12.1–2. Lillington-Martin Forthcoming suggests that Ioannina was born later, between 533 and 537. This later birth date for Ioannina would be consistent with the evidence of Procopius that she could not be older than 12 in 543, but is less likely given Antonina's more advanced age at the time (she would have been perhaps about 40 in 535) and the fact that Antonina was front and center in Procopius' narrative at the time but he says nothing about her

being pregnant or giving birth. Compare to Evert-Kappesowa 1964, 57, who argues Ioannina was born in 532. For Antonina being front and center in Procopius' various narratives of 535/536, see Chapter 4.

10. For more on the age and parentage of Photios and the unnamed daughter, see Chapter 1. On the ubiquity of domestic slaves in Byzantium and their role in families, see Leidholm 2022. Antonina's granddaughter was of marriageable age in 545: Procopius, *Secret History* 5.33. The role of mothers in educating their children: Herrin 2013, 91–96. Uriah the Hittite famously refused to spend the night at home with his wife Bathsheba while his comrades were engaged in war: see 2 Samuel 11.6–13. Evert-Kappesowa 1964, 58, also suggests personal reasons why Antonina must have been in Constantinople at this time.

11. Hermogenes arrived at Antioch on May 12: Theophanes, *Chronicle* AM 6021. On the lack of Roman desire to reignite hostilities at this time, see Stein 1949, 2.420, and Greatrex 1998, 160–165. Hermogenes' meeting with Kavad, and Kavad's demands: John Malalas, *Chronographia* 18.36, 44. The earthquake at Antioch in 528: John Malalas, *Chronographia* 18.27. On the history of Antioch in this period, see De Giorgi and Eger 2021, 190–234.

12. The movement of the army: Procopius, *Wars* 1.13.9. Rouphinos: Procopius, *Wars* 1.13.11, and John Malalas, *Chronographia* 18.50. Belisarius and Hermogenes share the command: Procopius, *Wars* 1.13.10. The possibility that Dara was undergoing repairs: Greatrex 1998, 170. The trench and the baths comment: Procopius, *Wars* 1.13.12–18. The location of the Battle of Dara, about 1.5 miles south of Dara itself: Lillington-Martin 2013, 604–606, although others locate the battle site just outside the walls of Dara, e.g., Whitby 2021, 128, and Greatrex 1998, 172. On the battle in general, see Greatrex 1998, 169–185, and Whately 2021, 52–56.

13. Numbers of each army and their dispositions: Procopius, *Wars* 1.13.13–24, and see Whately 2015, 396–398. The Persian attack on the Roman left wing: Procopius, *Wars* 1.13.25–28. The duels: Procopius, *Wars* 1.13.29–39, and see Leppin 2011, 131, for these duels, and Whately 2016, 166–171, on other duels in late antique battles.

14. For the letters and reinforcements, see Procopius, *Wars* 1.14.1–12, and commentary in Greatrex 2022, 1.14.1ff.

15. Belisarius addresses the army: Procopius, *Wars* 1.14.20–27. Stationing of army units: Procopius, *Wars* 1.14.28–33. The Battle of Dara is described by Procopius, *Wars* 1.14.34–54; John Malalas, *Chronographia* 18.50; and, more briefly, by Pseudo-Zachariah, *Historia Ecclesiastica* 9.3. Greatrex 1998, 184, describes Belisarius' victory at Dara as a "remarkable triumph" unequalled since 422.

16. For the Battle of Satala, see Procopius, *Wars* 1.15.1–17, and Greatrex 1998, 185–189.

17. The negotiations of 530 are reported in Procopius *Wars*, 1.16.1–10, and John Malalas, *Chronographia* 18.53–54. See also Greatrex 1998, 190–192. For Belisarius questioning the Samaritans, see John Malalas, *Chronographia* 18.54.

18. Persian invasion through Euphratesia: Procopius, *Wars* 1.17.1–2 and 1.18.1–3, and John Malalas, *Chronographia* 18.60. Size of Persian army: Procopius, *Wars* 1.18.1,

and Greatrex 1998, 195, but compare Rubin 1960, 185. Size and composition of Roman army: Procopius, *Wars* 1.18.5–7; John Malalas, *Chronographia* 18.60; and Whately 2015, 399–400 (compare to Hughes 2009, 59–60).

19. Greatrex 1998, 195–200, lays out the chronology of the campaign. The only source for the early campaign is John Malalas, *Chronographia* 18.60, which also records the disagreement between Sounikas and Belisarius. The demands of Roman officers to fight: Procopius, *Wars* 1.18.9–25. Greatrex 1998, 200, notes the possibility that officers might instigate their own attack without Belisarius.

20. The date of the Battle of Callinicum was Saturday, April 19, 531 (cf. Greatrex 1998, 201, contra Hughes 2009, 60, and Stanhope [Lord Mahon] 1848, 47, who both mistakenly date the battle to Sunday). Fasting: Procopius, *Wars* 1.18.23. For positioning of the two armies before the battle, see Procopius, *Wars* 1.18.26, 30, and John Malalas, *Chronographia* 18.60.

21. Two different accounts of the Battle of Callinicum are found in Procopius, *Wars* 1.18.26–50, and John Malalas, *Chronographia* 18.60. See interpretation in Rubin 1960, 286–287, and Greatrex 1998, 201–202 (who characterizes the attack on Sounikas and Simmas as diversionary). For the dense formation of infantry as a last line of defense, see Maurice, *Strategikon* 12.B.16, and Rance 2004, 280–284.

22. Procopius, *Wars* 1.18.50 suggests both sides had similar losses. Rubin 1960, 288, calls the Persian win a *Pyrrhussieg* (Pyrrhic victory), cf. Whitby 2021, 138. The inquiry of Konstantiolos: John Malalas, *Chronographia* 18.60–61. Emphases of Procopius' version: Procopius, *Wars* 1.18.4–50. Emphases of Malalas' version: John Malalas, *Chronographia* 18.60. Additional details are provided by Pseudo-Zachariah, *Historia Ecclesiastica* 9.4.

23. Differences on the aftermath of the battle are highlighted by Greatrex 1998, 206. Modern historians distrusting Procopius' version but accepting Malalas' uncritically: Jones et al. 1971, 3.186, and Hughes 2009, 63–64. But Greatrex 1998, 194–195, notes that suspicion of Procopius' account does not automatically make Malalas' version more trustworthy.

24. Konstantiolos reports to Justinian and the latter decides to sack Belisarius: John Malalas, *Chronographia* 18.60, confirmed also by Pseudo-Zachariah, *Historia Ecclesiastica* 9.6. Procopius, *Wars* 1.21.2, claims that Belisarius was recalled to be sent against the Vandals, but that was nearly two years away at this point, and is a transparent excuse to cover the sacking (see Cameron 1985, 158). Greatrex 1998, 194–195, suggests Malalas drew upon the report of Konstantiolos; see also Rubin 1960, 289. Belisarius' apparent inactivity during the inquiry: Greatrex 1998, 207.

25. The maxim is from Maurice, *Strategikon* 8.1.40. On Roman generals regularly being fired and reappointed in this period, see Parnell 2017, 83–96.

26. No source records Belisarius' activities between summer 531 and January 532. That he had his guardsmen with him is recorded by Procopius, *Wars* 1.24.40. *Chronicon Paschale* 621 names Belisarius as *magister militum* in January 532, an indication that he remained a general (although not General of the East) throughout this period.

The remaining engagements of the Roman-Persian war, the death of Kavad, and the pursuit of a negotiated peace with Khusro are covered by Greatrex 1998, 207–212. For Khusro's willingness to negotiate, see Börm 2007, 323–325.

27. The best modern account in English of the Nika Riot remains the masterful Greatrex 1997, but see also the more recent work of Meier 2003 and especially Pfeilschifter 2013, 178–210, for additional nuance. Sources for the Nika Riot: Procopius, *Wars* 1.24; John Malalas, *Chronographia* 18.71; *Chronicon Paschale* 620–629; Theophanes, *Chronicle* AM 6024; Pseudo-Zachariah, *Historia Ecclesiastica* 9.14; and Marcellinus Comes 532. Urban riots, especially when connected to hippodromes, were not at all uncommon in the sixth-century Roman world. See Parnell 2014 on riots in general and Parnell 2020b on the role of hippodromes in facilitating communication between emperor and people. For the use of the "Nika" chant before this riot, see Cameron 1973, 76–80.

28. The rioters burned down the headquarters of the city prefect: John Malalas, *Chronographia* 18.71, and the release of the convicts: Procopius, *Wars* 1.24.7. The rioters demand and receive the sacking of the three officials: Procopius, *Wars* 1.24.17, and John Malalas, *Chronographia* 18.71.

29. Greatrex 1997, 80–83, highlights the role of Justinian's incompetent vacillation in the escalation of the riot (compare Meier 2003, who argues that the vacillation was intentional rather than accidental). Belisarius and his guardsmen, here called a "troop of Goths," attack the rioters: John Malalas, *Chronographia* 18.71 and *Chronicon Paschale* 621. See Pfeilschifter 2013, 203–204, on the connection between "Goths" in this context and guardsmen. Greatrex 1997, 74, notes the difficulty of regular troops combating rioters in the open urban spaces.

30. The burning of central Constantinople: *Chronicon Paschale* 621–622 and John Malalas, *Chronographia* 18.71. The rush to Probos' house: *Chronicon Paschale* 622. The arrival of the Thracian soldiers: *Chronicon Paschale* 622–623. Hypatios and Pompey sent out: Procopius, *Wars* 1.24.19–21, and *Chronicon Paschale* 624. Pfeilschifter 2013, 191–194, argues that Hypatios and Pompey were sent out to make room in the palace for the newly arrived Thracian soldiers. Compare to the earlier argument of Greatrex 1997, 77–79. Justinian's appearance in the hippodrome with the Gospels: John Malalas, *Chronographia* 18.71 and *Chronicon Paschale* 623–624.

31. The acclamation of Hypatios: *Chronicon Paschale* 624 and John Malalas, *Chronographia* 18.71. Justinian contemplates flight and the speech of Theodora: Procopius, *Wars* 1.24.32–38; Theophanes, *Chronicle* AM 6024; and see Greatrex 1997, 78, and Potter 2015, 151–155.

32. The assault on the hippodrome: Procopius, *Wars* 1.24.40–54; John Malalas, *Chronographia* 18.71; *Chronicon Paschale* 626–627. The role of Narses: *Chronicon Paschale* 626 and see Brodka 2018, 37–46. Procopius plays up Belisarius' role in the attack and credits Justus and Boraides with seizing Hypatios (cf. Whitby 2021, 293). Both Malalas and the *Chronicon Paschale*, on the other hand, say that Belisarius seized Hypatios. Procopius likely exaggerates Belisarius' role in the slaughter (see

Brodka 2018, 51–53), as it seems clear from all three sources that Belisarius was tasked with arresting Hypatios, not with a general assault on the rioters. The execution of Hypatios and Pompey: Procopius, *Wars* 1.24.56.

33. The praise of Belisarius' regard for peasants: Pseudo-Zachariah, *Historia Ecclesiastica* 9.2, and Procopius, *Wars* 7.1.8. Contra to modern sensibilities, Procopius saw nothing wrong with the slaughter of the people in the hippodrome and thus wanted to connect his patron Belisarius to it (as suggested by Michael E. Stewart in a personal communication). On the death toll, see Stein 1949, 1.454 n. 2 and Greatrex 1997, 79, with dissenting view of Cameron 1976, 278.

CHAPTER 3

1. On the ups and downs of the careers of sixth-century generals, see Parnell 2012, 7–14.

2. On Belisarius' reappointment, see Jones et al. 1971, 3.187. *Codex Iustinianus*, Novel 155, is dated February 1, 533. Herrin 2020, 152, also connects Belisarius' appointment to Justinian's gratitude. For the Endless Peace, see Procopius, *Wars* 1.22.16–18. For the lengthy negotiations that led to the peace, as well as its terms, see Greatrex 1998, 213–218.

3. Historians who imagined Justinian to have a grand plan of reconquest: Jones 1964, 1.269–278; Barker 1966, 131–134; Norwich 1989, 205–227; Treadgold 1997, 178–184. For a recent summary of the revisionist position, see Heather 2018, 114–121, but also see Moorhead 1994, 63ff., and Leppin 2011, 149–158. The law of Justinian which describes bringing freedom to North Africa from the enemy Vandals is *Codex Iustinianus* 1.27.1.

4. For a summary of Vandal relations with the Eastern Romans, see Stein 1949, 1.319–327, 358–364 and 2.251–253, 311–313, and Treadgold 1997, 92–94, 152–153. See also Procopius, *Wars* 3.8.1–29.

5. For the Vandal persecution, see *Codex Iustinianus* 1.27.1.1–4. It is likely that at least some of the religious rhetoric of that law was not developed until after the Roman victory in this campaign, see Conant 2012, 306–310, and Cameron 1993. On the coup of Gelimer, see *Wars* 3.9.1–8, and Heather 2018, 116–7, 133–4. For the letters between Gelimer and Justinian, see *Wars* 3.9.9–24. On Justinian's friendly relations with Hilderic, see Conant 2012, 313–314.

6. John the Cappadocian's warning: Procopius, *Wars* 3.10.1–18. Whitby 2021, 177, suggests Justinian encouraged the revolt of Godas. The dream of the bishop: Procopius, *Wars* 3.10.18–34. Compare to a different religious vision recorded by Victor of Tunnuna 534.1.

7. On Justinian's requirement for loyalty in his generals, see Parnell 2012, 14–15. Belisarius receives the authority of an emperor: Procopius, *Wars* 3.11.18–20.

8. The makeup of Belisarius' expedition is described in Procopius, *Wars* 3.11.2–17. On the *foederati*, see Parnell 2017, 16–17; Koehn 2018b, 67–114; and Whately 2021, 108–114. For the size of the Army of the East, see Treadgold 1995, 60. Procopius

later mentions a unit of 300 of Belisarius' own guardsmen (*Wars* 3.17.1) and a group of 800 guardsmen, who might have all been Belisarius' or might not (*Wars* 3.19.23). For the increase in size of Belisarius' guards, see Chapter 5. For the size of the armies at Dara and Callinicum, see *Wars* 1.13.23, 1.18.5–7, and Whitby 2000, 292–93. Leo's Vandal expedition: *Wars* 3.6.1–2, Treadgold 1995, 189–192.

9. The naming of the expedition's officers: Procopius, *Wars* 3.11.5–17. The passage calls to mind the catalogue of ships and commanders in the second book of the *Iliad*.

10. The arrival of Heraclius' flotilla in 610: Kaegi 2003, 45–49. The blessing of Epiphanios: Procopius, *Wars* 3.12.1–2. The adoption of Theodosios: Procopius, *Secret History* 1.15–16. Evans 2011, 82, argues that Theodosios was baptized as an Arian Christian, but it is more likely that Theodosios came from an Arian family but now received Orthodox baptism. Given Belisarius' later close connections to the papacy, the general himself was most likely Orthodox (see Chapter 4). *Wars* 3.12.2 is explicit that the newly baptized Christian was one of the soldiers (τινα στρατιωτῶν). Theodosios, who is mentioned nowhere in the *Wars*, is never described in the *Secret History* as a soldier, only as a youth (τις νεανίας) in *Secret History* 1.15. That he was a young teenager at the time of his adoption is a hypothesis derived from comparing his description here (a youth) with that of the young Belisarius and Sittas (νεανία μὲν καὶ πρῶτον ὑπηνήτα, youths with their first beards) in *Wars* 1.12.21. Perhaps the lack of a beard for Theodosios here means he was slightly younger than a youth with his first beard. For further argument that Theodosios was not a soldier, and the implications of that, see Chapter 6.

11. Belisarius and Antonina set sail: Procopius, *Wars* 3.12.2. This is the first mention of Antonina in the *Wars* and could be taken as evidence that Belisarius married her just before the expedition set sail, but see Chapter 1 for an argument for an earlier marriage. Agrippina the Elder: Tacitus, *Annals* 1.69. Munatia Plancina: Tacitus, *Annals* 2.55. Praiecta: Procopius, *Wars* 4.24.3. Women in the sixth century: Brubaker 2004a. On female rarity, Whately Forthcoming argues that Roman campaign armies were primarily a male space.

12. Criticisms of their travel together: Procopius, *Secret History* 2.2 and 5.27. Casual references to Antonina's presence with Belisarius on campaign may be found in Procopius, *Wars* 3.20.1, 5.18.43, 6.7.3–4, and 7.28.4. Praiecta: Procopius, *Wars* 4.24.3. For more on the opinion of sixth-century Romans on the place of military wives, see Parnell 2022.

13. The departure from Constantinople occurred around the summer solstice, so in mid-June (Procopius, *Wars* 3.12.1). Both the Loeb and Kaldellis translations mistranslate θερινὰς τροπὰς as spring equinox. Compare Dijkstra and Greatrex 2009, 259 n. 113, who suggest the fleet actually departed in late June based on a passage from the chronicle of Michael the Syrian. I prefer Procopius' dating. For calculations of the length of travel in the ancient Roman world, including for the trip from Constantinople to Carthage, see http://orbis.stanford.edu/. The execution of the Huns: Procopius, *Wars* 3.12.6–22. The word Procopius uses for the

punishment (ἀνεσκολόπισε) is usually translated as impaled, but there is an argument to be made that the murderers were instead hanged from a *furca* in a form of crucifixion; see Cook 2015, 296–307. I am indebted to Toby Groom for this reference.

14. For the moldy bread incident and Antonina's water preservation, see Procopius, *Wars* 3.13.5–24. I am indebted to biologist Peter Avis and geologist Kristin Huysken for the scientific observations about Antonina's water preservation.

15. The spying of Procopius: Procopius, *Wars* 3.14.1–13, and on the friend's knowledge of the Vandalic navy's whereabouts, see Merrills 2017, 501–502. The last leg of the journey to Caput Vada: Procopius, *Wars* 3.14.14–17.

16. The deliberation of the officers and landing in Africa: Procopius, *Wars* 3.15. Belisarius and other sixth-century generals relied heavily on social networks of trusted officers to help them run their armies. Generalship in this period was at least partly collaborative (Parnell 2015a). The date of landfall in Africa is unknown, but was perhaps around September 1, based upon the distance between Caput Vada and Carthage, the pace of the army's march (*Wars* 3.17.7), and its arrival at Ad Decimum, south of Carthage, on September 13 (*Wars* 3.21.17–24).

17. The lecture of Belisarius and the capture of Syllectum: Procopius, *Wars* 3.16.1–11. The letter to the Vandals: *Wars* 3.16.12–14. Other historians have imagined a more limited goal than even the restoration of Hilderic: Roger Scott thought that Belisarius' primary job in this campaign was simply to "show the flag," see Scott 2012, VI, 8–10. The marching formation adopted by Belisarius had multiple benefits, see Stewart 2020, 109, and Maurice, *Strategikon* 7.1.11. For the pace of the march, see *Wars* 3.17.7. The route of the march: *Wars* 3.17.1–10. The actions of Gelimer and Ammatas: *Wars* 3.17.11–15.

18. The date of the battle is determined by the comment of Procopius, *Wars* 3.21.17–24, that the battle occurred the day before the Feast of St. Cyprian, which was at this time held on September 14. The length of the march is determined by dividing the distance between Caput Vada and Ad Decimum by the pace, which Procopius says was 80 stades a day (*Wars* 3.17.7). Seven stades was the equivalent of one Roman mile, and one Roman mile was roughly equivalent to 0.91 modern mile (see calculations in Greatrex 2022, Appendix 2). Thus 80 stades a day was approximately 10.4 modern miles per day. The victory of John over Ammatas: *Wars* 3.18.1–11. The defeat of Gibamund: *Wars* 3.18.12–19.

19. The initial stages of the Battle of Ad Decimum: Procopius, *Wars* 3.19.1–24. The apparent indecision of Gelimer: *Wars* 3.19.25, compare the analysis of Hughes 2009, 94. The conclusion of the battle: *Wars* 3.19.29–33.

20. The arrival of the infantry and the march to Carthage: Procopius, *Wars* 3.20.1–16. The language of Procopius ("the infantry with the wife of Belisarius came up") does not suggest that Antonina commanded the infantry on this march. This would have been quite unprecedented, although it is not impossible given her apparent authority over Belisarius' officers later in Italy (see Chapter 5). Evans 2011, 88,

says Antonina "brought up the infantry," which stretches the meaning of the passage. Praise for the peaceful occupation of Carthage: *Wars* 3.21.8. Carthage made safe: *Wars* 3.21.11–16, 23.19–21.

21. The reconnaissance of Diogenes: Procopius, *Wars* 3.23.1–18. On the use of personal guards in general during this period, see Schmitt 1994. On the assignment of guardsmen to critical missions on campaigns, see Parnell 2017, 163–165.

22. For these events and letters, see Procopius, *Wars* 3.24–25, quote at 3.25.13. The Vandals reunited and the outreach to the Berbers: *Wars* 3.25.1–9.

23. Procopius, *Wars* 4.1.1–2.7.

24. The disposition of the armies for the Battle of Tricamarum: Procopius, *Wars* 4.2.8–3.9. The strategies at the beginning of the battle mirror the instructions for first- and second-line troops in Maurice, *Strategikon* 3.12 and 3.15. Compare to discussion in Heather 2018, 52–54. The conclusion of the battle and storming of the camp: Procopius, *Wars* 4.3.10–28.

25. The pursuit of Gelimer and death of John: Procopius, *Wars* 4.4.1–19. John's epitaph: *Wars* 4.4.20. Pharas ordered to besiege Gelimer: *Wars* 4.4.22–32.

26. The dispatch of officers to seize Vandal lands: Procopius, *Wars* 4.5.1–10. On Belisarius' seizure of ports and islands, see the analysis of Lillington-Martin 2018, 170–179, compare Whitby 2021, 187 n. 26. Lilybaeum: Procopius, *Wars* 4.5.11–25, and for its history see 3.8.11–13.

27. The negotiations between Gelimer and Pharas: Procopius, *Wars* 4.6. On the interesting letters of Gelimer and Pharas and their implications, see Pazdernik 2006, 175–206, and Parnell 2015b, 814–820. The surrender of Gelimer: Procopius, *Wars* 4.7.

28. Procopius, *Secret History* 1.19. On corruption and extortion by Roman public officials of the time, see Jones 1964, 1.398–401, and Kelly 2004, 65–68. Evert-Kappesowa 1964, 63, imagines that Belisarius would have found such corruption quite natural. Belisarius was staggeringly wealthy after the Vandal War. He paid for expensive celebrations as consul in Constantinople (Procopius, *Wars* 4.9.15–16) and Syracuse (*Wars* 5.5.18), and by 540 he was allegedly maintaining 7,000 personal guardsmen at his own expense (*Wars* 7.1.20). On the wealth of Belisarius, see Appendix 3.

29. Scholars who accept Procopius' accusation as true: Gibbon 1776–1789, 4.204–205; Stanhope (Lord Mahon) 1848, 320–322, 426–427; Stein 1949, 2.286; Treadgold 2007, 182; Evans 2011, 82ff. More could be cited. Criticisms of Antonina's passion and Belisarius' infatuation: Procopius, *Secret History* 1.18, 1.20. On the nature of these smears, see Fisher 1978, 269–274; Cameron 1985, 70–74; James 2001, 16–17; and Neville 2019, 5–21. Leslie Brubaker's comment about Theodora, that Procopius made her "an ideal type, the perfect anti-woman, with all the qualities that late Roman culture valued in a woman inverted" (Brubaker 2004b, 94) also applies here to Antonina. The slander of the affair is explored in more detail in Chapters 4 and 6. On the wealth of Belisarius, see Appendix 3.

30. The accusations against Belisarius: Procopius, *Wars* 4.8.1–5. The decision to return: Procopius, *Secret History* 18.9; *Codex Iustinianus* 1.27.2.13–15 (which also describes the military commands Belisarius was required to establish in Africa). Procopius describes the beginning of the Vandal-Berber wars in *Wars* 3.8.1–9.8. The Romans would fight the Berbers long after Belisarius' departure (*Wars* 4.10ff.).

31. On the Roman triumph in general, see Beard 2007. For analysis of Belisarius' triumph in particular, see Beard 2007, 318–328, and Börm 2013, 63–91. Procopius describes the triumph: *Wars* 4.9.1–10. "Vanity of vanities" occurs repeatedly throughout Ecclesiastes, but first at 1.2. Perhaps Procopius was also thinking about Ecclesiastes 2.1–11, in which the author describes the futility of indulging himself by acquiring wealth and power. On Procopius' depiction of Gelimer, see Knaepen 2001, 383–403. It is worth noting that likely no one could hear Gelimer in the roar of the crowd, so this story is probably apocryphal. Belisarius and Gelimer prostrate before Justinian: Procopius, *Wars* 4.9.11–14, and see Pazdernik 2006 on the theme of servitude implied here.

32. The earliest contemporary dating for Belisarius' rank of patrician is 536 (Jones et al. 1971, 3.193–194). Antonina is also described as patrician in multiple sources as early as 537, including Procopius, *Secret History* 3.16; *Liber Pontificalis* 60; and Liberatus, *Breviarium* 22. If they were patricians by 536/7, the most likely reason for their promotion to this rank is the victory in Africa, so their elevation can be relatively safely dated to the second half of 534 (when they returned to Constantinople) or January 535 (when Belisarius entered into his consulship). For an overview of senatorial ranks, see Jones 1964, 1.528. The consular procession of Belisarius: Procopius, *Wars* 4.9.15–16.

CHAPTER 4

1. Procopius, *Wars* 5.5.6–7

2. Procopius, *Wars* 5.4.12–31. For Amalasuntha's difficult position and offer to Justinian, see *Wars* 5.3.10–12, 28. For alternative takes on Justinian's reasons for attacking first North Africa and Italy, see Heather 2018, 114–121, 147–153, and Lillington-Martin 2018, 170–179. Marcellinus Comes 476.2, and see Watts 2021, 122–125, for the idea that this might have reflected Justinian's own views.

3. The orders of Belisarius and number of his troops: Procopius, *Wars* 5.5.1–7. The actions of Peter and Mundus: *Wars* 5.6. Whitby 2021, 211, also argues that Justinian hoped for a peaceful transfer of power. Compare with Scott 2012, XIII, 27, who thinks that Belisarius' "7,000" (*sic*) troops were intended to completely drive the Goths from Italy. Sicily was well worth owning both as a revenue-generating island and as part of Justinian's strategy of controlling islands and trade routes in the western Mediterranean, see Lillington-Martin 2018, 175–177.

4. The enumeration of Belisarius' army: Procopius, *Wars* 5.5.2–4. 500–1,000 guardsmen was a relatively common complement for a prominent general in this period (Schmitt 1994, 162–163). We also know Belisarius had somewhere around this number by 537, when he is recorded using groups of 200 and 300 of his guardsmen in the siege of Rome (Procopius, *Wars* 5.27.1–14). On the later increase in size of Belisarius' unit of guardsmen to allegedly 7,000, see *Wars* 7.1.20. The other commanders probably also had guardsmen, though in smaller numbers: Whitby 2021, 210, suggests this could have brought the total expedition to nearly 10,000 men. The quote about Photios: Procopius, *Wars* 5.5.5. For Procopius foreshadowing use of names elsewhere, see Whately 2016, 125–131. On Belisarius' social network in Italy, see Parnell 2015a, 122–124.

5. The Vandal campaign and Antonina: Procopius, *Wars* 3.11.2–12, 3.12.2. We can be sure Antonina was present in 535 because she is later recorded in Sicily (Procopius, *Secret History* 1.15–27) and Rome (Procopius, *Wars* 5.18.43) without being mentioned as just arriving from Constantinople. So almost certainly she had simply been with Belisarius the whole time. On the connection between military matters and masculinity in this period, see Stewart 2016, 43–61.

6. The calculation of travel time between Constantinople and Sicily comes from http://orbis.stanford.edu/. Belisarius' subjugation of Sicily: Procopius, *Wars* 5.5.12–19.

7. Procopius, *Wars* 5.6.6–27. Compare with Frankforter 1996, 51–54, who argues that Procopius lies about all of this and Theodahad had no intention of ceding Italy but instead expected Justinian's recognition of his government.

8. Procopius, *Wars* 4.14.5–6. A popular recent treatment of the Late Antique Little Ice Age and its impact is Harper 2017, 249–259, but see Haldon et al. 2018a, 4–5. For the scientific perspective, see Büntgen et al. 2016.

9. The opening stages of the mutiny in Africa: Procopius, *Wars* 4.14.7–15.49. The mutiny would last years, with profound consequences for Roman control of the region. Jones et al. 1971, 3.1061, speculates that Procopius was in Carthage at the time on a mission for Belisarius. Ildiger had been present in Africa since 534; he is left in charge of Carthage at Procopius, *Wars* 4.15.49. The Sicilian mutiny is described briefly: *Wars* 4.15.48, compare the fanciful role for Antonina envisioned by Chassin 1957, 99. Lillington-Martin and Stewart 2021, 289, propose that Theodahad might have incited the mutiny in Sicily. The victory of the Goths in Dalmatia, Theodahad's response, and Justinian's order to Belisarius: Procopius, *Wars* 5.7.1–26.

10. The quote about Antonina's lust: Procopius, *Secret History* 1.21. The story about Makedonia and the two slaves: *Secret History* 1.21–27.

11. On the gender-specific smearing of Antonina in the *Secret History*, see Fisher 1978, 269–274; Cameron 1985, 70–74; James 2001, 16–17; and Neville 2019, 5–21. See Brubaker 2004b, 94, about similar slanders of Theodora. Procopius' absence: Procopius, *Wars* 4.14.39. The slander of Antonina might also be compared to the slander of Justinian in the *Secret History*. In his claim that Justinian was a

demon, Procopius provides several anecdotes (just as he does of the alleged affair of Antonina), without naming witnesses or claiming himself to have witnessed demonic activity (*Secret History* 12.14–32). The quote of Constantine: Procopius, *Secret History* 1.24. For the death of Constantine, see Chapter 5.

12. Invective working best when not easily falsifiable: Börm 2015, 330. Theodosios' wealth: Procopius, *Secret History* 1.32–33. Of course, Theodosios had not yet been to the palace of Ravenna at this point in the campaign. The *Secret History* was written around 548–550 with the benefit of hindsight. So in 536 his pilfered wealth must have come only from the palace of Carthage. Antonina's claim in Carthage: Procopius, *Secret History* 1.19. The arguments over Theodosios reach their conclusion in Chapter 6.

13. Procopius, *Wars* 5.8.1–4. On Ebrimuth's desertion, see also Jordanes, *Getica* 60.30–39, and Lillington-Martin and Stewart 2021, 287–288. A note on orthography: in this chapter as well as in Chapters 5 and 7, the names of Italian cities are rendered as they are spelled today if they are still inhabited (so Reggio rather than Rhegium, as Belisarius would have called it, and Milan rather than Mediolanum).

14. The debate over the surrender of Naples: Procopius, *Wars* 5.8.5–45. Preparations for the assault through the aqueduct: *Wars* 5.9.8–21. The conquest of Naples: *Wars* 5.9.22–10.37. Procopius might have deliberately understated the scale of slaughter at Naples, which is described in vivid detail in *Liber Pontificalis* 60.3.

15. Procopius, *Wars* 5.11.1–28. On Theodahad in general and the reasons for his demise in particular, see Vitiello 2014. On Vittigis' decision not to personally defend Rome at this point, see Stewart 2020, 19–20.

16. The entry into Rome: Procopius, *Wars* 5.14.14. On this interesting remark about the significance of this entry and other aspects of Roman memory of the fall of the Western Roman Empire in 476, see Kruse 2019. For Procopius, charging that barbarian kings allowed the city walls in their kingdoms to fall into disrepair was a way of showing that they did not care about urban life, see Merrills 2022, 185. For more on Belisarius' relationship with Rome, see Chapters 5 and 7.

17. Procopius, *Wars* 5.15–16. On the impossibly high number for the Gothic army, see Whately 2019, 266–269.

18. The fortification of the Salarian Bridge: Procopius, *Wars* 5.17.13–14, Lillington-Martin 2013, 616–621. Belisarius battles the Goths: Procopius, *Wars* 5.17.15–20, 5.18.1–29. A good modern account of the siege of Rome may be found in Whately 2019, 265–284.

19. Antonina persuades Belisarius to eat: Procopius, *Wars* 5.18.43. On her presence being unusual, see the discussion of the few other wives who accompanied their husbands on campaign in previous Roman history in Chapter 3.

20. Officers and gates: Procopius, *Wars* 5.19.1–18. Belisarius' defiance: *Wars* 5.20.18. It has been argued that these actions and speeches recorded by Procopius are an

attempt to portray the Italians as a passive, helpless people caught in a dispute be-tween the more martial Romans and Goths (Stewart 2017, 483–486).

21. For this battle, see Procopius, *Wars* 5.22–23. Gothic casualties: Procopius, *Wars* 5.23.26 and see Whately 2019, 267, and Whitby 2021, 223 n. 45.

22. Procopius, *Wars* 5.24.1–21. On Procopius' use of numbers here and elsewhere, see Whately 2019; Whately 2015; and Treadgold 2007, 210–218.

23. Procopius, *Wars* 5.25.3 mentions the θεράπαινα of the soldiers, and see Chassin 1957, 112, who notes the contrast between the other women being sent away and Antonina remaining.

24. Procopius, *Wars* 5.25.13, and Procopius, *Secret History* 1.14. In the latter, Procopius pledges to explain the deposition of Silverius in detail "in a later book," a promise he never kept.

25. *Liber Pontificalis* 60.7–8, trans. Raymond Davis, *The Book of Pontiffs*, 3rd edition (Liverpool: Liverpool University, 2001). For the dating of the *Liber*, see Richards 1979, 131–132; McKitterick 2016, 247.

26. Liberatus, *Breviarium* 22.22–25, 65–66, and 68–73, ed. E. Schwartz, *Abrégé de l'histoire des nestoriens et des eutychiens* (Paris: CERF, 2019), my translations. Victor of Tunnuna 542.1.21–23 and 28, ed. T. Mommsen, *MGH AA*, vol. XI, my translations.

27. Marcellinus Comes 537.1. Marcellinus finished the *Chronicle* in 534, and the portions after that year, including this passage, were compiled by an anonymous continuator. See Croke 2001. Procopius complained endlessly about Justinian and Theodora working together, see for example *Secret History* 4.21, 10.13, 14.8, 17.27, and 30.21–26. On Theodora's role in ecclesiastical affairs in Constantinople, see Potter 2015, 166–177. On an increasing acceptance of the involvement of imperial women in such matters, see Hillner 2019, 396–406.

28. On Monophysitism, see Frend 1972. On the Three Chapters controversy, see Richards 1979, 131–132, and further analysis in Chapter 8. The banishment of senators during the siege: Procopius, *Wars* 5.25.14, and see Evert-Kappesowa 1964, 69. The irregular appointment of Silverius: *Liber Pontificalis* 60.1.

29. *Liber Pontificalis* 61.2.

CHAPTER 5

1. Procopius, *Wars* 5.26.

2. The arrival of reinforcements and the first three sallies: Procopius, *Wars* 5.27.1–14. As Peter Heather has said about the Vandals, the Goths were "fighting a sixth-century war with a fifth-century army" (Heather 2018, 146). Vittigis' emulation of the tactic: Procopius, *Wars* 5.27.15–29.

3. Procopius, *Wars* 5.28–29.

4. 67 engagements: Procopius, *Wars* 6.2.37. The dispatch of Procopius and three small forces: *Wars* 6.4.1–8.

5. Antonina goes to Naples: Procopius, *Wars* 6.4.6. Antonina "assists" Procopius: *Wars* 6.4.20. Compare Whitby 2021, 225–226, who manages to describe this resupply operation without mentioning Antonina at all. As noted in the Introduction, it is possible that Procopius wrote the *Secret History* to ingratiate himself to an anti-Justinian (and therefore anti-Belisarius) clique, but anger at Antonina for this moment might have still molded the way he chose to frame his invective.

6. The arrival of the reinforcements and the covering engagement: Procopius, *Wars* 6.5. On the career of John, the nephew of Vitalian, see the entry for Ioannes 46 in Jones et al. 1971, 3.652–661, and Cosentino 2016, 121–122.

7. Procopius, *Wars* 6.6, 6.7.13.

8. Procopius, *Wars* 6.7.4–12.

9. The arrival of Ildiger: Procopius, *Wars* 6.7.15. The expedition of John: Procopius, *Wars* 6.7.25–34. Belisarius had sent 300 of his guards as one of the sallies in April 537 (Procopius, *Wars* 5.27.11). According to Procopius, the number of guards employed by Belisarius would eventually reach 7,000 by 540 (*Wars* 7.1.18–21). Even for a man of Belisarius' wealth, it is likely that he could have sustained such a large number of guards only on a short-term basis (See Appendix 3). On the plausibility of this figure, see Parnell 2012, n. 40.

10. Procopius, *Wars* 6.8.

11. Antonina's alleged hatred of Constantine: Procopius, *Secret History* 1.24–5 (and see Chapter 4). Antonina pushes for Constantine's execution: Procopius, *Secret History* 1.28–29. Evert-Kappesowa 1964, 68, finds the accusation ridiculous, pointing to the long period between Constantine's alleged slander of Antonina and his death. For the literary trope of powerful women carrying long grudges, see the caricature of Theodora in Procopius, *Secret History* 15.3–5, and Brubaker 2004b, 91. Marcellinus Comes 538.2.

12. Belisarius' social network: Parnell 2015a, 116–117. The reaction to Constantine's death: Procopius, *Secret History* 1.30. On the audience of the *Secret History* as men who were opposed to Justinian (and thus to Belisarius as well), see the Introduction.

13. Attempts to break into Rome: Procopius, *Wars* 6.9. John seizes Rimini: *Wars* 6.10.1–10.

14. The end of the siege of Rome: Procopius, *Wars* 6.10.13. Belisarius' promise not to surrender: *Wars* 5.20.18. Belisarius attacks the retreating Goths: *Wars* 6.10.14–20. John's insubordination: *Wars* 6.11. The inscription naming Belisarius is described in Jones et al. 1971, 3.223. It must date to about this time because it was the first opportunity to repair the aqueduct after Vittigis cut it in 537 (Procopius, *Wars* 5.19.13). Rimini and Milan besieged: *Wars* 6.12.

15. The capture of Todi and Chiusi: Procopius, *Wars* 6.13.1–4. Reinforcements under Narses: *Wars* 6.13.16–18. The war council: *Wars* 6.16.1–17.

16. The Rimini rescue operation: Procopius, *Wars* 6.16.21–24. The insubordination of Narses: *Wars* 6.18. Compare Brodka 2018, 86–92, who blames Belisarius for

not being willing to share power with Narses. The capture of Urbino: Procopius, *Wars* 6.19.

17. The Milan disaster: Procopius, *Wars* 6.21. Compare Brodka 2018, 101–102, who places the blame for this incident on Belisarius being too passive rather than on insubordination of John and slow transmission of orders. Whitby 2021, 229, argues that Belisarius was more cautious than Narses. The recall of Narses: Procopius, *Wars* 6.22.4. Chassin 1957, 141, imagines (probably fancifully) that Antonina kept Belisarius apprised of his enemies at the court, including Narses.

18. The siege of Fiesole and Osimo: Procopius, *Wars* 6.23.1–5. The inaction of Vittigis: *Wars* 6.24. The Frankish incursion: *Wars* 6.25. The surrender of Fiesole and Osimo: *Wars* 6.27.

19. On the history of Ravenna, see Herrin 2020 and Deliyannis 2010, and on its walls, see Christie and Gibson 1988. Negotiations with Vittigis: Procopius, *Wars* 6.28. Justinian's proposal: *Wars* 6.29.1–2. Vittigis and the Persians: *Wars* 6.22.17–20.

20. The frustration of Belisarius and the offer of the Goths: Procopius, *Wars* 6.29.3–20. Belisarius' deception and the sending away of the officers: *Wars* 6.29.21–30. Belisarius occupies Ravenna: *Wars* 6.29.31–41.

21. For these events, see Procopius, *Wars* 6.30. Whitby 2021, 303–304, concurs that the proposed treaty would not have resulted in a lasting peace.

22. Procopius, *Wars* 7.1.1–22. The estimate of the travel time between Ravenna and Constantinople is from http://orbis.stanford.edu/. On the decision to not grant Belisarius a triumph in 540, see Börm 2013. The Chalke mosaic: Procopius, *Buildings* 1.10.16, and see commentary by Herrin 2020, 158–159.

CHAPTER 6

1. Praise for Belisarius and his entourage: Procopius, *Wars* 7.1.4–6, my translation. The 540 invasion of Khusro: *Wars* 2.5–13. The defense of Bouzes: *Wars* 2.6.1–8, see also Jones et al. 1971, 3.255. For eastern soldiers probably being used in Italy, see Whitby 2021, 147. On the soldiers available to Bouzes in 540, see Whately 2021, 156–158. The defense of Germanos: Procopius, *Wars* 2.6.9–7.18. On the career of Germanos, see Cosentino 2016.

2. The journey of Belisarius: Procopius, *Wars* 2.14.8–13. The captured Vandals in the East: *Wars* 4.14.17. Shipping soldiers to foreign fronts for service was a typical Roman strategy.

3. The accusation against Antonina: Procopius, *Secret History* 2.1–3. The downfall of John: *Wars* 1.25.11–43, see also Potter 2015, 186–188. John's longevity was remarkable. Justinian's Praetorian Prefects of the East before John averaged seven months in office, and those in the position after John averaged two years in office. See the fasti table in Jones et al. 1971, 3.1473.

4. Praise for Antonina: Procopius, *Wars* 1.25.13, my translation. In Kaldellis 2014, 69, the compliment is translated "most crafty." The Greek word, ἱκανωτάτη, implies a

sense of sufficiency or competency and does not suggest a double-edged compliment, as might be assumed by the English "crafty." I have therefore preferred "most competent" here. The connection between Antonina's alleged affair and need to appease Theodora: Procopius, *Secret History* 1.13–14. Compare Potter 2015, 188, and Evans 2011, 148–155, who are both more willing to believe this connection.

5. Euphemia's discussion with Antonina: Procopius, *Wars* 1.25.16–17. A similar entrapment scheme was employed by Germanos to entrap Artabanes and his fellow conspirators in 549, see Procopius, *Wars* 7.31–32.

6. Procopius, *Wars* 1.25.18–25. Narses himself was a *spatharius* and probably had served with a unit of imperial guardsmen at some point, see Brodka 2018, 43–46.

7. Procopius, *Wars* 1.25.26–35. The date of May 541 is suggested by the legal evidence. John is referred to as Praetorian Prefect still on May 7, 541 (*Codex Iustinianus*, Novel 109), but his successor is addressed in a law of June 1 (Novel 111). See Jones et al. 1971, 3.633. John's dismissal is also reported in John Malalas, *Chronographia* 18.89 (where it is mistakenly dated to August 541) and Marcellinus Comes 544.3 (mistakenly dated to 544).

8. The rivalry of John and Theodora: Procopius, *Wars* 1.25.4–5; Procopius, *Secret History* 17.38; John Lydus, *On Magistracies* 3.69; and see Potter 2015, 139.

9. John's jealousy of Belisarius: Procopius, *Wars* 1.25.12. For John's roles in the Vandal War, see Chapter 3. Evert-Kappesowa 1964, 62, points this out as a reason for resentment between Belisarius and John. Antonina and the water supply: Procopius, *Wars* 3.13.5–24; Antonina and Belisarius eating: *Wars* 5.18.43; Antonina directing supplies: *Wars* 6.4.20 and 6.7.4. Marcellinus Comes 544.3 mentions that Belisarius received John's residence in Constantinople. Kaldellis 2014, 71 n. 167, suggests that this was "an indirect way of rewarding Antonina."

10. Most historians accept that Procopius left Belisarius' service sometime between 540 and 542. The narratives of campaigns after 540 are less detailed than those of earlier campaigns, suggesting Procopius was no longer an eyewitness. The two popular choices are 540 (Heather 2018, 12; Treadgold 2007, 184; Jones 1964, 1.266; Stein 1949, 2.711), and 542, when Belisarius was disgraced (Jones et al. 1971, 3.1062; Cameron 1985, 164, 188). I prefer the earlier dating because of the lack of concrete details here about the army reorganization and number of soldiers Belisarius was able to muster. Belisarius organizes the army: Procopius, *Wars* 2.16.2. Belisarius probably brought together scattered units and re-equipped them rather than merged or created new units, as there would not have been enough time for a complete reorganization. Thanks to Conor Whately for pointing this out. The spying operation: *Wars* 2.16.1, 2.16.3, and 2.15.35.

11. The war council: Procopius, *Wars* 2.16.6–19. The skirmish at Nisibis: *Wars* 2.18. The seizure of Sisauranon: *Wars* 2.19.1–25, and for its dating, see Greatrex 2022, 2.19.33.

12. The raid of Al-Harith: Procopius, *Wars* 2.19.26–30. The retreat of the Romans: *Wars* 2.19.31–46.

13. The accusation that Belisarius tarried to wait for Antonina: Procopius, *Secret History* 2.18, 22–24. Belisarius reviled: *Secret History* 2.21. On Roman conceptions of duty for husbands and the place of their wives, see Parnell 2022 and Cooper 2007, 152–160. Belisarius could have marched to Ctesiphon: Procopius, *Secret History* 2.25. Numerous passages of Maurice, *Strategikon* warn generals against taking unnecessary risks or advancing into enemy territory without adequate intelligence (7.1.3, 8.1.40, 8.2.56). The admission that Belisarius had other reasons to retreat: Procopius, *Secret History* 2.19. Whitby 2021, 150 n. 114, concurs that the reasons given in the *Wars* were enough to cause Belisarius to retreat.

14. Antonina in Constantinople and harassing Photios: Procopius, *Secret History* 2.1–5. Belisarius' speech to Photios: *Secret History* 2.6–11. The arrest of Antonina and denouement of the argument: *Secret History* 3.1–29.

15. The contrast between Belisarius' virtues in *Wars* and vices in *Secret History*: Stewart 2021. Procopius' use of negative stereotypes like the hateful mother: Fisher 1978, 275; Cameron 1985, 70–74; Brubaker 2004b, 91–94; and Neville 2019, 14–19. A sampling of historians who have accepted the story of Antonina's affair uncritically: Evans 2011, 153–157; Hughes 2009, 192–194; Stein 1949, 2.495–496; Stanhope (Lord Mahon) 1848, 320–322; Gibbon 1776–1789, 4.207–209. The chronology: Procopius, *Secret History* 2.15, *Wars* 2.19.49, *Secret History* 3.5. To paraphrase Brubaker, to say that the text "tells us next to nothing" about actual events in this period would be unfair (Brubaker 2004b, 101). Compare Börm 2015, 330, who argues that invective divorced from reality is ineffective.

16. Photios' wealth and Belisarius' lost wealth: Procopius, *Secret History* 2.7–9. Photios brings Theodosios' money: *Secret History* 3.5. Photios' rage: *Secret History* 1.32. On the birth of Ioannina, see Chapter 2, and on the adoption of Theodosios, see Chapter 3. Evert-Kappesowa 1964, 64, also points out the role that money played in this family argument.

17. The military career of Photios: Procopius, *Wars* 5.5.5, 5.10.5; Liberatus, *Breviarium* 22; Procopius, *Secret History* 2.1. Belisarius' pride in Photios: *Secret History* 2.7. Antonina's favoritism of Theodosios: *Secret History* 2.3–4, 1.18, 1.21.

18. It is possible that in creating this slander, either Photios himself or Procopius was influenced by the story of Euripides' *Hippolytus*, in which a woman lusts after her stepson. The *Hippolytus* was quite popular in this period (Bowersock 2006, 55–59). However, there are no obvious connections between the language Procopius used to describe the alleged affair of Antonina and Theodosios and the language Euripides used in the play. The fate of Photios is described at Procopius, *Secret History* 3.27–29, and see Jones et al. 1971, 3.1038.

19. The winter travel to Constantinople: Procopius, *Secret History* 3.4, 3.12, and *Wars* 2.19.49. The torture and imprisonment of Photios: *Secret History* 3.12–29. He remained a monk for all of Justinian's reign. Much later, Photios was dispatched by Justin II to crush a Samaritan and Jewish revolt (John of Ephesus, *Ecclesiastical*

History 3.1.32). See Jones et al. 1971, 3.1038–1039, and Chapter 8. The death of Theodosios: Procopius, *Secret History* 3.19–20.

20. There is an avalanche of modern accounts of the Justinianic Plague. For general works, see Harper 2017, Little 2006, and Sarris 2020. Important recent articles include Meier 2016, Mordechai and Eisenberg 2019, Mordechai et al. 2019, Greatrex 2020, Meier 2020, and Sarris 2022. The plague is also discussed in more general works of the period, for example Potter 2015, 190–193.

21. John of Ephesus records the plague hitting Jerusalem (Joh. Eph. in the *Chronicle of Zuqnīn*, ed. Witakowski, 1996, 99). Evagrius describes its impact on Antioch (Evagrius, *Ecclesiastical History* 4.29). Marcellinus Comes records it in Italy, Illyricum, and the East (543.2). The Procopius quote: *Wars* 2.22.3. 10,000 people per day: Procopius, *Wars* 2.23.2. 16,000 in one day: Joh. Eph. in the *Chronicle of Zuqnīn*, ed. Witakowski 1996, 87. Reactions: Procopius, *Wars* 2.23.17–18. The plague features in the work of most historians of the period, see also John Malalas, *Chronographia* 18.92, and Corippus, *Iohannis* 3.343–400.

22. Death toll estimates: Mordechai 2019, 25546 and 25553, and Meier 2020, 174–175. Works that downplay the long-term impacts include Mordechai and Eisenberg 2019, Mordechai et al. 2019, and Haldon et al. 2018b. Works that emphasize the long-term impacts include Harper 2017, Little 2006, Meier 2016, Meier 2020, Sarris 2020, and Sarris 2022. Heather 2018 is an account of "war and empire in the age of Justinian" in which the Justinianic Plague is barely mentioned (306–307) and not at all discussed in the context of military operations. Whitby 2021, 306, allows that the plague caused "considerable short-term disruption." Whitby 1995, 93–99, and Whately 2021, 209–214, attempt to assess the impact of the plague on military recruitment.

23. Khusro's 542 invasion: Procopius, *Wars* 2.20.1–18. Belisarius' rushed travel: *Wars* 2.20.20. Travel estimate is from http://orbis.stanford.edu/.

24. The army is mustered: Procopius, *Wars* 2.20.21–28 and commentary in Greatrex 2022, 2.20.24. The display for Abandanes: *Wars* 2.21.1–8. Perhaps these 6,000 might have been picked specifically because they were healthy, to advertise to Abandanes that they were not suffering from the plague (Hughes 2009, 197). The withdrawal of Khusro: Procopius, *Wars* 2.21.9–33. Perhaps Belisarius' subordinates commissioned fortification work at nearby Cyrrhus (near Zaytūnak in north-western Syria) about this time. An inscription on the city gate at the site acclaims Belisarius as general. The inscription is described in Jones et al. 1971, 3.223.

25. Praise: Procopius, *Wars* 2.21.28. Criticism: Procopius, *Secret History* 3.31. Hughes speculates that Khusro's army was infected, but Belisarius' army was not, and this is why the Roman general did not want to engage in combat (Hughes 2009, 197–198). This is plausible, but not any more plausible than both armies being infected. On the impact of the plague in Persia, see Bonner 2020, 191–195.

26. Procopius, *Secret History* 4.1–4. For Belisarius' past disagreement with Peter, see the section "In the East Again," above, and *Wars* 2.18.1–26. Perhaps John the

Glutton had reason to seek revenge on Belisarius as well. He had co-commanded the 1,200 guardsmen who raided Mesopotamia and failed to return to Belisarius in 541 (*Wars* 2.19.26–30). If Belisarius had reprimanded John for this, it would have given John motive to turn on the general in 542.

27. The downfall of Belisarius: Procopius, *Secret History* 4.13–17. The version in the *Wars*: Procopius, *Wars* 2.21.34. Belisarius sets out for Italy in Spring 544: Procopius, *Wars* 7.9.23–7.10.1. Confirmation of downfall: Marcellinus Comes 545.3.

28. For the claim that Belisarius' guardsmen numbered 7,000, see Procopius, *Wars* 7.1.20. On the wealth of Belisarius, see Appendix 3. Belisarius not convicted: Procopius, *Secret History* 4.13. The death of Theodosios: *Secret History* 3.20.

29. Belisarius restored due to Antonina: Procopius, *Secret History* 4.20–30. Procopius claims that Belisarius was subordinate to Antonina in some way in all of the following passages of the *Secret History*: 1.20, 1.26, 1.39, 3.1–2, 4.41, and 5.27. On the growing view in the later Roman Empire that the husband should have more authority than the wife, as opposed to the more equal marriages of the earlier Roman Empire, see Cooper 2007, 152–160. The wife interceding for the husband: Procopius, *Secret History* 4.19, emphasis added. On the inversion of the social order of husband and wife in the *Secret History*, see Fisher 1978, 269–275; Brubaker 2004b, 85–94; and Stewart 2021, 11–15.

30. Evert-Kappesowa 1964, 65–66, doubts that Belisarius was restored only because of Antonina's intervention. For a complete review of Justinian's reputation for mercy, see Parnell 2020a. The continued employment of plotters: Procopius, *Buildings* 1.1.16. For Artabanes, see Parnell 2020a, 16–17; Stewart 2020, 163–192; and Procopius, *Wars* 4.28.29–43, 7.31.2–32.51, and 7.39.8. Clemency in time: *Codex Iustinianus*, Novel 129, trans. Miller and Sarris 2018, 859, with my own modifications and emphasis added.

31. The oath of Belisarius: Procopius, *Wars* 6.29.19–20 (see Chapter 5). The restoration of Belisarius' wealth: Procopius, *Secret History* 4.31–35, and see Appendix 3. His appointment as *comes sacri stabuli* and assignment to Italy: *Secret History* 4.39; *Wars* 2.21.34, 7.9.23; Marcellinus Comes 545.3; and Evagrius, *Ecclesiastical History* 4.21.

32. The betrothal of Ioannina: *Secret History* 4.36–37. On Anastasios' parentage and relation to Theodora, see Cameron 1978, 269–272. For speculation on Ioannina's year of birth, which is not directly recorded in any of the primary sources, see Chapter 2. It probably was not assumed that this betrothal would lead to a wedding immediately, as indicated by the fact that Belisarius and Antonina promptly set off on a new campaign after the engagement. Antonina's refusal to go to the East: *Secret History* 4.38–39. Compare to Evans 2011, 168, and Herrin 2013, 86.

CHAPTER 7

1. For a more detailed account of the years 540–543 in Italy, see Procopius, *Wars* 7.1–9, and commentary in Stein 1949, 2.564–576, and Heather 2018, 251–259.

2. For numbers of soldiers in the previous campaigns, see Chapters 3 and 4, and for 544, see Procopius, *Wars* 7.10.1. On the impact of the plague, see Chapter 6. Examinations of the plague's effect on the Roman military have focused on whether it impeded recruitment in the longer term (Whitby 1995, 93–99; Whately 2021, 209–214), which it seems not to have done, but have not addressed the deaths of experienced soldiers and the time lag required to recruit and train new ones in the short term. Belisarius' departure in 544 would fit right in that time frame in which the army would have lost veteran soldiers to the plague in 542/543 and not yet been able to replace them all.

3. The recruiting drive: Procopius, *Wars* 7.10.2 and see Whately 2021, 198. The idea that Belisarius would rebel: Procopius, *Secret History* 4.39–40.

4. Antonina's first mention in this campaign: Procopius, *Wars* 7.19.7. The accusation of infatuation: Procopius, *Secret History* 4.41. See also *Wars* 7.1.11, where Procopius praises Belisarius for never touching a woman other than his wife.

5. Procopius, *Wars* 7.10.3–11.1. See Stanhope (Lord Mahon) 1848, 342, and Whitby 2021, 236, on Totila's concern at Belisarius' arrival.

6. Belisarius dispatches his forces: Procopius, *Wars* 7.11.11–39. On the comparison of this moment to the siege of Rome in 537, see Hughes 2009, 213. On the San Vitale mosaics and the identification of Belisarius and Antonina within them, see Andreescu-Treadgold and Treadgold 1997, 719. The authors' identification of Ioannina and her betrothed Anastasios on the panels is less likely, being based in even more layers of guesswork (720). Other historians more cautiously point out that the identity of Belisarius and Antonina is not confirmed, with some going as far as to call it "fanciful" (Herrin 2020, 437 n. 18). However, following the arguments of Andreescu-Treadgold and Treadgold, it seems more plausible than fanciful: Belisarius and Antonina were in the city at the time, were the city's main connection to Justinian and Theodora, and would have wished to shore up their authority by broadcasting their connection to the imperial couple.

7. Belisarius' letter to Justinian: Procopius, *Wars* 7.12.1–11. Vigilius' letter to Auxanius: *Patrologia Latina* 69.27. A second letter in August 546 also credited Belisarius' assistance (*Patrologia Latina* 69.37). These letters are evidence of a prolonged relationship between Belisarius and the pope he helped to install (Chapter 4). See further interactions between Belisarius and Vigilius in Chapter 8. Totila seizes cities: Procopius, *Wars* 7.12.12–20.

8. John's sojourn in Constantinople: Procopius, *Wars* 7.12.11, *Secret History* 5.8–12. Justinian's negligence: *Wars* 8.26.7. Compare Hughes 2009, 215, who totes up the problems the empire faced in 545, along with Stanhope (Lord Mahon) 1848, 384–386, and Heather 2018, 253, 264. Meier 2004 argues that Justinian's enthusiasm for the wars in the West waned in the 540s and his focus turned to religious matters, which would also explain a hesitancy to send reinforcements. Totila besieges Rome: Procopius, *Wars* 7.13.1–11. On the start date of the siege, see Stein 1949,

2.578 n. 2. Belisarius regrets being in Ravenna: Procopius, *Wars* 7.13.13–19, and sends Phokas and Valentinos: 7.15.1.

9. Famine and profiteering in Rome: Procopius, *Wars* 7.15.2–16, 7.16–17, and compare Stanhope (Lord Mahon) 1848, 350–354. John's reinforcements: Procopius, *Wars* 7.13.20. Procopius provides the travel time for the two options in *Wars* 7.18.4. Otranto to Rome is a distance of some 380 miles, and if this took 40 days, it would suggest the soldiers were walking around 10 miles a day. This mirrors the travel pace for the army in Africa, which marched 10 miles a day to get to Carthage (see Chapter 3). The army in Italy was smaller and could probably move more quickly, and certainly not slower (as implied by Procopius saying it would take more than 40 days). So, Procopius probably exaggerates the slowness of the land option. The army splits up: Procopius, *Wars* 7.18.1–4 and Marcellinus Comes 547.2–3.

10. The abortive march of John: Procopius, *Wars* 7.18.5–29. Antonina accused of seeking the murder of John: Procopius, *Secret History* 5.7–14. Evans 2011, 185–186, swallows this story whole. Evert-Kappesowa 1964, 68, rejects this accusation against Antonina as hearsay. On other problems with this story, including Procopius' assertion that John was far below Iustina and Germanos in rank, see Cosentino 2016, 121–122; Stewart Forthcoming; and Lin 2021, 132–133. Stein 1949, 2.580, refers contemptuously to John's insubordination and ego in the context of 546.

11. Totila's wooden defense of the Tiber: Procopius, *Wars* 7.18.8–10. Belisarius' relief fleet and plan: *Wars* 7.19.1–11. Antonina's previous supply effort on the Tiber: *Wars* 6.7.5–12 (see Chapter 5).

12. The relief operation and Belisarius' illness: Procopius, *Wars* 7.19.12–33. Approximately 50% of patients hospitalized for stroke develop fever (Wrotek et al. 2011). Compare to Stein 1949, 2.583–584; Stanhope (Lord Mahon) 1848, 358–360; Hughes 2009, 220; and Whitby 2021, 239, all of whom focus on Isaac's failure and downplay the issue of Belisarius' health. Evans 2011, 193, says Belisarius "panicked" or was perhaps "manic depressive," which ignores the physical symptoms presented by Procopius.

13. The immense role played by John the Armenian in the Vandal War is described in Chapter 3. The fall of Rome and its tiny population: Procopius, *Wars* 7.20. The diplomatic exchange between Totila and Justinian: *Wars* 7.21. On the timing of this embassy and Totila's diplomatic strategy, see Cristini 2020, 35–38. Totila's near destruction and then evacuation of Rome: *Wars* 7.22.1–19 and Marcellinus Comes 547.5.

14. Cristini 2020, 33–35, argues that Totila did understand the symbolic importance of holding Rome, but does not offer an explanation for why the Gothic king abandoned the city (41). Belisarius reconnoiters Rome: Procopius, *Wars* 7.23.8–11. The rebuilding and repopulating of Rome: *Wars* 7.24.2–7, see also Evagrius, *Ecclesiastical History* 4.21. Procopius praises the act: *Wars* 7.24.1. Belisarius defends

Rome from Totila: *Wars* 7.24.8–34. On Totila's fury and justification of his actions, see Pazdernik 2015.

15. On Belisarius' garrisoning of Rome preventing him from undertaking offensive operations, see Stanhope (Lord Mahon) 1848, 378–379. Belisarius sends letters to Justinian: Procopius, *Wars* 7.27.1. Totila and John's operations: *Wars* 7.25–26. The arrival of the reinforcements: *Wars* 7.27.2–3.

16. Belisarius sails from Rome with 900 soldiers: Procopius, *Wars* 7.27.12–17. The ambush at Crotone: *Wars* 7.28.

17. The army assembles at Otranto: Procopius, *Wars* 7.30.1–2, 9. To get to 5,000 total, we start with the fact that Valerianos had about 1,000 guardsmen, Varazes had about 800 soldiers, and the new infantry numbered 2,000. It is unclear how many soldiers Belisarius and John each had. We know Belisarius had 900 men before Crotone, and presumably much fewer after his cavalry were ambushed there—so perhaps a few hundred. John might have had about 1,000 soldiers, although this is speculation. Antonina sets off for Constantinople: *Wars* 7.30.3.

18. Rusciane besieged: Procopius, *Wars* 7.29.21, 7.30.5. The failed rescue operation and the fall of Rusciane: *Wars* 7.30.9–24. The sixth-century Roman navy was not well equipped for amphibious assaults, and, as seen in Chapter 3, the troops were skittish about such operations. See Murray 2012, 69–142, for the requirements for successful assaults of this kind, which were more common in the Hellenistic navies some eight centuries earlier.

19. The decision for Belisarius to return to Rome: Procopius, *Wars* 7.30.15. The murder of Konon: *Wars* 7.30.7, and see Stein 1949, 2.588–589, and Lillington-Martin and Stewart 2021, 303–304. Belisarius' religious endowments in Rome: *Liber Pontificalis* 61.2.

20. The death of Theodora: Procopius, *Wars* 7.30.4; John Malalas, *Chronographia* 18.104. The two versions of the recall: Procopius, *Wars* 7.30.25, *Secret History* 5.16. Stein 1949, 2.589, Hughes 2009, 228, and Evans 2011, 198, all prefer the *Wars* version.

21. Belisarius leaves a garrison in Rome: Procopius, *Wars* 7.36.1. Belisarius' travel: *Wars* 7.32.19. The exact date of Belisarius' departure and the length of his journey is unknown. Procopius says he commanded in Italy for five years (*Wars* 7.35.1, *Secret History* 5.1), so he must have stayed until the beginning of 549. See Stein 1949, 2.590 n. 4 from 589 for further discussion. The conspiracy of Artabanes: *Wars* 7.31–32, quote at 7.32.38. For more on what the conspiracy of Artabanes reveals about the relationship of Justinian and Belisarius, see Stewart 2020, 176–192, and Lin 2021, 133. Belisarius arrives in Constantinople: *Wars* 7.35.1; Evagrius, *Ecclesiastical History* 4.21.

22. Gregory of Tours, *History of the Franks* 3.32. Gregory errs in suggesting that Belisarius was defeated by a Frankish general who conquered all of Italy. The many critiques of Procopius may be found, in order, in *Wars* 7.35.1, *Secret History* 5.1, 4.42, and 5.4.

23. Evert-Kappesowa 1964, 66, also rejects the accusations of Procopius. Compare Whitby 2021, 309, who suggests that Belisarius "could not cope with Totila's tactics." Stanhope (Lord Mahon) 1848, 384–386, blames Justinian for not reinforcing Belisarius, accusing the emperor of laziness, procrastination, and a fickle temper. Compare Hughes 2009, 229–230, and Evans 2011, 197. On the Balkan threat of the Lombards and Gepids, see Procopius, *Wars* 7.34.40–47; Whitby 2021, 267–270; and, more generally, Sarantis 2016, 227–324. Roger Scott makes a powerful argument for Justinian's lack of prioritization for all wars in the West, including the one in Italy: Scott 2012, VI, 11–16. Totila's victories: *Wars* 7.36.1–15. Narses' army: *Wars* 8.21. Narses' victory over Totila at Busta Gallorum showed that one major victory in a pitched battle would initiate the beginning of the end for Gothic resistance: *Wars* 8.30–32 and see Rance 2005. For a brief summary of these events, see Stein 1949, 2.592–604, and Heather 2018, 265–268.

CHAPTER 8

1. For the betrothal of Ioannina and Anastasios, see Chapter 6. The tale of the breaking off of the engagement is found in Procopius, *Secret History*, 5.18–27. It is repeated essentially verbatim by Evans 2011, 199, and Stanhope (Lord Mahon) 1848, 409–410.

2. On gendered tropes, see Fisher 1978, 273; Garland 1999, 13; and Brubaker 2004b, 94. Powerful women and subordinate men: Fisher 1978, 269–270; James 2001, 16–17; and Stewart 2021, 11–15. For other instances of the theme of subordination, see Procopius, *Secret History* 1.13, 1.39, 2.2, 3.1–2, 4.29–30, and 4.41.

3. Stanhope (Lord Mahon) 1848, 409, argues that Belisarius and Antonina never approved of the engagement but felt unable to refuse Theodora. Cameron 1978, 270–272, argues that Anastasios was a son of Theodora's illegitimate daughter, and therefore of no use politically to Antonina once Theodora was dead. Some historians, such as Evans 2011, 200, have argued that Ioannina and Anastasios were eventually reunited, but there is no historical evidence for this.

4. Belisarius recalled because of Persian war: Procopius, *Wars* 7.30.25, see also Stein 1949, 2.589. Belisarius reappointed General of the East: Procopius, *Wars* 8.21.1 (ἀλλὰ καὶ στρατηγὸν τῆς ἑῴας ὄντα, τῶν βασιλικῶν σωματοφυλάκων ἄρχοντα καταστησάμενος, αὐτοῦ κατεῖχεν). For the Count of the Protectors title, see Stein 1949, 2.822–823. The reappointment as a reward: Hughes 2009, 232; Stanhope (Lord Mahon) 1848, 410; and Jones 1964, 1.290.

5. The first five-year truce: Procopius, *Wars* 2.28.10–11. Roman invasion of Lazica: *Wars* 2.29.10. The attempt of Yazdgushnasp is described in *Wars* 2.28.31–37. This event has sometimes been dated to 547 (e.g., Stein 1949, 2.503–504; Greatrex 2022, 2.28.31–44), but 548 is also possible based on the context. 548 seems more likely if Khusro used the attempt on Dara as a feint to distract Justinian from the increased hostilities in Lazica (see Bonner 2020, 200–201). The five-year extension: *Wars*

8.15.1–12. Belisarius is titled only ex-consul and patrician in Vigilius, *Dum in Sanctae Euphemiae* 1, discussed in more detail below.

6. For Belisarius' preparation for war in spring 541, see Chapter 6. It would have taken about eight days for a messenger from Dara to arrive to Belisarius in Constantinople, if he was stationed there. See Chapter 6 for a comparison of travel times from the capital to the East.

7. Belisarius denied additional glory: Evans 2011, 199, 204; Hughes 2009, 241; and Stanhope (Lord Mahon) 1848, 419. Chassin 1957, 188–200, goes even further by absurdly suggesting that Belisarius was in disgrace between 548 and 559. On standard terms of service, see *Codex Theodosianus* 7.20.4; Jones 1964, 1.635; and Southern and Dixon 1996, 87. Bessas: Procopius, *Wars* 8.11.40. Liberius: *Wars* 7.39.7. Narses: see the discussion in Jones et al. 1971, 3.926.

8. Admiration for Belisarius: Procopius, *Wars* 7.35.3, 8.21.3. The first seven books of the *Wars* were distributed around 551, just in time to make headlines for Belisarius' retirement. See the Introduction, Cristini 2021, and Greatrex 2014. Belisarius mocked: Procopius, *Secret History* 5.27. Belisarius held in honor: *Wars* 8.21.1. Belisarius filling advising gap of Theodora: Hughes 2009, 228.

9. For Belisarius and Antonina's role in the election of Vigilius, see Chapter 4. For an overview of the struggle between Vigilius and Justinian, see Sotinel 2005, 280–284, and Stein 1949, 2.648–666.

10. The first group of officials: Vigilius, *Dum in Sanctae Euphemiae* in Schwartz 1940, 1; translation by Price 2009, 1.170–171. The visits of this group in August 551 and January 552: Vigilius, *Dum in Sanctae Euphemiae* in Schwartz 1940, 4; translation by Price 2009, 1.170–173, and see Stein 1949, 2.648–650; Leppin 2011, 304; and Lin 2021, 124–125. The list of officials in May 553: Acts of the Council of Constantinople of 553, ACOec iv I, p. 27; translation by Price 2009, 1.214. The group summoned by Vigilius: Acts of the Council of Constantinople of 553, ACOec iv I, p. 185; translation by Price 2009, 2.76. Belisarius is mentioned first in each of these lists.

11. The invasion of Zabergan: John Malalas, *Chronographia* 18.129, and, on the battle with Sergios, see Whitby 2021, 276. For more on Zabergan's invasion and Roman relations with the Kutrigurs and other Huns in general, see Sarantis 2016, 325–374. Descriptions of Belisarius at the time: Agathias, *Histories* 5.15.7; John Malalas, *Chronographia* 18.129. For the death of Procopius, see Treadgold 2007, 191; Cameron 1985, 12–15; Jones et al. 1971, 3.1066.

12. Belisarius gathers 300 soldiers: Agathias, *Histories* 5.16.2. On the frequency of appearance of units of 300 soldiers in the Gothic war, see Whately 2015, 409–411. Belisarius commandeers horses, orders trees dragged behind the army: John Malalas, *Chronographia* 18.129. Strategy maxims about preventing the enemy from accurate reconnaissance may be found in Maurice, *Strategikon* 7.2.3 and 7.2.8. The battle and aftermath: Agathias, *Histories* 5.19–5.20. Agathias' hyperbolic praise: *Histories* 5.15.8.

13. Rumors of jealousy of Belisarius: Agathias, *Histories* 5.20.4–6. These rumors sound suspiciously like those Procopius recorded after Belisarius' conquest of the Vandals (Procopius, *Wars* 4.8.1–3, and see Chapter 3) and during the capture of Ravenna (*Wars* 6.29.7 and see Chapter 5). Justinian repairs Long Wall and pays off Zabergan: John Malalas, *Chronographia* 18.129; Agathias, *Histories* 5.23.8.

14. The plot is recorded in John Malalas, *Chronographia* 18.141 and repeated in Theophanes, *Chronicle* AM 6055.

15. Whitby 2021, 298–299, agrees it is unlikely Belisarius actually participated in the plot. Historians who argue that Justinian was jealous of Belisarius: Whitby 2021, 12; Evans 2011, 199; Stein 1949, 2.539; Stanhope (Lord Mahon) 1848, 419–422; and Hughes 2009, 241. On the 564 edict on Aphthartodocetism, see Evagrius, *Ecclesiastical History* 4.39; Jones 1964, 1.298; Stein 1949, 2.686–689; and Treadgold 1997, who describes the edict as showing "a touch of senility" (214).

16. The restoration of Belisarius: John Malalas, *Chronographia* 18.147 and Theophanes, *Chronicle* AM 6055. For more on Justinian's mercy toward his generals, and Belisarius in particular, see Chapter 6.

17. The deaths of Belisarius and Justinian: Theophanes, *Chronicle* AM 6057 and see commentary by Lin 2021, 139. Antonina potentially outliving Belisarius: *Patria Constantinopolitana* 3.117 and see Chapter 9.

18. The Abbot Photios and his service to Justin II: Theophanes, *Chronicle* AM 6058; John of Ephesus, *Ecclesiastical History* 3.1.31–32. On the possibility that he was tasked with slaying the other Justin, see Mango, Scott, and Greatrex 1997, 355 n. 4. The length of Photios' authority: John of Ephesus, *Ecclesiastical History* 3.1.32. See also Jones et al. 1971, 3.1038–1039.

CHAPTER 9

1. The medieval reception of the works of Procopius are neatly described by Croke 2019, 5–13. The origins of the *Patria*: Kazhdan 1991, 3.1598; Knös 1960, 265. The quote is from *Patria Constantinopolitana* 2.17, my translation. Antonina's fate: *Patria Constantinopolitana* 3.117.

2. Text of the *Novel of Belisarius*: Bakker and van Gemert 1988. A more complete summary of the novel may be found in Knös 1960, 241–242, who also argues for its development as a popular folk song. The origin of the blinding tradition and the Alexios name: Knös 1960, 280. The use of the *Secret History* in the early modern West: Croke 2019, 13–89.

3. The version of Raphael Maffei: Knös 1960, 242 n. 1. Raphael's translation of the *Wars* and the publication of the *Secret History* by Nicolò: Croke 2019, 30–32, 74–89.

4. Jakob Bidermann (1607) *Belisarius*, reprinted Berlin: DeGruyter, 1966. Belisarius is shown begging in only one (Bidermann 1607) of five works of fiction (Jean Rotrou, *Le Belisaire* 1643; William Philips, *Belisarius: A Tragedy* 1758; Jean-François Marmontel, *Belisaire* 1767; Gaetano Donizetti, *Belisario* 1836), but in

three (Francois-Andre Vincent, *Belisarius* 1776; Jean-Francois Peyron, *Belisarius Receiving Hospitality from a Peasant* 1779; Jacques-Louis David, *Belisarius Begging for Alms* 1781) of four works of art (Jean-Baptiste Stouf, *Belisarius* 1791).

5. Further works of neoclassical art with Belisarius as a subject followed after 1791, including Antoine Denis Chaudet, *Belisarius and His Guide* (1794) and François Gérard, *Belisarius* (1797).

6. Gaetano Donizetti, *Belisario* (1836).

7. Quotes from Oldmixon 1722, 52–53; Gibbon 1776–1789, 4.313; Stanhope (Lord Mahon) 1848, 432–433. Among others, the following later historians explicitly reject the blinding story as ahistorical: Diehl 1901, 167; Stein 1949, 2.285; Knös 1960, 265; Barker 1966, 199–200; Hughes 2009, 241; Evans 2011, 207.

8. Quotes from Gibbon 1776–1789, 4.369 and 4.203. A small sample of historians who accept the *Secret History* accusations: Stanhope (Lord Mahon) 1848, Diehl 1901, Stein 1949, Barker 1966, Hughes 2009, and Evans 2011.

9. Graves 1938, reprinted 1982, 544–563.

10. The Belisarius Series begins with Drake and Flint 1998 and ends with Drake and Flint 2006. Kastenellos 2012. Judicator's album: https://judicatormetal.bandc amp.com/album/let-there-be-nothing. The band's vocalist and songwriter, John Yelland, explained his inspiration for the album to Jeremy J. Swist in a 2020 interview: https://heavymetalclassicist.home.blog/2020/12/28/date-album-belisa rio-an-interview-with-judicator/. For more on the heavy metal reception of this period, see Swist 2021. The playlist for the Epic History TV documentary videos may be found here: https://www.youtube.com/playlist?list=PLUOc2qodFHp_ HvRHG7Kib4hbuaqavf85V. Full disclosure: I was a consultant for the series.

APPENDIX 3

1. Procopius, *Secret History* 4.31–33. The figure in the *Secret History* is given in *kentenaria*, which equaled 100 pounds. Paul receives 1,000 pounds of gold from Anatasios: John Lydus, *On Magistracies* 3.48. On the annual income of senators during this period, see Jones 1964, 1.554–557, and Hendy 1985, 201–203. For the cost of the Endless Peace, see Procopius, *Wars* 1.22.3, and for Phocas' expenditure on Hagia Sophia, see John Lydus, *On Magistracies* 3.76.

2. General's salary: Treadgold 1995, 152. Poverty wage: Treadgold 1995, 118. 2021 Federal Poverty Guidelines: https://aspe.hhs.gov/topics/poverty-economic-mobility/poverty-guidelines/prior-hhs-poverty-guidelines-federal-register-referen ces/2021-poverty-guidelines.

3. Cavalryman's salary: Treadgold 1995, 152. 7,000 guardsmen: Procopius, *Wars* 7.1.20. The rumor that Belisarius had kept portions of the two treasuries: Procopius, *Secret History* 4.34.

Bibliography

PRIMARY SOURCES

Acts of the Council of Constantinople of 553. Edited by Eduard Schwartz. *Acta Conciliorum Oecumenicorum*, Tome 4, vol. 1. Berlin, 1971. Translated by Richard Price. *The Acts of the Council of Constantinople of 553*. 2 vols. Liverpool: Liverpool University Press, 2009.

Agathias. *The Histories*. Edited by Rudolf Keydell. Berlin: De Gruyter, 1967. Translated by Joseph Frendo. Berlin: De Gruyter, 1975.

Chronicon Paschale. 2 vols. Edited by Ludwig Dindorf. *Corpus scriptorum historiae Byzantiae*. Berlin, 1832. Translated by Michael Whitby and Mary Whitby. *Chronicon Paschale 284–628 AD*. Liverpool: Liverpool University Press, 1989.

Codex Justinianus. 3 vols. Edited by Paul Krueger. Berlin: Apud Weidmannos, 1886–1888. Translated by D. Miller and P. Sarris. *The Novels of Justinian: A Complete Annotated English Translation*. 2 vols. Cambridge: Cambridge University Press, 2018.

Corippus, Flavius Cresconius. *Iohannidos seu De bellis Libycis libri VIII*. Edited by Iacobus Diggle and F. R. D. Goodyear. London: Cambridge University Press, 1970. Translated by George W. Shea. *The Iohannis, or, De Bellis Libycis*. Lewiston, NY: Edwin Mellen Press, 1998.

Evagrius Scholasticus. *Ecclesiastical History*. Edited by J. Bidez and L. Parmentier. London: Methuen, 1898. Translated by Michael Whitby. *Ecclesiastical History*. Liverpool: Liverpool University Press, 2000.

John of Ephesus. *The Third Part of the Ecclesiastical History of John Bishop of Ephesus*. Translated by R. Payne Smith. Oxford: Oxford University Press, 1860. Also translated by Witold Witakowski, *Pseudo-Dionysius of Tel-Mahre Chronicle, Known also as the Chronicle of Zuqnin*. Liverpool: Liverpool University Press, 1996.

Liber Pontificalis. Edited by L. Duchesne. *Le Liber Pontificalis*. 2 vols. Paris, 1886–1892. Translated by Raymond Davis. *The Book of Pontiffs*, 3rd edition. Liverpool: Liverpool University Press, 2010.

Liberatus. *Breviarium*. Edited by E. Schwartz. *Abrégé de l'histoire des nestoriens et des eutychiens*. Paris: CERF, 2019.

Lydus, John. *De Magistratibus*. Edited and translated by Anastasius Bandy. Philadelphia: American Philosophical Society, 1982.

Malalas, John. *Chronographia*. Edited by Ioannes Thurn. Berlin: Walter de Gruyter, 2000. Translated by Elizabeth Jeffreys, Michael Jeffreys, and Roger Scott. *The Chronicle of John Malalas*. Melbourne: Australian Association for Byzantine Studies, 1986.

Marcellinus Comes. *The Chronicle*. Edited by Theodore Mommsen. MGH, Auctores Antiquissimi, vol. 11. Berlin: Apud Weidmannos, 1894. Translated by Brian Croke. *The Chronicle of Marcellinus: A Translation and Commentary*. Sydney: Australian Association for Byzantine Studies, 1995.

Maurice. *Maurice's Strategikon: Handbook of Byzantine Military Strategy*. Translated by George T. Dennis. Philadelphia: University of Pennsylvania Press, 1984.

Patria Constantinopolitana. Edited by Theodor Preger. *Scriptores Originum Constantinopolitanarum*, vol. 2. Leipzig: B.G. Teubner, 1907.

Procopius of Caesarea. *The Anecdota*. Edited by H. B. Dewing. Cambridge, MA: Harvard University Press, 1914. Translated by Anthony Kaldellis. *The Secret History With Related Texts*. Indianapolis: Hackett Publishing, 2010.

Procopius of Caesarea. *The Buildings*. Edited and translated by H. B. Dewing. Cambridge, MA: Harvard University Press, 1940.

Procopius of Caesarea. *The History of the Wars*. 5 vols. Edited by H. B. Dewing. Cambridge, MA: Harvard University Press, 1914–1940. Translated by Anthony Kaldellis. *The Wars of Justinian*. Indianapolis: Hackett Publishing, 2014.

Pseudo-Zachariah. *Historia Ecclesiastica*. Edited and translated by E. W. Brooks. CSCO Scr. Syr. 38–39, 41–42. Paris, 1919–1924.

Theophanes Confessor. *Chronographia*. 2 vols. Edited by C. de Boor. Leipzig, 1883–1885. Translated by Cyril Mango, Roger Scott, and Geoffrey Greatrex. *The Chronicle of Theophanes Confessor*. Oxford: Clarendon Press, 1997.

Victor of Tunnuna. *Chronicon*. Edited by Theodore Mommsen. MGH, Auctores Antiquissimi, vol. 11. Berlin: Apud Weidmannos, 1894.

Vigilius. *Dum in Sanctae Euphemiae*. Edited by Eduard Schwartz. *Vigiliusbriefe*. SBAW. PH, Heft 2. Munich, 1940. Translated by Richard Price. *The Acts of the Council of Constantinople of 553*. 2 vols. Liverpool: Liverpool University Press, 2009.

Zachariah of Mitylene. *Syriac Chronicle*. Translated by F. J. Hamilton and E. W. Brooks. London: Methuen, 1899.

SECONDARY SOURCES

Amory, Patrick. 1997. *People and Identity in Ostrogothic Italy, 489–554*. Cambridge: Cambridge University Press.

Andreescu-Treadgold, Irina, and Warren Treadgold. 1997. "Procopius and the Imperial Panels of S. Vitale." *The Art Bulletin* 79.4: 708–723.

Bakker, Willem, and Arnold van Gemert. 1988. Ἱστορία τοῦ Βελισαρίου: Κριτικὴ ἔκδοση τῶν τεσσάρων διασκευῶν με εισαγωγή, σχόλια καὶ γλωσσάριο. Athens: Morphotiko Idryma Ethnikes Trapezes.

Barker, John W. 1966. *Justinian and the Later Roman Empire*. Madison: University of Wisconsin Press.

Bassett, Sarah. 2004. *The Urban Image of Late Antique Constantinople*. Cambridge: Cambridge University Press.

Beard, Mary. 2007. *The Roman Triumph*. Cambridge, MA: Belknap Press of Harvard University Press.

Betancourt, Roland. 2020. *Byzantine Intersectionality: Sexuality, Gender, and Race in the Middle Ages*. Princeton, NJ: Princeton University Press.

Bidermann, Jakob. 1607. *Belisarius*. Reprinted Berlin: DeGruyter, 1966.

Bonner, Michael R. Jackson. 2020. *The Last Empire of Iran*. Piscataway: Gorgias Press.

Börm, Henning. 2007. *Prokop und die Perser*. Stuttgart: Franz Steiner Verlag.

Börm, Henning. 2013. "Justinians Triumph und Belisars Erniedrigung. Überlegungen zum Verhältnis zwischen Kaiser und Militär im späten Römischen Reich." *Chiron* 43: 63–91.

Börm, Henning. 2015. "Procopius, His Predecessors, and the Genesis of the *Anecdota*: Antimonarchic Discourse in Late Antique Historiography." In *Antimonarchic Discourse in Antiquity*. Edited by Henning Börm, 305–346. Stuttgart: Franz Steiner Verlag.

Bowersock, G. W. 2006. *Mosaics as History: The Near East from Late Antiquity to Islam*. Cambridge, MA: Belknap Press.

Brodka, Dariusz. 2004. *Die Geschichtsphilosophie in der spätantiken Historiographie: Studien zu Prokopios von Kaisareia, Agathias von Myrina und Theophylaktos Simokattes*. Frankfurt: Peter Lang.

Brodka, Dariusz. 2018. *Narses: Politik, Krieg und Historiographie im 6. Jahrhundert n. Chr.* Berlin: Peter Lang.

Brubaker, Leslie. 2004a. "The Age of Justinian: Gender and Society." In *The Cambridge Companion to the Age of Justinian*. Edited by Michael Maas, 427–447. Cambridge: Cambridge University Press.

Brubaker, Leslie. 2004b. "Sex, Lies, and Intertexuality: The Secret History of Prokopios and the Rhetoric of Gender in Sixth Century Byzantium." In *Gender in the Early Medieval World: East and West 300-900*. Edited by L. Brubaker and J. M. H. Smith, 83–101. Cambridge: Cambridge University Press.

Büntgen, Ulf, Vladimir Myglan, Fredrik Ljungqvist, et al. 2016. "Cooling and Societal Change During the Late Antique Little Ice Age from 536 to around 660 AD." *Nature Geoscience* 9: 231–236.

Cameron, Alan. 1973. *Porphyrius the Charioteer*. Oxford: Oxford University Press.

Cameron, Alan. 1976. *Circus Factions: Blues and Greens at Rome and Byzantium*. Oxford: Oxford University Press.

Cameron, Alan. 1978. "The House of Anastasius." *Greek, Roman, and Byzantine Studies* 19: 259–276.

Cameron, Averil. 1985. *Procopius and the Sixth Century*. Berkeley: University of California Press.

Cameron, Averil. 1993. "The Byzantine Reconquest of N. Africa and the Impact of Greek Culture." *Graeco-Arabica* 5: 153–165.

Cameron, Averil. 2014. *Byzantine Matters*. Princeton, NJ: Princeton University Press.

Cesaretti, Paolo. 2008. "All'ombra di una preterizione: Proc. *Aed.* I 1,1." *Rivista di studi bizantini e neoellenici* 45: 153–178.

Chassin, Lionel Max. 1957. *Bélisaire, généralissime byzantin (504–565)*. Paris: Payot.

Christie, Neil and Sheila Gibson. 1988. "The City Walls of Ravenna." *Papers of the British School at Rome* 56: 156–197.

Conant, Jonathan. 2012. *Staying Roman: Conquest and Identity in Africa and the Mediterranean, 439–700*. Cambridge: Cambridge University Press.

Cook, John Granger. 2015. *Crucifixion in the Mediterranean World*. Tübingen: Mohr Siebeck.

Cooper, Kate. 2007. *The Fall of the Roman Household*. Cambridge: Cambridge University Press.

Cosentino, Salvatore. 2016. "Il patrizio Germano e la famiglia imperiale nel VI secolo." In *Studi Bizantini in Onore di Maria Dora Spadaro*. Edited by T. Creazzo, C. Crimi, R. Gentile, G. Strano, 115–130. Rome: Acireale.

Cristini, Marco. 2020. "The Diplomacy of Totila (541–552)." *Studi Medievali* 61.1: 29–48.

Cristini, Marco. 2021. "Procopius of Caesarea." In *Biographisch-Bibliographisches Kirchenlexikon Online*. https://www.bbkl.de/index.php/frontend/lexicon/P/Pr/procopius-of-caesarea-85574 (first published online: May 2021).

Croke, Brian. 2001. *Count Marcellinus and His Chronicle*. Oxford: Oxford University Press.

Croke, Brian. 2005. "Justinian's Constantinople." In *The Cambridge Companion to the Age of Justinian*. Edited by Michael Maas, 60–86. Cambridge: Cambridge University Press.

Croke, Brian. 2019. "Procopius, from Manuscripts to Books: 1400–1850." *Histos* Supplement 9: 1–173.

Dagron, Gilbert. 1974. *Naissance d'une capitale: Constantinople et ses institutions de 330 à 451*. Paris: Presses Universitaires de France.

Dagron, Gilbert. 2011. *L'hippodrome de Constantinople: jeux, peuple et politique*. Paris: Gallimard.

De Giorgi, Andrea U., and A. Asa Eger. 2021. *Antioch: A History*. London: Routledge.

Deliyannis, Deborah. 2010. *Ravenna in Late Antiquity*. Cambridge: Cambridge University Press.

Detschew, Dimiter. 1957. *Die thrakischen Sprachreste*. Wien: R.M. Rohrer.

Diehl, Charles. 1901. *Justinien et la civilization byzantine au vie siècle*. Paris: E. Leroux.

Dijkstra, Jitse, and Geoffrey Greatrex. 2009. "Patriarchs and Politics in Constantinople in the Reign of Anastasius (with a Reedition of *O.Mon.Epiph.* 59)." *Millennium* 6: 223–264.

Donizetti, Gaetano. 1836. *Belisario*. Torino: Tipografia Favale. https://archive.org/deta ils/balisairegrandopoodoni/mode/2up.

Drake, David, and Eric Flint. 1998. *An Oblique Approach*. Wake Forest: Baen Books.

Drake, David, and Eric Flint. 2006. *The Dance of Time*. Wake Forest: Baen Books.

Evans, J. A. S. 2002. *The Empress Theodora: Partner of Justinian*. Austin: University of Texas Press.

Evans, J. A. S. 2011. *The Power Game in Byzantium: Antonina and the Empress Theodora*. London: Continuum.

Evert-Kappesowa, Halina. 1964. "Antonine et Bélisaire." In *Byzantinische Beiträge*. Edited by J. Irmscher, 55–72. Berlin: Akademie-Verlag.

Fisher, Elizabeth A. 1978. "Theodora and Antonina in the Historia Arcana: History and/or Fiction?" *Arethusa* 11: 253–279.

Frankforter, A. Daniel. 1996. "Amalasuntha, Procopius, and a Woman's Place." *Journal of Women's History* 8.2: 41–57.

Frend, W. H. C. 1972. *The Rise of the Monophysite Movement: Chapters in the History of the Church in the Fifth and Sixth Centuries*. Cambridge: Cambridge University Press.

Garland, Lynda. 1999. *Byzantine Empresses: Women and Power in Byzantium, AD 527–1204*. London: Routledge.

Gibbon, Edward. 1776–1789. *The History of the Decline and Fall of the Roman Empire*. 6 vols. London: Strahan & Cadell.

Graf, Fritz. 1997. *Magic in the Ancient World*. Translated by Franklin Philip. Cambridge, MA: Harvard University Press.

Graves, Robert. 1938. *Count Belisarius*. Reprinted New York: Farrar, 1982.

Greatrex, Geoffrey. 1997. "The Nika riot: a reappraisal." *Journal of Hellenic Studies* 117: 60–86.

Greatrex, Geoffrey. 1998. *Rome and Persia at War, 502–532*. Leeds: Francis Cairns.

Greatrex, Geoffrey. 2014. "Perceptions of Procopius in Recent Scholarship." *Histos* 8: 76–121.

Greatrex, Geoffrey. 2020. "Procopius and the Plague in 2020." *Boletín de la Sociedad Española de Bizantinística* 35: 5–12.

Greatrex, Geoffrey. 2022. *Procopius of Caesarea:* The Persian Wars. *A Historical Commentary*. Cambridge: Cambridge University Press.

Haldon, John, et al. 2018a. "Plagues, Climate Change, and the End of an Empire: A Response to Kyle Harper's *The Fate of Rome* (1): Climate." *History Compass* 16.12: 1–13.

Haldon, John, et al. 2018b. "Plagues, Climate Change, and the End of an Empire: A Response to Kyle Harper's *The Fate of Rome* (3): Disease, Agency, and Collapse." *History Compass* 16.12: 1–10.

Harper, Kyle. 2017. *The Fate of Rome: Climate, Disease, and the End of an Empire*. Princeton, NJ: Princeton University Press.

Harvey, Susan A. 2001. "Theodora the 'Believing Queen': A Study in Syriac Historiographical Tradition." *Hugoye: Journal of Syriac Studies* 4.2: 209–234.

Heather, Peter. 2018. *Rome Resurgent: War and Empire in the Age of Justinian.* New York: Oxford University Press.

Hendy, Michael F. 1985. *Studies in the Byzantine Monetary Economy, c. 300–1450.* Cambridge: Cambridge University Press.

Herrin, Judith. 2013. *Unrivalled Influence: Women and Empire in Byzantium.* Princeton, NJ: Princeton University Press.

Herrin, Judith. 2020. *Ravenna: Capital of Empire, Crucible of Europe.* Princeton, NJ: Princeton University Press.

Hillner, Julia. 2019. "Imperial Women and Clerical Exile in Late Antiquity." *Studies in Late Antiquity* 3.3: 369–412.

Howard-Johnston, James. 2000. "The Education and Expertise of Procopius." *Antiquité Tardive* 8: 19–30.

Hughes, Ian. 2009. *Belisarius: The Last Roman General.* Barnsley: Pen & Sword Military.

Humphrey, John. 1986. *Roman Circuses: Arenas for Chariot Racing.* Berkeley: University of California Press.

Isaac, Benjamin. 1992. *The Limits of Empire: The Roman Army in the East.* Oxford: Clarendon Press.

James, Liz. 2001. *Empresses and Power in Early Byzantium.* London: Leicester University Press.

Jireček, Konstantin. 1886. "Archäologische Fragmente aus Bulgarien." *Archäologisch-epigraphische Mitteilungen aus Österreich-Ungarn* 10: 43–104.

Jireček, Konstantin. 1911. *Geschichte der Serben.* Gotha: F.A. Perthes.

Jones, A. H. M. 1964. *The Later Roman Empire, 284–602: A Social, Economic and Administrative Survey.* 3 vols. Oxford: Blackwell.

Jones, A. H. M., J. R. Martindale, and J. Morris. 1971–1992. *The Prosopography of the Later Roman Empire.* 3 vols. Cambridge: Cambridge University Press.

Kaldellis, Anthony. 2004. *Procopius of Caesarea: Tyranny, History, and Philosophy at the End of Antiquity.* Philadelphia: University of Pennsylvania Press.

Kaldellis, Anthony. 2009. "The Date and Structure of Prokopios' *Secret History* and His Projected Work on Church History." *Greek, Roman, and Byzantine Studies* 49: 585–616.

Kaldellis, Anthony. 2019. *Romanland: Ethnicity and Empire in Byzantium.* Cambridge, MA: Belknap Press of Harvard University Press.

Kastenellos, Paul. 2012. *Antonina: A Byzantine Slut.* Apuleius Books.

Kazhdan, Alexander, ed. 1991. *The Oxford Dictionary of Byzantium.* 3 vols. New York: Oxford University Press.

Kaegi, Walter E. 2003. *Heraclius: Emperor of Byzantium.* Cambridge: Cambridge University Press.

Kelly, Christopher. 2004. *Ruling the Later Roman Empire.* Cambridge, MA: Belknap Press of Harvard University Press.

Knaepen, Arnaud. 2001. "L'image du roi vandale Gélimer chez Procope de Césarée." *Byzantion* 71: 383–403.

Knös, Börje. 1960. "La légende de Bélisaire dans les pays grecs." *Eranos: Acta Philologica Suecana* 58: 237–280.

Koehn, Clemens. 2018a. "Justinian στρατηγόσ." In *Le monde de Procope* (*The World of Procopius*). Edited by Geoffrey Greatrex and Sylvain Janniard, 215–228. Paris: Éditions de Boccard.

Koehn, Clemens. 2018b. *Justinian und die Armee des frühen Byzanz.* Berlin: De Gruyter.

Koritarov, Vasil. 1990. *Sapareva bani@@a.* Sofia: Izd-vo na Otechestveni@@ia front.

Kruse, Marion. 2019. *The Politics of Roman Memory: From the Fall of the Western Empire to the Age of Justinian.* Philadelphia: University of Pennsylvania Press.

Leidholm, Nathan. 2022. "Parents and Children, Servants and Masters: Slaves, Freedmen, and the Family in Byzantium." In *The Routledge Handbook on Identity in Byzantium*, edited by Michael Edward Stewart, David Alan Parnell, and Conor Whately, 263–281. London: Routledge.

Leppin, Hartmut. 2011. *Justinian. Das Christliche Experiment.* Stuttgart: Klett-Cotta Verlag.

Lillington-Martin, Christopher. 2012. "Hard and Soft Power on the Eastern Frontier: A Roman Fortlet Between Dara and Nisibis, Mesopotamia, Turkey, Prokopios' Mindouos?" *The Byzantinist* 2012.2, 4–5.

Lillington-Martin, Christopher. 2013. "Procopius on the Struggle for Dara in 530 and Rome in 537–538: Reconciling Texts and Landscapes." In *War and Warfare in Late Antiquity*. Edited by A. Sarantis and N. Christie, 599–630. Leiden: Brill.

Lillington-Martin, Christopher. 2018. "Procopius, πάρεδρος/*quaestor*, *Codex Justinianus*, 1.27 and Belisarius' Strategy in the Mediterranean." In *Procopius of Caesarea: Literary and Historical Interpretations*. Edited by Christopher Lillington-Martin and Elodie Turquois, 157–185. London: Routledge.

Lillington-Martin, Christopher. Forthcoming. "Joannína: Belisarius' Only Daughter?" In *Historiography and Characterisation in Procopius of Caesarea* (forthcoming PhD diss.). Coventry.

Lillington-Martin, Christopher, and Michael Edward Stewart. 2021. "Turning Traitor: Shifting Loyalties in Procopius' *Gothic Wars.*" Βυζαντινά Σύμμεικτα 31: 281–305.

Lin, Sihong. 2021. "Justin under Justinian: The Rise of Emperor Justin II Revisited." *Dumbarton Oaks Papers* 75: 121–142.

Little, Lester, ed. 2006. *Plague and the End of Antiquity: The Pandemic of 541–750.* Cambridge: Cambridge University Press.

Maas, Michael, ed. 2005. *The Cambridge Companion to the Age of Justinian.* Cambridge: Cambridge University Press.

Mango, Cyril. 1981. "Daily Life in Byzantium." *Jahrbuch der Österreichischen Byzantinistik* 31: 337–353.

Marmontel, Jean-François. 1767. *Belisaire.* Paris: S. Joseph.

McKitterick, Rosamond. 2016. "The Papacy and Byzantium in the Seventh- and Early Eighth-Century Sections of the *Liber Pontificalis.*" *Papers of the British School at Rome* 84: 241–273.

Meier, Mischa. 2003. "Die Inszenierung einer Katastrophe: Justinian und der Nika Aufstand." *Zeitschrift für Papyrologie und Epigraphik* 142: 273–300.

Meier, Mischa. 2004. *Das andere Zeitalter Justinians: Kontingenzerfahrung und Kontingenzbewältigung im 6. Jahrhundert n. Chr.* Göttingen: Vandenhoeck & Ruprecht.

Meier, Mischa. 2016. "The 'Justinianic Plague': The Economic Consequences of the Pandemic in the Eastern Roman Empire and Its Cultural and Religious Effects." *Early Medieval Europe* 24: 267–292.

Meier, Mischa. 2020. "The 'Justinianic Plague': An 'Inconsequential Pandemic'? A Reply." *Medizinhistorisches Journal* 55.2: 172–199.

Meier, Mischa, and Federico Montinaro, eds. 2022. *A Companion to Procopius of Caesarea*. Leiden: Brill.

Merrills, Andy. 2017. "Rome and the Vandals." In *The Sea in History: The Ancient World*. Edited by Philip de Souza, Pascal Arnaud, and Christian Buchet, 496–508. Suffolk: Boydell and Brewer.

Merrills, Andy. 2022. "Contested Identities in Byzantine North Africa." In *The Routledge Handbook on Identity in Byzantium*. Edited by Michael Edward Stewart, David Alan Parnell, and Conor Whately, 181–197. London: Routledge.

Moorhead, John. 1994. *Justinian*. London: Routledge.

Mordechai, Lee, and Merle Eisenberg. 2019. "Rejecting Catastrophe. The Case of the Justinianic Plague." *Past and Present* 244: 3–50.

Mordechai, Lee, et al. 2019. "The Justinianic Plague. An Inconsequential Pandemic?" *PNAS* 116: 25546–25554.

Mulvin, Lynda. 2004. "Late Roman Villa Plans: The Danube-Balkan Region." *Late Antique Archaeology* 2.1: 377–410.

Murray, William M. 2012. *The Age of Titans: The Rise and Fall of the Great Hellenistic Navies*. Oxford: Oxford University Press.

Neville, Leonora. 2019. *Byzantine Gender*. York: Arc Humanities Press.

Norwich, John Julius. 1989. *Byzantium: The Early Centuries*. New York: Knopf.

Oldmixon, John. 1722. *The Life of Belisarius a Roman general under Justinian the Great: With Some Parallels to the Late Duke of Marlborough*. London: J. Robert.

Parnell, David Alan. 2012. "The Careers of Justinian's Generals." *Journal of Medieval Military History* 10: 1–16.

Parnell, David Alan. 2014. "Spectacle and Sport in Constantinople in the Sixth Century." In *Companion to Sport and Spectacle in Greek and Roman Antiquity*. Edited by Paul Christesen and Donald Kyle, 633–645. Malden: Wiley-Blackwell Press.

Parnell, David Alan. 2015a. "The Social Networks of Justinian's Generals." *Journal of Late Antiquity* 8.1: 114–135.

Parnell, David Alan. 2015b. "Barbarians and Brothers-in-Arms: Byzantines on Barbarian Soldiers in the Sixth Century." *Byzantinische Zeitschrift* 108.2: 809–826.

Parnell, David Alan. 2017. *Justinian's Men: Careers and Relationships of Byzantine Army Officers, ca. 518–610*. London: Palgrave-Macmillan.

Parnell, David Alan. 2020a. "Justinian's Clemency and God's Clemency." *Βυζαντινά Σύμμεικτα* 30: 11–30.

Parnell, David Alan. 2020b. "The Emperor and His People at the Chariot Races in Byzantium." *The International Journal of the History of Sport* 37: 233–245.

Parnell, David Alan. 2022. "A War of Words on the Place of Military Wives in the Sixth-Century Roman Army." In *The Routledge Handbook on Identity in Byzantium*. Edited by Michael Edward Stewart, David Alan Parnell, and Conor Whately, 363–376. London: Routledge.

Payne, Richard E. 2015. *A State of Mixture: Christians, Zoroastrians, and Iranian Political Culture in Late Antiquity*. Oakland: University of California Press.

Pazdernik, Charles. 1997. "A Dangerous Liberty and a Servitude Free from Care: Political *Eleutheria* and *Douleia* in Procopius of Caesarea and Thucydides of Athens" (unpublished PhD diss.). Princeton.

Pazdernik, Charles. 2000. "Procopius and Thucydides on the Labors of War: Belisarius and Brasidas in the Field." *Transactions of the American Philological Association* 130: 149–187.

Pazdernik, Charles. 2006. "Xenophon's Hellenica in Procopius' Wars: Pharnabazus and Belisarius." *Greek, Roman, and Byzantine Studies* 46: 175–206.

Pazdernik, Charles. 2015. "Belisarius' Second Occupation of Rome and Pericles' Last Speech." In *Shifting Genres in Late Antiquity*. Edited by Geoffrey Greatrex and Hugh Elton, 207–218. Farnham: Ashgate.

Pfeilschifter, Rene. 2013. *Der Kaiser und Konstantinopel. Kommunikation und Konfliktaustrag in einer spätantiken Metropole*. Berlin: De Gruyter.

Philips, William. 1758. *Belisarius: A Tragedy*. London: J. Staples.

Potter, David. 2015. *Theodora: Actress, Empress, Saint*. Oxford: Oxford University Press.

Puk, Alexander. 2014. *Das römische Spielewesen in der Spätantike*. Millennium-Studien 48. Berlin: De Gruyter.

Rance, Philip. 2004. "The *Fulcum*, the Late Roman and Byzantine *Testudo*: the Germanization of Roman Infantry Tactics?" *Greek, Roman, and Byzantine Studies* 44: 265–326.

Rance, Philip. 2005. "Narses and the Battle of Taginae [Busta Gallorum] 552: Procopius and Sixth-Century Warfare." *Historia: Zeitschrift für Alte Geschichte* 54.4: 424–472.

Rance, Philip. 2010. "The *De Militari Scientia* or Müller Fragment as a Philological Resource. Latin in the East Roman Army and Two New Loanwords in Greek: *palmarium* and **recala*." *Glotta, Zeitschrift für griechische und lateinische Sprache* 86: 63–92.

Richards, Jeffrey. 1979. *The Popes and the Papacy in the Early Middle Ages, 476–752*. London: Routledge & Kegan Paul.

Rotrou, Jean. 1643. *Le Belisaire*. Paris: Antoine de Sommaville et Augustin Courbé.

Roueché, Charlotte. 2008. "Entertainments, Theatre, and Hippodrome." In *The Oxford Handbook of Byzantine Studies*. Edited by Elizabeth Jeffreys, 677–684. Oxford: Oxford University Press.

Rubin, Berthold. 1960. *Das Zeitalter Justinians*. Berlin: Water de Gruyter.

Sarantis, Alexander. 2016. *Justinian's Balkan Wars: Campaigning, Diplomacy, and Development in Illyricum, Thrace and the Northern World, AD 527–565*. Leeds: Francis Cairns.

Sarris, Peter. 2006. *Economy and Society in the Age of Justinian*. Cambridge: Cambridge University Press.

Sarris, Peter. 2020. "Climate and Disease." In *Companion to the Global Early Middle Ages*. Edited by Erik Hermans, 511–538. Leeds: Arc Humanities Press.

Sarris, Peter. 2022. "New Approaches to the 'Plague of Justinian.'" *Past and Present* 254.1: 315–346.

Schmitt, Oliver. 1994. "Die Buccellarii: Eine Studie zum militärischen Gefolgschaftswesen in der Spätantike." *Tyche* 9: 147–174.

Scott, Roger. 2012. *Byzantine Chronicles and the Sixth Century*. Farnham: Ashgate.

Signes Codoñer, Juan. 2005. "Der Historiker und der Walfisch: Tiersymbolik und Milleniarismus in der Kriegsgechichte Prokops." In *Zwischen Polis und Provinz und Peripherie: Beiträge zur byzantinischen Geschichte und Kultur*. Edited by L. M. Hoffmann, 37–58. Wiesbaden: Harrassowitz.

Smith, Steven D. 2019. *Greek Epigram and Byzantine Culture: Gender, Desire, and Denial in the Age of Justinian*. Cambridge: Cambridge University Press.

Sotinel, Claire. 2005. "Emperors and Popes in the Sixth Century: The Western View." In *The Cambridge Companion to the Age of Justinian*. Edited by Michael Maas, 267–290. Cambridge: Cambridge University Press.

Southern, Pat, and Karen Ramsey Dixon. 1996. *The Late Roman Army*. New Haven, CT: Yale University Press.

Stanhope, Philip Henry (Lord Mahon). 1848. *The Life of Belisarius*. 2nd edition. London: John Murray.

Stein, Ernest. 1949. *Histoire du Bas-Empire*. 2 vols. Paris: Desclée de Brouwer.

Stewart, Michael Edward. 2016. *The Soldier's Life: Martial Virtues and Manly Romanitas in the Early Byzantine Empire*. Leeds: Kismet Press.

Stewart, Michael Edward. 2017. "The Danger of the Soft Life: Manly and Unmanly Romans in Procopius' Gothic War." *Journal of Late Antiquity* 10.2: 473–502.

Stewart, Michael Edward. 2020. *Masculinity, Identity, and Power Politics in the Age of Justinian*. Amsterdam: Amsterdam University Press.

Stewart, Michael Edward. 2021. "Bashing Belisarius: Polemical Characterizations in Procopius' *Secret History*." *Acta Classica Supplementum* 11: 245–264.

Stewart, Michael Edward. Forthcoming. "Finding Mr. or Mrs. Right: Marriage Alliances in the Age of Theodora." In *Seminars of the Interuniversity Center for the History and Archaeology of the Early Middle Ages* (SCISAM) 10. Edited by Francesco Borri and Cristina La Rocca. Turnhout: Brepols.

Swist, Jeremy J. 2020. "Date album Belisario: An Interview with Judicator." *Heavy Metal Classicist* (blog): https://heavymetalclassicist.home.blog/2020/12/28/date-album-belisario-an-interview-with-judicator/.

Swist, Jeremy J. 2021. "Headbanging to Byzantium: The Reception of the Byzantine Empire in Heavy Metal Music." In *İstanbul'da Bu Ne Bizantinizm! / What Byzantinism is this in Istanbul!* Edited by E. Alışık, 200–229. Istanbul: İstanbul Araştırmaları Enstitüsü Yayınları.

Theodoropoulos, Panagiotis. 2021. "Did the Byzantines call themselves Byzantines? Elements of Eastern Roman Identity in the Imperial Discourse of the Seventh Century." *Byzantine and Modern Greek Studies* 45.1: 25–41.

Tougher, Shaun. 2010. "Having Fun in Byzantium." In *A Companion to Byzantium.* Edited by Liz James, 135–146. Chichester: Wiley-Blackwell.

Treadgold, Warren. 1995. *Byzantium and Its Army, 284–1081.* Stanford: Stanford University Press.

Treadgold, Warren. 1997. *A History of the Byzantine State and Society.* Stanford: Stanford University Press.

Treadgold, Warren. 2007. *The Early Byzantine Historians.* New York: Palgrave Macmillan.

Vacalopoulos, Apostolos. 1963. *A History of Thessaloniki.* Thessaloniki: Institute of Balkan Studies.

Vespignani, Giorgio. 2010. "Costantinopoli Nuova Roma come modello della *urbs* regia tardoantica." *Reti Medievali Rivista* 11.2: 117–136.

Vitiello, Massimiliano. 2014. *Theodahad: A Platonic King at the Collapse of Ostrogothic Italy.* Toronto: University of Toronto Press.

Watts, Edward J. 2021. *The Eternal Decline and Fall of Rome: The History of a Dangerous Idea.* Oxford: Oxford University Press.

Webb, Ruth. 2008. *Demons and Dancers: Performance in Late Antiquity.* Cambridge, MA: Harvard University Press.

Whately, Conor. 2015. "Some Observations on Procopius' Use of Numbers in Descriptions of Combat in Wars Books 1–7." *Phoenix* 69.3: 394–411.

Whately, Conor. 2016. *Battles and Generals: Combat, Culture, and Didacticism in Procopius' Wars.* Leiden: Brill.

Whately, Conor. 2019. "Procopius on the Siege of Rome in AD 537/538." In *Brill's Companion to Sieges in the Ancient Mediterranean.* Edited by J. Armstrong and M. Trundle, 265–284. Leiden: Brill.

Whately, Conor. 2021. *Procopius on Soldiers and Military Institutions in the Sixth-Century Roman Empire.* Leiden: Brill.

Whately, Conor. Forthcoming. "Women and the Military in the Age of Justinian." In *Women and the Roman Army: Changed Perspectives and Current Work.* Edited by Elizabeth Greene and Lee Brice. Cambridge: Cambridge University Press.

Whitby, Michael. 1995. "Recruitment in Roman Armies from Justinian to Heraclius (ca. 565–615)." In *The Byzantine and Early Islamic Near East III: States, Resources, and Armies.* Edited by Averil Cameron, 61–124. Princeton, NJ: Darwin Press.

Whitby, Michael. 2000. "The Army, c. 420–602." In *The Cambridge Ancient History*, vol. 14: *Late Antiquity: Empire and Successors, AD 425–600.* Edited by Averil Cameron,

Bryan Ward-Perkins, and Michael Whitby, 288–314. Cambridge: Cambridge University Press.

Whitby, Michael. 2021. *The Wars of Justinian*. Yorkshire: Pen & Sword Military.

Wrotek, Sylwia E., Wieslaw E. Kozak, David C. Hess, and Susan C. Fagan. 2011. "Treatment of Fever After Stroke: Conflicting Evidence." *Pharmacotherapy* 31: 1085–1091.

Index

For the benefit of digital users, indexed terms that span two pages (e.g., 52–53) may, on occasion, appear on only one of those pages.

Figures are indicated by f following the page number